For five decades some of the best and brightest artistic talents have been employed to design and create original and outstanding sleeves for vinyl and CD albums. In the pages of this book you will find more than 250 of those designs, arranged chronologically, and by musical genre from 1956 to 2005.

In an age where music is increasingly delivered direct to the consumer via internet download with no packaging and thus no visual art attached, the sleeves contained in this book have acquired a historical importance. Many are already rare and difficult to find, with collectors and specialists fighting over good condition copies and paying high prices for them. Some of the album sleeves in this book represent the precious part of the whole package, with the sleeve being far more interesting than the music contained on the vinyl.

That is because sleeve designers have not only reflected the visual approach of the many and varied musical and youth cult styles to emerge since 1956, but have also helped to define and even begin them, too.

Throughout the book are quotes from various designers, photographers and people for whom the album cover has played a big part in their lives. There are sleeves for rare and unsuccessful (in terms of sales) records, and there are sleeves for albums which sold in their millions. All of them have one thing in common, however: they are all graphically, artistically and culturally important.

THE GREATEST ALBUM COVERS OF ALL TIME

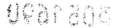

This edition first published in 2008 by
Collins & Brown
10 Southcombe Street
London
W14 0RA

An imprint of Anova Books Company Ltd

Distributed in the United States and Canada by
Sterling Publishing Co, 387 Park Avenue South, New York,
NY 10016-8810, USA

ISBN 978-1-84340-481-1

First published in the United Kingdom in 2005

A CIP catalogue for this book is available from the British Library.

10 9 8 7 6

Produced by Essential Works

www.essentialworks.co.uk

All entries on pages 10-115 by Barry Miles unless otherwise
stated; pages 116-253 Johnny Morgan unless otherwise stated.
Design by Kate Ward for Essential Works

Reproduction by Rival Colour Ltd, UK
Printed and bound by 1010 Printing International Ltd, China

This book can be ordered direct from the publisher at
www.anovabooks.com

THE GREATEST ALBUM COVERS OF ALL TIME

BARRY MILES,
GRANT SCOTT &
JOHNNY MORGAN

COLLINS & BROWN

PICTURE CREDITS: 10 RECORDS/UK 173; 4AD 181 (bottom); ALLEGRO 57; A&M RECORDS/US/UNIVERSAL 59 (right); ABC RECORDS/US 96 (right); ABC-PARAMOUNT/US 30 (left); ACE 35 (top); ANIMAL RECORDS (CHRYSALIS)/US 159 (bottom); APPLE CORPS LTD/UK 52, 53, 70 (bottom); ARGO RECORDS/UK 17; ARISTA/SONY 35, 192, 247; ARTEMIS 249 (bottom); ASYLUM/US 95; ATLANTIC/US 28, 34 (top), 39, 49, 70 (top); BEGGARS BANQUET/UK 159 (top); BELLA UNION 179; BIZARRE RECORDS/US/RYKODISC 68, 92; BLUE NOTE/US/EMI 27, 31, 40, 47, 118; CAPITOL US 11, 12, 20, 35 (bottom); CBS/SONY/US 175; CHARLY/SPECIALTY/US 34; CHARLY/UK 120, 122; CHARLY/VEEJAY 59 (left); CHRYSALIS RECORDS/UK 93, 183 (top); COLUMBIA/CBS/SONY 111 (right); COLUMBIA/CBS/US 150 (bottom); COLUMBIA/SONY/US 77, 237; COLUMBIA/US 29, 64 (top), 65, 66, 84, 91, 94, 99, 101 (left), 149, 213 (top); COMMAND-PROBE/US 76; CONTEMPORARY RECS/FANTASY JAZZ 30 (right); CREATION RECORDS/UK/SONY 189 (right); CREATION/SONY 188; DEBUT/FONTANA/US 43; DECAY/MANIFESTO 163; DECCA/UK 14, 63; DEF JAM RECORDS, CBS RECORDS/US 170, 171, 207; DOMINO RECORDINGS/UK 220; DUOPHONIC UHF DISKS 219; EG RECORDS/UK/WARNER 161; ELEKTRA /US WARNER 69, 97; EMI HARVEST/UK 104, 105; EMI/UK 166, 209 (right); EMI/US 13; EMPEROR NORTON 229; EPIC 239, 252 (top); EPIC/UK 151 (bottom);

EPIC/US 125; EPIC/US SONY 165, 201 (bottom), 211; FACTORY/UK/LONDON/WARNER 141, 145, 146, 147; FFRR/LONDON/UNIVERSAL 231; FONTANA/BOPLICITY 46 (left); FONTANA/VERVE 41; GEFFEN/US 182, 195, 196, 197, 199, 201 (top), 251 (bottom); GREENSLEEVES 131; GRITRECORDS/US 236; GROVE-ISLAND RECORDS/UK 130; ILLEGAL RECORDS/UK/EMI 158; IMMEDIATE/UK/SANCTUARY 71, 75 (right); IMPULSE!/VERVE/US 42 (bottom), 44; INTERNATIONAL RECORDS SYNDICATE (IRS)/A&M 153 (left); ISLAND RECORDS/UK 82, 85, 100, 108, 127, 128 (right); 150 (top), 152, 155, 180; K7 218, 227, 232; KAMERA RECORDS/UKCASTLE/SANCTUARY 162 (top); LIBERTY/US 15; LICKING FINGERS 253 (bottom); LIVERPOOL TATE GALLERY/UK 243 (right); MATADOR RECORDS/US 233, 249 (top); MATADOR RECORDS/US/BEGGARS 174 (bottom), 181 (top), 253 (top); MAVERICK/WARNERS 230 (bottom); MCA RECORDS/US 204, 212 (top), 213 (bottom); MERCURY/US 117, 134 (left); MERCURY/VERVE 48; MERGE 193 (left); MPS RECORDS/GERMANY/VERVE 46 (right); NEMS/UK/ANAGRAM/CHERRY RED 136 (bottom); NIXA/UK 21; NONESUCH 242, 243 (left); NONESUCH/WARNER 241, 248; NOTHING/INTERSCOPE/US 203; ONE LITTLE INDIAN 185, 186, 187; PANKAY RECORDS/UK 228; PARLOPHONE/UK 18, 51, 73, 245; PHILIPS/UK 60, 61; POLYDOR 138 (right); POLYDOR/UM/US 74; PRESTIGE/FANTASY JAZZ 24, 42 (top); PRIORITY RECORDS/US ISLAND RECORDS/UK 208;

PROHIBITED RECORDS/FRANCE 252 (bottom); RADAR RECORDS-WEA/UK 140 (bottom); RADARSCOPE/ WARNER/US/CHARLY 75 (left); RADIO ACTIVE RECORDS/US 189 (left); RCA/UK 83, 115 (top), 134 (right); RCA/US 33, 58; REPRISE RECORDS/US 101 (right), 109; ROLLING STONE RECORDS/UK/EMI 129; ABCKO THE ROLLING STONES 88; PROMOTONE BV: THE ROLLING STONES 87, 89; ROUGH TRADE/UK 251 (top); ROUGH TRADE/UK/WARNER 157 (right); RUFFTOWN/US 238; SANCTUARY RECORDS/UK 111 (left); SELECT 56; SELF IMMOLATION/SOME BIZARRE/US 162 (bottom); SHANACHIE 128 (left); SIRE/US 136 (top), 151 (left), 156, 157 (left), 209 (left); SONY 123 (left), 235; SONY/INVICTUS 124 (right); SONY MUSIC ENTERTAINMENT/COLUMBIA/US 205 (right); SONY/US COLUMBIA 45; SOUL JAZZ RECORDS/UK 244; SOUTHBOUND/ACE 124 (left), (bottom); STIFF/UK 137, 138 (left); SUB POP 200; TOO PURE 190; TRACK/UK 64 (bottom), 67 (left), 96 (left); UNITED ARTISTS/MGM/BMG/SONY 123 (right); UNIVERSAL RECORDS/US 119, 212 (bottom), 121 (bottom); VERTIGO/GERMANY 113; VERVE/US 25, 26, 55, 67 (right); VICTOR/PRESTIGE 23; VIRGIN/UK 110, 114, 115 (bottom), 133, 139, 140 (top), 153 (right), 191, 215, 217; VIRGIN/US 250; WARNER BROS/US 81, 107, 121 (top), 167, 174 (top), 183, 205 (left); WARNER CHAPPEL/UK 193 (right); WARP 221; WARP RECORDS 230 (top); XL RECORDINGS 216, 225, 226; ZOMBA RECORDS, RCA/SONY 169

Contents

Introduction

In an age of music downloads, where the product is delivered straight to the consumer without packaging, the fact that the same product was once delivered in huge, cardboard sleeves and was made of black, shiny vinyl, seems strange and archaic. Yet it was not even a generation ago that music was pressed onto 12" vinyl and sold in shops. It was not even half a generation ago that music was pressed onto 12cm CDs instead of the vinyl and sold in shops. Both methods of getting music to consumers required a tangible format and thus a visual presence to make the product look as original and different as possible from all of the others in the store.

Today the battlegrounds for consumers of recorded music tend to be television channels and radio or, occasionally, printed media. Previously, the record shop was this battleground. Oddly, the music business of the early 21st century seems to have come full circle and mirrors the music business of the early 1950s. Before Elvis Presley rocked the world – and even for a time after, too – musical entertainers predominantly recorded and released singles. These were usually sold either as 78rpm slabs of shellac or as 45rpm slices of vinyl and contained two songs. Today, once again, musical entertainers are building careers (albeit often extremely short-lived ones) by "releasing" singles. That is, putting one recorded song at a time onto websites for download. There are still record shops in existence of course, but they increasingly sell movies, mobile telephones and even books alongside CDs (with usually no more than a dozen 12" vinyl singles also being stocked, for DJ use).

The point of this apparent ramble through the state of recorded music sold now and back in the 1950s is to put into context what this book represents. For anyone reading this book in, say, 2016, the idea that there were once music shops that sold only unwieldy slabs of vinyl on which bands and singers had pressed a series of "songs" that were meant to be listened to as a whole, rather than as separate and individual numbers, is going to seem positively weird. Conversely, to many of the people reading this book ten years earlier it seems very odd indeed that record shops packed full of only vinyl albums no longer exist.

For the generation of first rock and rollers, the Baby Boomers who were there at the birth of rock music, the 12" vinyl album is more than just a record. Every album they owned is etched in song into their memory, and all that is needed to prompt reminiscences of a particular time is the sight of the sleeve that contained a particular treasure.

This book is a musical history lesson. It is part catalogue, part palimpsest and part art journal. It offers a visual journey through six decades of recorded pop music – "pop" is used in its original, abbreviated form here, as shorthand for popular – and takes in as many of the dominant genres of pop music in each decade as time and space allows. The title of this book might be The Greatest but in truth it should be Some Of The Greatest, because there just isn't the space to fully do justice to the breadth and imagination of the people who, between 1956 and 2006, created some of the wittiest, sharpest, smartest and most bizarre art to ever be mass produced. We have attempted to put together a kind of scrapbook of fifty years' worth of popular music development, with that development being represented by the artwork and design that has been used to sell it.

There will undoubtedly be many album sleeves not included in this book that people will consider to be huge oversights. It should be pointed out, for instance, that there is not one Yes, Led Zeppelin or Electric Light Orchestra album sleeve. This is because none of the authors (nor the editor) considers them to be of any great artistic or cultural worth. In other words, they made no great artistic or graphic impact on anything in the field of album art that came after. Such sleeves all look very much like a product of their time, rooted in early and mid-1970s pomposity, oozing delusions of grandeur but looking like the jacket for a silly sci-fi novel. But hopefully we have given good critical reasons for the inclusion of all 250+ sleeves that you will find here. All of which have significant artistic worth or cultural impact.

The sleeves are not here simply because they look nice, however – they are here because they are important. And this importance does not necessarily extend to the music that the sleeve is selling, indeed in some cases the records are terrible but the cover sublime. We have also found quite a few great albums with equally classic sleeves, of course. Frank Sinatra, The Beatles, the Rolling Stones, Factory Records and Sonic Youth each have a stand-alone section, for instance, one in each decade from the 1950s through to the 1990s. These artists (and in the 1980s, a record company, Factory) have created truly astounding and influential music and this has been reflected in their album artwork and design. It is no coincidence that the band members took active roles in creating their sleeves.

While at first there was a temptation to skew the volume of actual covers included here towards the 1960s and 1970s, we have attempted to offer as fair a representation of each decade (and the musical genres spawned by each) as possible. In reality this has meant that the slimmest "chapters" are the 1950s, when album production was in its infancy, and the 1980s, when the major change in format from vinyl to CD that the music industry forced upon designers seems to have stumped them for a while. We were pleasantly surprised, however, by how many great sleeves have been created in the last fifteen years. In the 1990s it seems that designers and artists got to grips fully with the smaller CD booklet format to create some truly innovative work.

What will happen to the art of album cover design in the future remains to be seen. As with most things, there are those who cling to the conventions and skills of the past. They will continue to design 12" sleeves in the hope that the rare "album" is recorded for sequential listening and released as a CD and vinyl item. And at least until the music industry can find a way to make downloading music pay as well as selling actual tangible product, CDs will continue to be released and they will always require packaging.

For anyone thinking of taking it up as a career then, this book could be useful. Enjoy.

Mal Peachey (Editor)

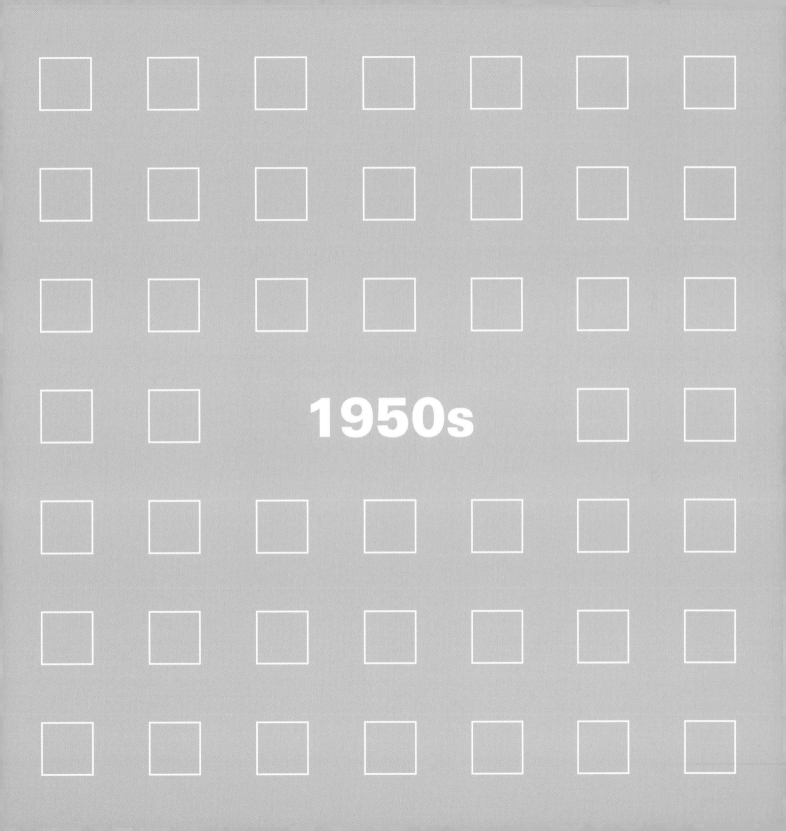

1950s

1950s Pop

Although the long-playing record had been introduced by Columbia in 1948, it wasn't until the mid-1950s that the industry began to recognize the marketing possibilities of the 12-inch record that played at 33⅓ rpm. Originally the format had been thought most suitable for classical music because of the length of the pieces involved. The Pop market continued to be dominated by three-minute songs released on 78 rpm shellac singles. Bing Crosby was still the world's most successful singer in the mid-1950s, despite Frank Sinatra having been the first teenage scream dream a decade earlier, and Crosby's records were all singles. Columbia had been the recording home to both, but Sinatra had been "let go" in 1952 when he was going through a downturn in popularity. To Columbia's and Bing's regret, no doubt, Frank was on the verge of the greatest comeback in the history of Pop music. He was the first major artist to take advantage of the 12-inch album format, and the first to use the packaging to its fullest advantage.

Because albums until 1954 tended to be compilations of hit singles, the covers were almost universally plain: the name and picture of the singer were often the only features to be found on the front.

There were also orchestral versions of hits released in the album format in the early 1950s, however, and because there was no "star" to sell the album, the sleeve design had to be more inventive. Alex Steinweiss, the art director for Columbia, is usually credited with the idea of creating original artwork in order to sell records. His work drew upon classical painting, modern art and cartoons of the era, and created the "look" of pre-1950s Pop albums – all high colour, fizzing graphics and angular images.

Jim Flora drew his own covers for RCA Victor in the late 1940s and early 1950s, making the lettering a part of the design. His covers were cartoonish and made the albums look fun too. When he left RCA in 1956 he became a children's book illustrator.

Dutch photographer Paul Huf's pictures of women in surreal surroundings were used by designer Herry van Borssum Waalkes on light classical recordings on the then new Philips label in the mid-1950s. The covers are now regarded as classics of high camp.

In the Pop market, though, no recording artist was more involved in the process of sleeve design than Frank Sinatra. In fact it was for that, rather than his singing, that he won his very first Grammy Award. [JM]

▶ Songs for Young Lovers / Frank Sinatra

RELEASED 1955 | CAPITOL | USA | SLEEVE DESIGN BY ROTHSCHILD | PHOTOGRAPHY BY KEN VEEDER | ART DIRECTION FRANK SINATRA | ALBUM PRODUCED BY VOYLE GILMORE

It wasn't Sinatra's first album for Capitol, the label that had given him his second stab at singing for a living, but it was the most important he had released up to that date. In 1954 Frank Sinatra was just beginning to turn his life around. After taking the best deal that Capitol (launched in 1942 by Sinatra's friend, the singer-songwriter Johnny Mercer) could make, he declined a big advance in favour of total artistic control, including deciding how the covers would look. The first Capitol Sinatra 10-inch album had been *Swing Easy*, which showed not the skinny kid who made the girls scream, but a suited and hatted, smiling Frank. But for this, his first themed release, he opted for a more adult look. Alone, cool-looking with hat and cigarette, standing under a dim (if short) street lamp he watches unsmiling as happy couples walk by. It was the debut of a new, serious Sinatra, heard for the first time singing standard American songs as if they were Blues numbers. [JM]

Frank Sinatra
Songs for Young Lovers

VIOLETS FOR YOUR FURS
MY FUNNY VALENTINE • THE GIRL NEXT DOOR
A FOGGY DAY • LIKE SOMEONE IN LOVE
I GET A KICK OUT OF YOU • LITTLE GIRL BLUE
THEY CAN'T TAKE THAT AWAY FROM ME

Accompanied by NELSON RIDDLE

▲ Sings for Only the Lonely / Frank Sinatra

RELEASED 1958 | CAPITOL | USA | SLEEVE ART DIRECTED BY FRANK SINATRA | PAINTING NICK VOLPE | ALBUM PRODUCED BY VOYLE GILMORE

Sinatra won his first Grammy Award for this album, but not for the music: he won it for the album design. Apparently based on a painting that Frank had done of himself as a crying clown, it reflects the air of loneliness that permeates the album. As with his previous Capitol releases, *Only the Lonely* is a concept album, the concept being, in his words, "for losers like me". He meant losers in love, having just parted with second wife Ava Gardner.

▶ Great covers encapsulate the music inside and so it was with Frank Sinatra's No One Cares, with its melancholic early morning bar scene

ALAN EDWARDS, MUSIC PR

▲ Come Fly with Me / Frank Sinatra

RELEASED 1958 | CAPITOL | USA | SLEEVE ART DIRECTED BY FRANK SINATRA | ILLUSTRATION BY UNKNOWN | ALBUM PRODUCED BY VOYLE GILMORE

Arguably the most successful album of Sinatra's Capitol period, its striking, painted cover image evoking the new idea of Jetset living, the sleeve for *Come Fly with Me* was as whole a concept as the music. All the songs involved travel, with the back cover laid out with a flight log, flight plan and pilot handbook (naming Sinatra as Pilot, and arrangers Billy May and Nelson Riddle as Co-Pilots) all printed in a script font. [JM]

▶ No One Cares / Frank Sinatra

RELEASED 1959 | CAPITOL | USA | SLEEVE ART DIRECTED BY FRANK SINATRA | ALBUM PRODUCED BY DAVE CAVANAUGH

Frank sits alone at a bar, happy couples smiling around him. He's in his soon-to-be-trademark white mac and dark trilby, a cigarette in one hand and booze in the other. The album title sits perfectly balanced above the crowd. The red and dark blue lighting reflects the singer's mood and Gordon Jenkins' lush string arrangements for a bunch of Blues songs, including Stormy Weather and I Don't Stand a Ghost of a Chance. Frank's not smiling. Hell, he's not even looking at the camera. [JM]

◀ Glamorous Holiday / Frank Chacksfield

RELEASED 1958 | DECCA | UK | PHOTOGRAPHY BY HANS WILD

A classic release from the days when album buyers were mostly adults and wanted to spend their evenings listening to sophisticated continental music like this. A concept album, one side features songs headed "Evening in Paris" and the other, "Evening in Rome". The sleeve reflects this idea literally, right down to the airliner and the title *Glamorous Holiday* which reassures the buyer that this is quality stuff. Are the girls stewardesses or about to go on holiday? Somehow they have managed to get hold of the queue signs and are welcoming us on board. Albums like this remind us how lucky we are that the 1950s are over.

◀ Black Coffee / Peggy Lee

RELEASED 1956 | DECCA | USA | ALBUM PRODUCED BY MILT GABLER

Originally recorded in 1953 as a 10-inch, this was probably the most successful of Peggy Lee's concept albums, and her own favourite. She approached it as a sultry late-night Jazz album and it was so successful that three years later Decca had her add four extra tracks to expand it to the new 12-inch format. The design reflects the original concept, literally, with a cup of black coffee along with the pot it came in. This is late-night seduction music so we also have a red rose. There are no people, and the lady has even removed her pearl necklace so it looks as if the rose worked – or maybe it was the music and the coffee.

▶ Julie / Julie London with the Jimmy Rowles Orchestra

RELEASED 1958 | LIBERTY | USA | ALBUM PRODUCED BY BOBBY TROUP

Produced by her husband, this was one of more than thirty albums by the star of the dream sequence in *The Girl Can't Help It*. Though lacking the range of Sarah Vaughan or Ella Fitzgerald, Julie London was a master of the understated torch song. Trapped in an era when female singers were automatically "songbirds", "broads" or worse, London's albums were fronted by a series of provocative sleeves, of which, in purely design terms, *Julie* is one of the best. This type of cover is quintessentially of the period, right down to light green backdrop used in soft-core cheesecake shots by the newly emergent *Playboy*, *Nugget*, *U* and other men's magazines. The late 1950s modern chair gives the sleeve that sophisticated edge necessary to make it acceptable for family viewing (and listening).

julie

JULIE LONDON

LRP 3096

LIBERTY
REG U S PAT OFFICE
SPECTRA-SONIC-SOUND
THE ULTIMATE IN HI-FI

PRINTED IN U.S.A.

15

1950s Exotica

The 1950s saw widespread acceptance of the long-playing record and exotic new forms of stereo and hi-fidelity recording, often emblazoned across the front of the record sleeve. For years Decca had a pair of ears on its records. With the advent of stereo came a number of records that did nothing but test your stereo set-up. People bought recordings of tennis matches, just to hear the sound of the ball being hit from one speaker to the other, and orchestral musical was often recorded with bizarre degrees of separation between the lead violin on the left speaker and the kettle drum on the right. Pop artists were still largely represented by singles, and the newly emergent long-player focused largely on Broadway musicals and humour acts. Many of the latter, recorded at famous cafés or nightclubs, brought the live performance into the homes of people who may never have even visited the big city.

Also popular were spoken-word records by poets; it was regarded as amazing that you could hear Robert Frost or Dylan Thomas's actual voice in your split-level living room. You could get "actual business letters dictated at various speeds" too – the field was wide open. The album designers were often the same people who had previously packaged the original "albums", which consisted of 12-inch 78 rpm shellac discs housed in a sturdy book with "pages" of individual card sleeves for each part of the symphony or musical piece. The front covers were smartly embossed, just like a family Bible. When vinyl took over, and the same symphony could be housed on one record, the designers continued to treat the front sleeve like a book, scattering the lettering all over it. But it was soon decided that the title and artist's name should go at the top, to be easily seen when people flipped through the racks. Then it was realized the sleeve was a strong marketing tool, being studied for hours by fans, so special photographs began to feature, such as the one of Lonnie Donegan included here.

A whole school of graphics seemingly emerged and disappeared, styled to produce amusing drawings for sleeves. Andy Warhol's mother, Julia Warhola, was one such quirky designer, specializing in curly lettering and exotic birds. While areas such as Jazz quickly established a style, the "miscellaneous" end of the market, – sound-effects albums, recordings of steam trains, bird calls and poetry – had no such formula, and out of the chaos often came truly innovative design.

▶ **Under Milk Wood by Dylan Thomas / The BBC Cast**
RELEASED 1954 | ARGO RECORDS | UK | SLEEVE DESIGNED BY OLGA LEHMANN | ALBUM PRODUCED BY DOUGLAS CLEVERDON
Olga Lehmann decided that the only possible sleeve for such a record was an illustratration of the play script. So we have blind Captain Cat looking out over a small Welsh seaside town at the morning activities of Myfanwy Price, Willy Nilly the postman, Butcher Beynon, and the husbands of Mrs Ogmore-Pritchard who "Dust the china, feed the canary, sweep the drawing room floor; and before you let the sun in, mind he wipes his shoes". It is in the design tradition of book jackets rather than album sleeves, leaning in the direction of the far superior work of Eric Ravilious. As such this is a period piece, a nervous cross between book publishing and the music business.

SONGS FOR SWINGIN' SELLERS

mono

PARLOPHONE LONG PLAYING 33⅓ R.P.M. RECORD

SONGS FOR SWINGIN' SELLERS

WANTED

▲ Songs for Swingin' Sellers / Peter Sellers

RELEASED 1959 | PARLOPHONE | UK | PHOTOGRAPHY BY KEN PALMER | ALBUM PRODUCED BY GEORGE MARTIN

This was recorded back in the days when George Martin was best known as a producer of comedy records, while Sellers was famous for his work with the Goons and in films. It was unusual in the 1950s (and early 1960s) for EMI to spend more than £20 on an album sleeve, but here they seem to have pulled out the stops and arranged a special shoot to create a sleeve in keeping with the irreverent tone of the record. (It is a parody of Sinatra's *Songs for Swingin' Lovers*.) Mort Sahl's brand of "sick humour" was then popular, which probably resulted in this slightly cruel image. The addition of the 1950s record player is a touch of genius.

▶ Robert Frost Reads His Poetry / Robert Frost

RELEASED 1957 | CAEDMON | USA | SLEEVE DESIGNED BY MATTHEW LEIBOWITZ | ALBUM PRODUCED BY UNKNOWN

Recorded in his Cambridge, Massachusetts, home, this album of Frost reading his work is cited in the sleeve notes as "the definitive" recording. The poet published only one major work after this (*In the Clearing*, 1962), and died in 1963. For the cover, Matthew Leibowitz, an award-winning advertising designer, chose a painting by the artist Ben-Zion (born Benzion Weinman in 1897 in Ukraine). The horse is reminiscent both of Picasso's *Guernica* and the early work of Mark Rothko, who like Zion had been a member of the Group of Ten artists formed in 1936 in New York. It is an unusual piece for Ben-Zion, being colourful and figurative. He made his reputation painting dark, brooding works that were abstract and reflective of his Jewish roots. The sky, grass and rolling horse hint at the rural peace of Massachusetts, but are also symbolic of the darker, underlying images of death to be found in Frost's poems.

Robert

FROST

reads
his
poetry

Langspeling 33⅓ R.P.M. Recording

Caedmon TC 1060

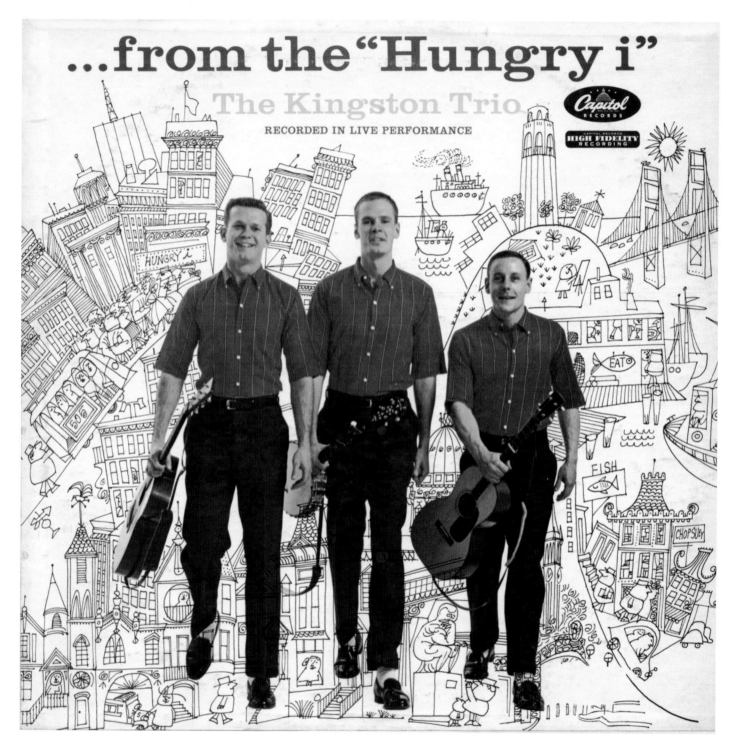

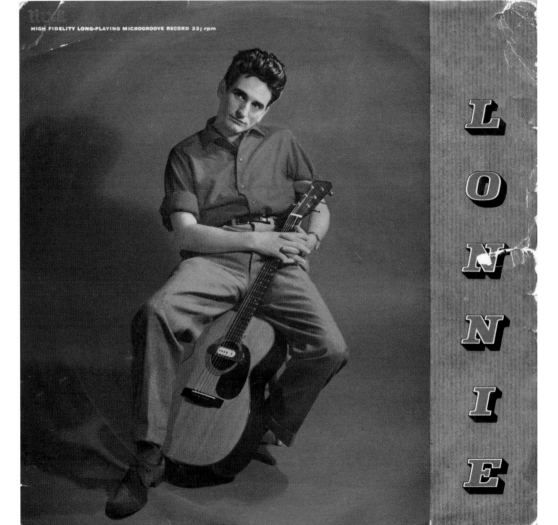

◀ The Kingston Trio from the "Hungry I" / The Kingston Trio
RELEASED 1959 | CAPITOL | USA | SLEEVE ILLUSTRATION BY FRANK PAGE | ALBUM PRODUCED BY VOYLE GILMORE

A live recording from San Francisco's famous Hungry I nightclub featuring an all new set-list. Anyone who was expecting to hear Tom Dooley was disappointed. Cunningly the record company did not print a track-list on the sleeve; you had to buy the album to find out what was on it, though some tracks were mentioned in the sleeve notes. The sleeve tells it all: three preppy college boys bringing folk music to the middle classes in matching shirts, socks and loafers. Frank Page's drawing of San Francisco's tourist sights is supposed to be "hip", imitating, as it does, the work of Siné. Something went wrong in the production department though, and the drawing shows through their legs and two of their instruments, although one guitar was successfully masked.

▲ Lonnie / Lonnie Donegan and His Skiffle Group
RELEASED 1958 | NIXA | UK | SLEEVE DESIGNED BY PETER CLAYTON | PHOTOGRAPH BY RON COHEN | PRODUCED BY ALAN FREEMAN AND MICHAEL BARCLAY

By the time Donegan's second album (with dubious typography typical of the era) was released, skiffle was sweeping Britain. Crucial in the birth of British Rock 'n' Roll, it inspired everyone – including The Beatles – to pick up a guitar and begin making music. Lonnie, king of skiffle, was already succumbing to the pop image makers. He doesn't look very comfortable – his right suede Hush Puppy is tucked awkwardly behind his guitar and the high-cut slacks seem to be belted uncomfortably tight. This is the new moody Lonnie with the beginnings of a pompadour, as if he was contemplating a move into Rock 'n' Roll.

21

1950s **Jazz**

In the 1950s the best art to be found in people's houses was often in their record rack. It was the most innovative period ever for modern Jazz, and equally for the sleeves that housed the music. In 1956 Reid Miles joined Blue Note Records and, over 15 years, designed almost five hundred sleeves for them. The 1950s was also the era of the Beat Generation and Abstract Expressionist painters, and a new open, cool sense of design evolved, inspired by the hard-edged mobiles of Alexander Calder and Colorfield painting of Elsworth Kelly, Kenneth Noland and Frank Stella, as well as the clean contours of Bauhaus and Italian Futurism.

Modern Jazz sleeves reflected this sometimes difficult music, making it more accessible, giving it credibility from an artistic viewpoint, and making the albums desirable objects to own. Reid Miles's designs set the tone for sleeves for a decade and more. The images were often large; there seemed to be plenty of white space (though often the whole sleeve had a tone over it); there was room to breathe. Most of all they were not fussy; the typography was bold and, crucially, part of the design itself, the shape of the letters often providing the main design element.

And Miles was not alone: notable sleeves were produced by Burt Goldblatt for Savoy and Bethlehem Records, while David Stone Martin's sleeves for Verve were often witty and shared the energy of the music. Jim Flora's sleeves for Columbia in the 1940s and RCA Victor in the 1950s showed a distinct influence of Joan Miro and Paul Klee, with their stick writing connected with little blobs.

Then there were designers such as Tom Hannan, whose work for Blue Note and Prestige was often worthy of framing. The work of another Prestige designer, Esmond Edwards, who was also a photographer, showed similar influences to of Reid Miles, as well as being influenced by Miles himself. Another key designer was Paul Bacon, who noteably worked for Blue Note and Riverside record labels. Bacon's work was familiar to millions of readers through the more than seven thousand book jackets he designed, even though his name is relatively obscure. William Claxton's Jazz sleeves were also highly regarded, though he is much better known for his superb Jazz photography. Over fifty years later, in the era of the CD, the influence of Reid Miles and such can still be seen in music packaging.

▶ **Thelonius Monk and Sonny Rollins / Thelonius Monk and Sonny Rollins**
RELEASED 1954| PRESTIGE RECORDS | USA | SLEEVE DESIGNED BY TOM HANNAN | ALBUM PRODUCED BY RUDY VAN GELDER
Tom Hannan designed many of Sonny Rollins's sleeves for Prestige, including *Tenor Madness* (1956) and *Saxophone Colossus* (1956), both of which are superb. But the early Thelonius Monk and Sonny Rollins is the most redolent of the period, the black ink calligraphy suggesting the fascination with Zen Buddhism and Japanese calligraphy then sweeping Greenwich Village. The design itself in simple red and black could be by Franz Klein or Alexander Calder or any of the New York school of painters then causing excitement at the Museum of Modern Art. Hannan took this excitement and literally transferred it to the sleeve. It is challenging (like the music), beautiful (like the music) and very, very modern.

PRESTIGE LP 707
HI-FI

HANNAN

thelonious Monk
Sonny Rollins

THE YOUNG BLOODS

woods/byrd

Esquire

32-060

▲ **The Young Bloods /
Woods and Byrd**
RELEASED 1957 | PRESTIGE |
USA | ALBUM PRODUCED BY
RUDY VAN GELDER
An early hard bop date, recorded
in November 1956, featuring co-
leaders Donald Byrd on trumpet
and Phil Woods on alto. This was

a period when photographers
were delighting in the special
effects that could be obtained by
a slightly longer exposure than
usual which, particularly if you
were photographing a saxophone,
is what this looks like, and makes
a wonderful series of squiggles
on the page. In keeping with the

subject, it also looks like an
explosion. The hard honking of
these young musicians is reflected
in this energetic sleeve which
the designer probably hoped
would be brighter and have
more contrast but still stands
as a good example of non-Blue
Note Jazz design of the period.

▶ **Ella Fitzgerald Sings
Gershwin Vol 2 / Ella
Fitzgerald**
RELEASED 1959 | VERVE | USA |
SLEEVE DESIGNED BY SHELDON
MARKS | ARTWORK BY BERNARD
BUFFET | ALBUM PRODUCED BY
NORMAN GRANZ
The second part of a uniform
series, all with Buffet sleeves.
There was an unfortunate
period in the late 1950s when
Bernard Buffet was hugely
popular, viewed by the public
at large as the acceptable face
of modern art. His work was
easily recognizable: the spiky
lines, the dismal greys, browns
and neutral tones suggested the
more superficial aspects of
Sartre's existentialism and the
alienation felt by the post-war
generation. Though his early
work was highly regarded,
success overwhelmed him:
the work became more
stylized, more commercial
and the signature – which was
the bit everyone wanted – got
bigger and bigger. What had
he to do with Ella Fitzgerald?
They were both modern artists –
otherwise, nothing.

Ella Fitzgerald sings Gershwin   Vol. Two

HIS MASTER'S VOICE
LONG PLAY 33⅓ R·P·M RECORD

mono

Bernard Buffet

Verve A PANORAMIC TRUE HIGH FIDELITY RECORD MG V 4003

THE JAZZ MESSENGERS AT THE CAFE BOHEMIA   VOLUME 1 BLUE NOTE

HORACE SILVER   HANK MOBLEY   ART BLAKEY   KENNY DORHAM   DOUG WATKINS

◀ Ella and Louis / Ella Fitzgerald and Louis Armstrong
RELEASED 1956 | VERVE | USA | PHOTOGRAPHY BY PHIL STERN | ALBUM PRODUCED BY NORMAN GRANZ
Vogue photographer Phil Stern, famous for his iconic images of James Dean, Marilyn Monroe, Marlon Brando and other Hollywood stars, took forty sleeves for Verve Records. One of the very best was the photo shoot done with Ella Fitzgerald and Louis Armstrong. Instead of choosing one of the famous ones of the two of them at the microphone, he opted for a posed shot of Ella and Louis at rest. It is an intimate picture, taken in the studio, and they appear to be taking a well-earned break from work. A poignant shot, it is as if we are interrupting a reverie. This must be one of the first albums not to have the names of the artists on the front, which is a measure of their fame.

▲ The Jazz Messengers At the Café Bohemia Volume 1 / The Jazz Messengers
RELEASED 1955 | BLUE NOTE | USA | SLEEVE DESIGN BY JOHN HERMANSADER | PHOTOGRAPHY BY FRANCIS WOLFF | ALBUM PRODUCED BY ALFRED LION | RECORDED LIVE AT THE CAFE BOHEMIA, ON SHERIDAN SQUARE IN GREENWICH VILLAGE IN 1955
It is hard to imagine how daring it was to use typography in this way in the mid-1950s. Blowing up the letters so large that they became design elements, valuable for their shape as well as for what they said, causing the word to run on the next line – shocking! The series of fairly conventional portrait shots of the line-up, combined with the great shout of the typography, gave this set (originally two volumes, with a third added later) a powerful identity that is still strong half a century later.

CHANGE OF THE CENTURY
ORNETTE COLEMAN

MONO | LTZ-K 15199

An ATLANTIC recording

ornette coleman   change of the century

ATLANTIC FULL dynamics-frequency SPECTRUM

MINGUS AH UM / CHARLES MINGUS
BETTER GIT IT IN YOUR SOUL / GOODBYE PORK PIE HAT / BOOGIE STOP SHUFFLE / SELF-PORTRAIT IN THREE COLORS / OPEN LETTER TO DUKE / BIRD CALLS / FABLES OF FAUBUS / PUSSY CAT DUES / JELLY ROLL

COLUMBIA

◀ **Change of the Century /
Ornette Coleman**
RELEASED 1959 | ATLANTIC |
USA | PHOTOGRAPHY BY LEE
FRIEDLANDER | ALBUM PRODUCED
BY NESUHI ERTEGUN

Lee Friedlander, now better known for his street photography, his nudes and more surrealistic work, began his career working for Atlantic Records in the late 1950s and was responsible for some of their most memorable sleeve images. His portraits were usually taken close-up; not close enough to distort but close enough to see every hair and every pore on his subject's face. But despite this intimacy, the pictures rarely looked posed. Some, in fact, were of his subjects in action. This is a wonderful portrait, beautifully lit, three-quarter life-size, making us want to know what new boundaries this man had opened up, what new challenges he had posed for his listeners. Quite a few, as it turned out.

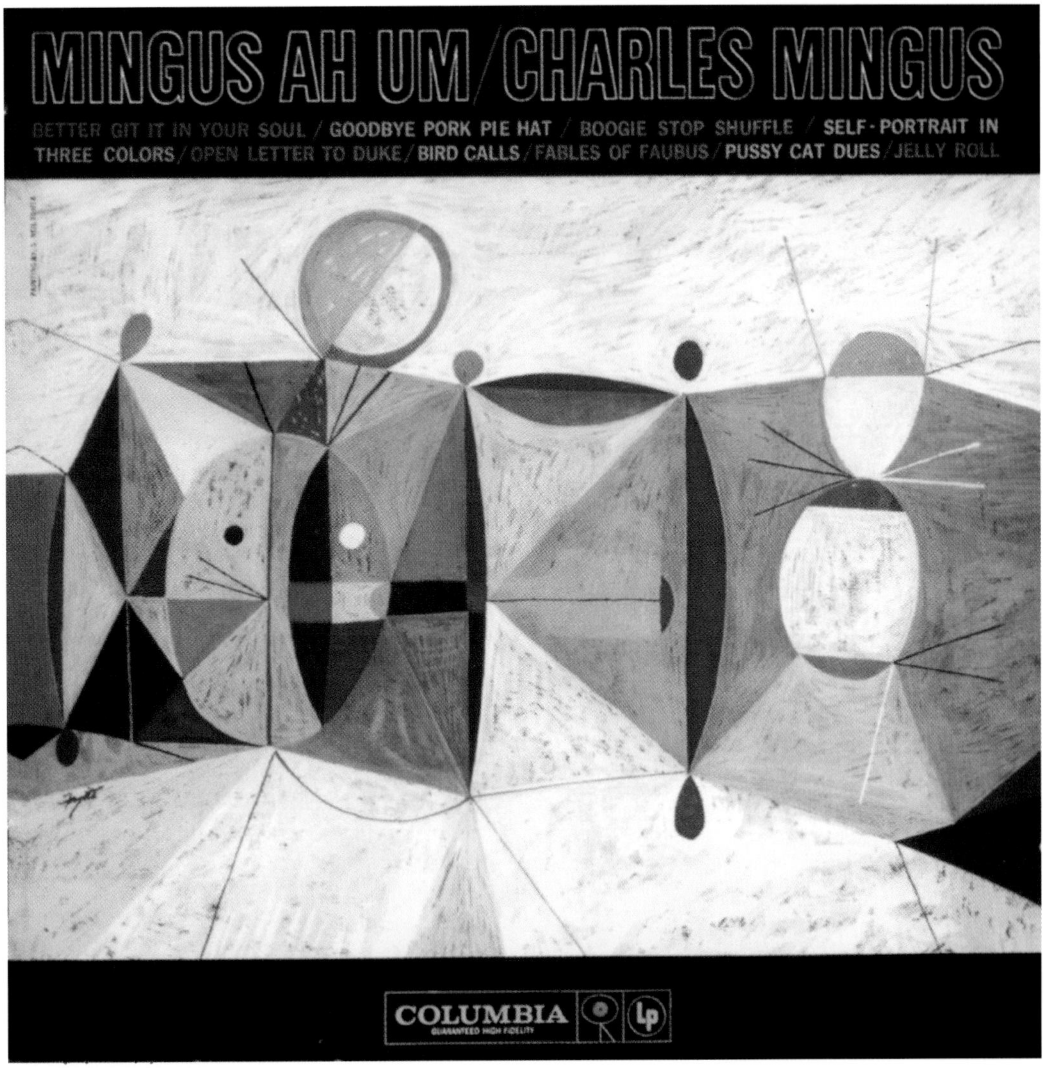

▲ **Mingus Ah Um /
Charles Mingus**
RELEASED 1959 | COLUMBIA / USA |
SLEEVE DESIGNED AND PAINTED BY
S. NEIL FUJITA | ALBUM PRODUCED
BY TEO MACERO

In the late 1950s, Jazz and modern art seemed to go together, particularly if the Jazz was modern and the art was abstract. This sleeve art is a painting by Neil Fujita, director of design and packaging at Columbia Records from 1954 to 1960, who painted similar sleeves for Miles Davis and Dave Brubeck. It was when there was still a debate over where the album title should be on a sleeve, and it was Fujita who first dictated that the type be placed in the top third of the cover to ease identification by record buyers. His paintings owe a lot to Paul Klee who was very popular at the time, and though very decorative they reflect the sound blocks of the music.

▼ This Is How I Feel About Jazz / Quincy Jones

RELEASED 1957 | ABC-PARAMOUNT | USA | SLEEVE DESIGN BY BOB CROZIER | PHOTOGRAPHY BY ALAN FONTAINE | ALBUM PRODUCED BY CREED TAYLOR

Bob Crozier's designs always had a clean modern feel to them, and also a relationship to the record that they housed. Here we have a first album by big-band arranger Quincy Jones, with Quincy himself looking smooth in front of a collage made from torn photographer's backdrop paper, created in the days before reliable photographic superimposition, and decades before Photoshop. The lettering is energetic and the sleeve has an upbeat, serious feel to it; very modern for 1957.

▼ Looking Ahead! / The Cecil Taylor Quartet

RELEASED 1959 | CONTEMPORARY RECORDS | USA | SLEEVE DESIGN BY GUIDI/TRI-ARTS | PHOTOGRAPHY BY DENNIS STOCK | ALBUM PRODUCED BY NAT HENTOFF

A calm-looking sleeve for one of the most controversial pianists of the time: drummers walked out mid-song; club owners threw him out after ten bars. The well composed cover shot uses strong colour contrast, almost as if it were a black-and-white photo, suggesting a power within. You would never suspect that this thoughtful looking man, with his serious spectacles, played music so radical that UK Jazz critic Benny Green questioned whether it was even music, let alone Jazz.

▶ Kenny Burrell / Kenny Burrell

RELEASED 1957 | BLUE NOTE | USA | SLEEVE DESIGN BY REID MILES | ARTWORK BY ANDY WARHOL | PRODUCED BY ALFRED LION

A solo guitar album with a design by Reid Miles executed by Andy Warhol, then working in New York as a commercial artist. This is early Warhol showing the influence of Ben Shahn, whose social realist art was popular in the 1950s – the foreshortening of the figure is a Shahn device. It has been suggested that the blotted line technique aped David Stone Martin, but Paul Klee is as likely an influence. Warhol designed for I Miller Shoes, and the drawing reflects fashion illustration more than anything else.

KENNY BURRELL BLUE NOTE 1543

RED MILES

Andy Warhol

1950s Rock 'n' Roll

On May 17, 1954, the Supreme Court declared that racial segregation in public schools violated the US Constitution, heralding the end of racial discrimination in America. Also that spring, an obscure doo-wop record called Sh-Boom by the Chords crossed over from the R 'n' B charts to top the Los Angeles Pop charts and become the first ever Rock 'n' Roll hit. It signalled a flood of black doo-wop and R 'n' B records making the Pop charts. Rock 'n' roll was here to stay. The original artists were black: Chuck Berry, Fats Domino, Bo Diddley, Little Richard, the Platters. Then in 1955 the film *Blackboard Jungle* was released, with a song by Bill Haley and His Comets over the opening credits. The kids had never heard anything like it, ripping cinemas to pieces as the establishment declared Rock 'n' Roll to be bad! Then there came another, even more potent, crossover.

In 1956 the young Elvis Presley left the Country-Rockabilly Sun label and cut Heartbreak Hotel for RCA, and from then on nothing could stop Rock 'n' Roll. It was dance music for the kids, the rhythm more important than the words – which caused everyone from Sinatra on down to dismiss it as a passing fad.

No other sleeves have been studied so intently, except possibly the Beatles', than those of the few proper Rock 'n' Roll albums of the 1950s. Their images burned into teenage consciousness: Elvis's iconic haircut and sneer, his gyrating hips on the eponymous *Elvis Presley* album, Little Richard's screaming mouth, sweat running down his face. And Gene Vincent, looking like a dressed-up juvenile delinquent.

Rock 'n' Roll had emerged from the South, of course, and the black, rollicking vulgarity of R 'n' B. In order to sell it to white folk, men like Johnny Otis and the doo-wop groups had to be presented as smart and unthreatening. So the doo-wop acts posed standing in line, fingerpopping, arranged shortest to the highest, the gloomy tall guy with the deep voice in the back, doing the handwave or synchronized kick. Only whites could show that Rock 'n' Roll was the music of rebellion, could reveal that the very phrase really meant sexual intercourse, but not many did. Mostly we had Buddy Holly peering through his specs, or the Crickets on *Chirpin' Crickets* forming a tableaux with their guitars. These were the innocent days of Rock 'n' Roll, or appeared to be on the few major label album sleeves released.

▶ **Elvis Presley / Elvis Presley**
RELEASED 1956 | RCA | USA | PHOTOGRAPHY BY WILLIAM "RED" ROBERTSON | ALBUM PRODUCED BY SAM PHILLIPS
One of the greatest Rock 'n' Roll sleeves of all time. Colonel Tom Parker hired the Robertson & Fresh commercial studio to photograph Elvis Presley's appearance on *The Andy Griffith Show*, held at Fort Homer Hesterly Armory in Tampa, Florida, on July 31, 1955. Elvis's name appeared at the bottom of the bill. Robertson took the photographs and his partner Harry Fresh did the darkroom work. The album credit to William "Popsie" Randolph refers to the pictures on the back. Presley's wild gyrations had struck fear into the hearts of the puritans and Robertson's original photograph was heavily cropped by RCA to make the image even more suggestive. Then they added the pink and green lettering, unlike anything RCA had ever done before. Designer Ray Lowry called his sleeve for The Clash's 1977 *London Calling* "a genuine homage to the original unknown, inspired genius who created Elvis Presley's first Rock 'n' Roll record", paying tribute to "the strange potency of the pink and green lettering and the sheer vibrancy of the Elvis picture".

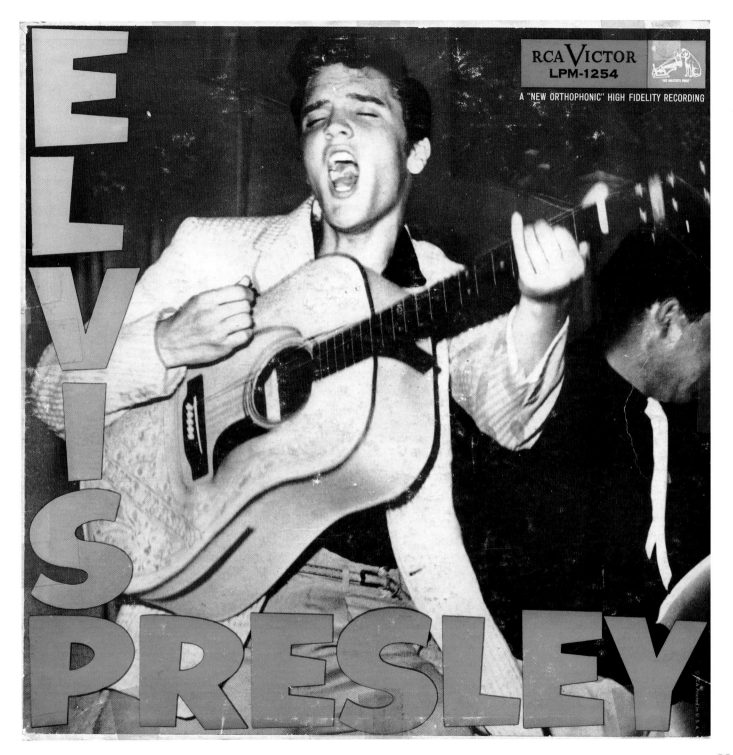

ELVIS PRESLEY

RCA VICTOR
LPM-1254
A "NEW ORTHOPHONIC" HIGH FIDELITY RECORDING

33

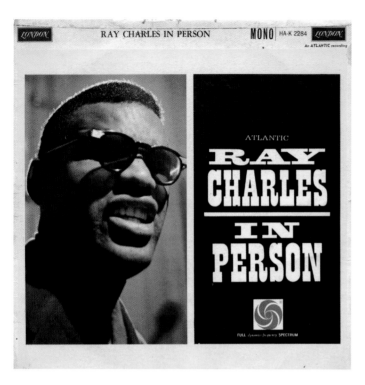

◀ Ray Charles in Person / Ray Charles

RELEASED 1959 | ATLANTIC | USA | PHOTOGRAPHY BY LEE FRIEDLANDER | ALBUM PRODUCED BY IVAN MILES | SUPERVISION BY ZENAS SEARS

An astonishing live recording of a concert from May 1959 when seven thousand people braved the rain at the Herndon Stadium in Atlanta, Georgia, and Ray Charles delivered one of the finest performances of his career. Fortunately the radio station WAOK captured it for posterity using a portable tape recorder and just one little microphone. Anyone hoping to have a "cool pad" in the early 1960s was required to have a copy of this sleeve as a "deck" for rolling up on. It's also good for keeping a record in. Just on the cusp of the 1960s, with typical period lettering, its dramatic picture shows Ray Charles looking young, energetic and soulful. Hipsters also admired the design of Ray's shades which were much copied. An unspeakably cool album from the Beatnik era which also straddled Soul/R 'n' B and Rock 'n' Roll.

◀ Here's Little Richard / Little Richard

RELEASED 1957 | SPECIALTY | USA | SLEEVE DESIGN BY THADD ROARK AND PAUL HARTLEY

Little Richard made his own demo record of Tutti Frutti and sent it to Specialty. It quickly became a hit and was followed by Long Tall Sally, Slippin' and Slidin', Rip It Up, Ready Teddy, All Around the World, and the title track from the movie *The Girl Can't Help It*. This was the album that gathered all the hits in one place, one of the greatest dance albums of all time. In the 1950s, albums were usually bought by middle-class adults, the only people who could afford them. *Here's Little Richard* was aimed entirely at the kids who bought the singles, with a sleeve as strong and direct as Richard's vocal style: the powerful unadorned black-and-white lettering and a live action shot rather than a posed portrait. This is Richard letting out one of his trademark squeals, pomp in place, sweat breaking out, energy personified.

Johnny Otis Rock 'n' Roll Hit Parade Volume One / Johnny Otis, His Orchestra and Entertainers

RELEASED 1957 | DIG | USA | ALBUM PRODUCED BY JOHNNY OTIS

A classic piece of 1950s Rock 'n' Roll design from Dig Records, with swinging hepcats playing up a storm, complete with two 'gators wailing on the horn and saxophone, and a cat and 'gator swinging from the crazy lettering that makes up Johnny's name. The King of Rock 'n' Roll wears a crown, even if he does look a little sinister in the photograph, with his "imperial" goatee that was copied by Frank Zappa, his number one fan. We are assured that this is a hi-fi recording and a list of the titles helps to clutter the front in case the potential buyer should not bother to turn the thing over. (Most of these were hits for other people.)

> This was one of the first records I bought. It wasn't until much later I discovered that the guitar Gene was holding had a large hole on the sound box, caused when Blue Caps drummer Dickie Harrell threw a cherry bomb during one of their live performances

DEREK HENDERSON, AUTHOR OF "GENE VINCENT, A COMPANION"

Gene Vincent Rocks! And the Blue Caps Roll / Gene Vincent and the Blue Caps

RELEASED 1958 | CAPITOL | USA | SLEEVE DESIGN BY CAPITOL ART DEPARTMENT | ALBUM PRODUCED BY KEN NELSON

Despite Be-Bop-A-Lula being a hit, by 1958 Gene Vincent was considered just another Elvis wannabe, at least in America. Two years later he'd be welcomed as a Rock 'n' Roll hero by the Teddy Boys and rockers of the UK who loved the hard-drinking, limping, leather-clad redneck as one of their own. For his first album, *Blue Jean Bop*, Vincent and his Blue Caps had worn clean, smart-looking shirts and obviously blue caps. For this, the unsuccessful second album, someone at Capitol decided to push the Elvis comparison as far as they could. There's a hint of the first Elvis album in the photo – taken at Capitol's Studio A by a staff photographer. Vincent's gaunt face, greasy quiff and intense, eyes-closed stance are somehow meaner and more threatening than the young Elvis's exuberant pose. That the photo is taken from underneath doesn't make it a "nicer" picture. Neither does the bizarre green shirt and matching cravat Vincent seems uneasy wearing. The title and graphics are perfectly placed and extremely modern. [JM]

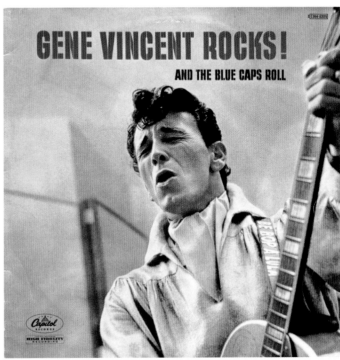

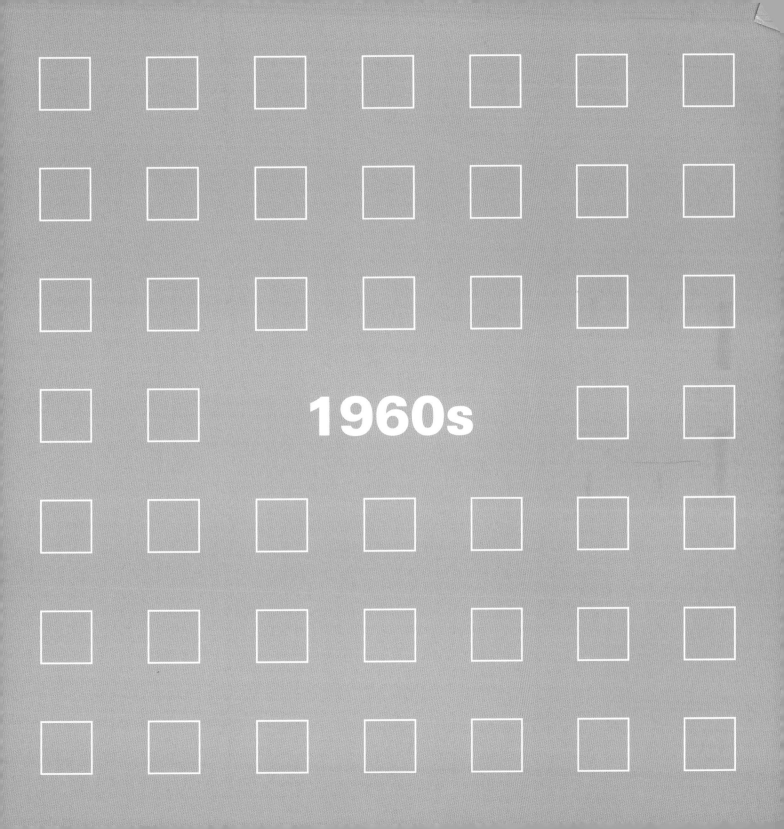

1960s

1960s Jazz

Ornette Coleman determined the major new trend in Jazz in the 1960s. His music was "the shape of Jazz to come", though many fellow musicians were wary of what he was doing. His album sleeves also made a link between his work and the wider art world, often as provocative as his playing. There were other new trends in the 1960s, from the "Third Stream" of the Modern Jazz Quartet to the bossa nova. John Coltrane revolutionized sax playing with his "sheets of sound", while Miles Davis tried all manner of experiments but always sounded lyrical.

George Russell's tonal organization, Cecil Taylor's deconstructed piano and Gill Evans's sound clusters all explored areas previously unknown. Some Jazz musicians were accommodating the requirements of symphony orchestras while, others were pushing the limits of the avant garde. It was a turbulent era, beginning at a time when mixed-race groups were still forbidden to perform in the American South.

In addition to playing NAACP benefits, Jazz composers such as Charles Mingus introduced political lyrics to their music, openly challenging the Southern racists – Fables of Faubus being a good example. The short-lived Kennedy era brought Jazz musicians to the White House and by mid-decade there were mixed-race Jazz festivals and the musicians could all stay in the same hotel. Even the avant garde had become more acceptable, and Cecil Taylor appeared on The Ed Sullivan Show.

Despite this, US Jazz musicians still found a deeper appreciation of their work in Europe, and made frequent transatlantic tours, some settling permanently. As a consequence, the 1960s also saw the development of European Jazz, often by musicians that had previously accompanied visiting Americans.

The 1960s was the second golden era of Jazz sleeve art; following on from Blue Note (which went from strength to strength in terms of its innovatory sleeve design) came the Impulse! label, with its generous gatefolds and stunning colour photography. And the tradition of albums utilizing expert sleeve notes continued, featuring a wealth of scholarship unmatched today. Jazz sleeves were still a genre separate from Rock or Pop, and were closer, if anything, to book design, such as the work of Roy Kuhlman for Grove Press, or film posters and opening credits. It was an exciting decade for both music and album cover design.

▶ **Free Jazz A Collective Improvisation by the Ornette Coleman Double Quartet / The Ornette Coleman Double Quartet**
RELEASED 1960 | ATLANTIC | USA | SLEEVE DESIGNED BY LORING EUTEMEY | ALBUM PRODUCED BY TOM DOWD | SUPERVISION BY NESUHI ERTEGUN
Literally a double quartet: two reeds, two trumpets, two basses, two drummers – that was the form of the piece. This is collective, free improvisation with sometimes all eight musicians improvising at the same time. The result is discordant, difficult and exhilarating. It was entirely appropriate to pair this complex exercise in free-form with Jackson Pollock's equally free-form work White Light which, though it dates to 1954, was associated in the public mind with daring experimentation and so gave an indication of what the album was about. The full painting is visible on the inner sleeve with just a tantalizing glimpse visible from the front through a die cut (which was invariably misaligned).

FREE JAZZ
A COLLECTIVE IMPROVISATION BY THE ORNETTE COLEMAN DOUBLE QUARTET

ATLANTIC 1364
FULL *dynamics-frequency* SPECTRUM

the
**ornette coleman
trio
at the
"golden circle"
stockholm**
volume two

THE FINEST IN JAZZ SINCE 1939
4225 BLUE NOTE

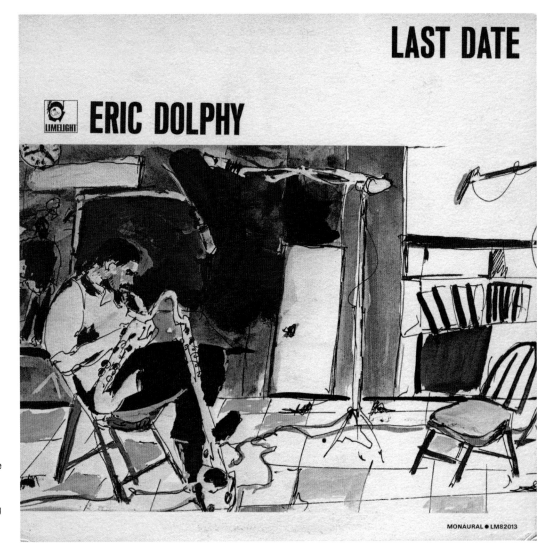

LAST DATE

ERIC DOLPHY

LIMELIGHT

MONAURAL ● LM82013

◄ **The Ornette Coleman Trio at the "Golden Circle" Stockholm Volume Two / The Ornette Coleman Trio**

RELEASED 1965 | BLUE NOTE | USA | SLEEVE DESIGNED BY REID MILES | PHOTOGRAPH BY FRANCIS WOLFF | ALBUM PRODUCED BY RUNE ANDREASSON

One of the most satisfying of Reid Miles's Blue Note designs. The group photograph is perfectly composed and the image and text are in perfect harmony with each other. The colours of the lettering are subtle and clearly just as Miles wanted them. "I've always been very definitive," he once said. "I see things in black-and-white terms. As far as I'm concerned, there are no shades of grey." The inclusion in the trio of bassist David Izenson (left in the photo) peering away from Coleman in the centre who, as the leader, stares at the camera while drummer Charlie Moffett peers the other way, is the physical embodiment of the black-and-white definition of the music. Unlike the other two musicians, Izenson never achieved a great level of fame – a point made in the sleeve notes – and this is his finest moment. It is one of Coleman's too.

▲ **Last Date / Eric Dolphy**

RELEASED 1964 | LIMELIGHT | USA | SLEEVE DESIGNED BY THE COMMITTEE: Z. JASTRZEBSKI, DESMOND STROBEL AND JAMES SCHUBERT | ILLUSTRATED BY Z. JASTRZEBSKI

Recorded on June 2, 1964 in Hilversum, Holland, the last recording of Dolphy before his fatal heart attack in Berlin 27 days later. The album ends with him saying: "When you hear music, after it's over, it's gone in the air. You can never capture it again." This is a classic Limelight label sleeve, an ink sketch of Dolphy in the recording studio, the artist making the most of the sinuous shapes of the bass clarinet and alto saxophone, the musician framed by the microphone stands and booms. Note how the sax and clarinet bleed into Dolphy and the floor, the muted but distinct colours and clashing lines perfectly reflecting his music.

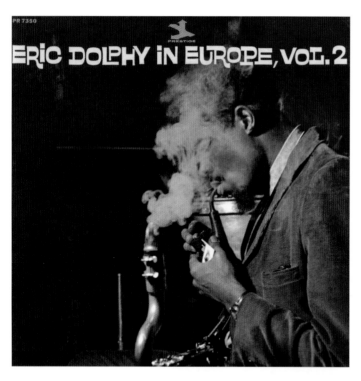

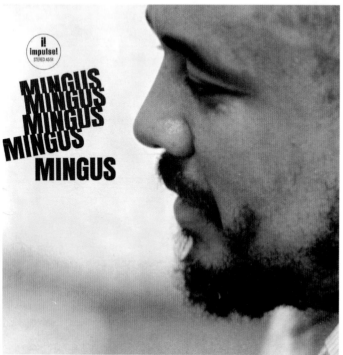

◀ In Europe Vol. 2 / Eric Dolphy

RELEASED 1965 | PRESTIGE | USA | SLEEVE DESIGNED BY DON SCHLITTEN | PHOTOGRAPH BY BURT GOLDBLATT | A LIVE PERFORMANCE RECORDED IN THE LECTURE HALL OF THE COPENHAGEN STUDENTS ASSOCIATION IN SEPTEMBER 1961 | NO PRODUCER CREDITED

Goldblatt's image of Dolphy makes several visual jokes: the pipe is shaped like an alto sax, looking as if he's playing a tiny horn; and the smoke he exhales billows out just enough to look as if it's coming from the instrument slung around his neck. Like many photographers, Goldblatt went for Dolphy's profile, catching him in a rare moment of reflection which contrasts with the excited yellow 1960s lettering dancing across the top of the sleeve.

◀ Mingus Mingus Mingus Mingus Mingus / Charles Mingus

RELEASED 1963 | IMPULSE! | USA | SLEEVE DESIGNED BY JOE LEBOW | PHOTOGRAPH BY JOE ALPER | ALBUM PRODUCED BY BOB THIELE

Charles Mingus could be a difficult character but Joe Alper's photograph shows a gentle, relaxed man; the only word to describe the look on his face would be tender. An over-life-size detail of a profile balances against a block of typography, one each side of the square. It's tempting to speculate that the number of times Mingus's name is repeated in the title was determined by the weight of the lettering on the page. It is obviously an early 1960s design, wide open, lots of space, adventurous and daring: a precursor of what was to come.

▶ At The Café Montmartre / Cecil Taylor

RELEASED 1963 | DEBUT/FONTANA | USA | SLEEVE DESIGNED BY FONTANA ART DEPARTMENT | PHOTOGRAPH BY LENNART STEEN | ALBUM PRODUCED BY ANDERS STEFANSEN

Steen's moody shot of Cecil Taylor evokes the atmosphere of late-night Jazz clubs, cigarette smoke, strong drinks, cool Jazz. This particular Café Montmartre was in Copenhagen, where the Cecil Taylor Trio (Jimmy Lyons on alto, Arthur Murray drums) had an extended residency. The thoughtful, contemplative image of Taylor contrasts strongly with the explosive violence of his piano playing. The typography is dominant, straightforward, less consciously artistic than on Blue Note albums but still makes a strong design statement. This, combined with the brooding portrait, manages to give the listener a pretty idea of the type of music contained within. An archetypal early 1960s Jazz sleeve.

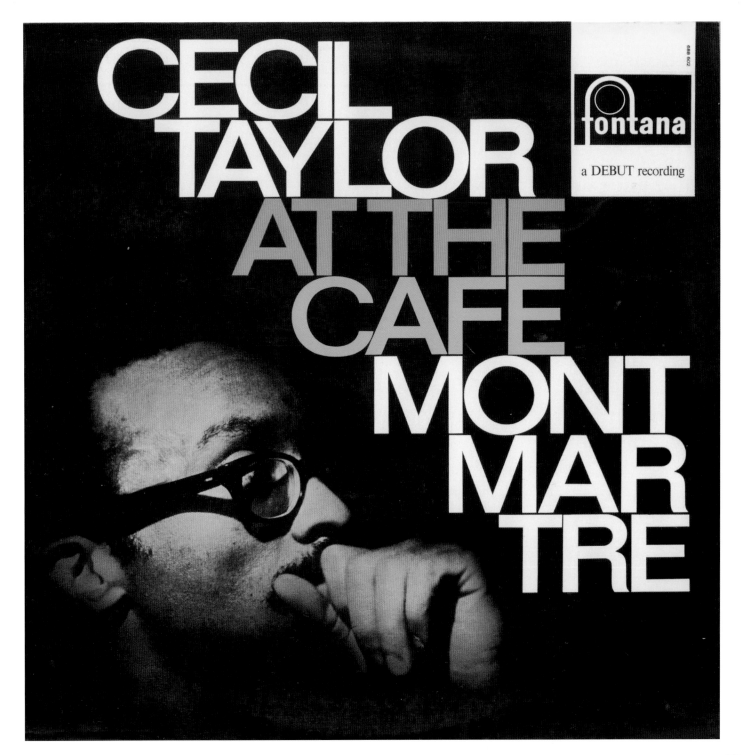

CECIL
TAYLOR
AT THE
CAFE
MONT
MAR
TRE

fontana

a DEBUT recording

688 602

into
the hot
the
gil evans
orchestra

impulse!
MONO A-9

**◀ Into the Hot /
The Gil Evans Orchestra**
RELEASED 1961 | IMPULSE! | USA | SLEEVE | DESIGNED BY ROBERT FLYNN | VICEROY | PHOTOGRAPH BY ARNOLD NEWMAN | ALBUM PRODUCED BY CREED TAYLOR
Legend has it that Gil Evans found himself with booked studio time and no project to record so he turned the sessions over to Cecil Taylor and John Carisi who each recorded three tracks. Curiously, even though Gil Evans had nothing to do with the record, his photograph is on the sleeve and on the fold-out, with no mention of Cecil Taylor or John Carisi except in the detailed sleeve notes by Nat Hentoff. Taking the sleeve as a separate artifact, this is an exceptionally clean and crisp Impulse! design. The subtle difference in colour between the title's lettering and that of the act, and the extreme composition, with Evans's musical score balancing the Impulse! logo and the vast empty space of the middle ground, was daring for its time. The title is a parody of Evans's own *Out of the Cool* and the deep red backdrop is no doubt about Evans finally going to hell.

▲ Monk / Thelonius Monk
RELEASED 1965 | COLUMBIA RECORDS | USA | SLEEVE PHOTOGRAPH BY W. EUGENE SMITH | PRODUCED BY TEO MACERO
Monk had a reputation as a mysterious, difficult figure, liable to get up and walk around his piano in the middle of a piece, not replying when spoken to, and completely wrapped up in his own music. Not for nothing was his middle name "Sphere", the music of the spheres was forever playing in his head and *Life* photographer Eugene Smith's shot shows him in just such a reflective mood. Smith studied subjects in painstaking detail before shooting a single frame, and this portrait, with its stage lighting combined with the stark white lettering on the black ground, gives us a powerful insight into the creative genius that was Monk.

▼ Coleman Hawkins Swing! / Coleman Hawkins

RELEASED 1964 | FONTANA | UK | SLEEVE DESIGN BY THE PHILIPS RECORDS DESIGN DEPT | PHOTOGRAPH BY UNKNOWN | ALBUM PRODUCED BY VARIOUS

In 1961 Dutch music and electrical company Philips launched a new label designed to re-release some of its back catalogue in a cheap but "hip" format. This album contains fourteen recordings made by the tenor giant in the 1930s but the cover doesn't betray the fact that the records' contents are anything but contemporary. The lithe, denim-clad girl dancing to the Hawk's sound looks as if she's dancing on a podium at a disco. The jaunty placement of the record's title references the beginning of the "Swinging" scene that was then developing. Also in the Popular Jazz Series was *Cookin' with Zoot Sims* and its awful cover has a girl wearing a chef's hat and jeans, bending over holding a frying pan. [JM]

▼ Girl Talk / Exclusively for My Friends / Oscar Peterson Trio

RELEASED 1968 | MPS RECORDS | GERMANY | SLEEVE DESIGN BY HANS B. PFITZER | PHOTOGRAPH BY SEPP WERKMEISTER | ALBUM PRODUCED BY HANS GEORG BRUNNER-SCHWER

A beautifully composed shot of a little girl playing with balloons, is hardly usual for a Jazz album, but importantly dates from 1968 when the ghetto was exploding. Contrast it with *Things Fall Apart* by The Roots (page 213) and the girl fleeing the cops during the 1965 Watts riots. This world view focusses on innocence and beauty: the philosophy of the 1960s before things got nasty.

▶ The Cat Walk / Donald Byrd

RELEASED 1961 | BLUE NOTE | USA | DESIGNED BY REID MILES | PHOTOGRAPH BY FRANCIS WOLFF | ALBUM PRODUCED BY RUDY VAN GELDER

A Blue Note sleeve where you have to see the 12-inch original to get the full impact. Typography is carefully placed, like a piece of concrete poetry, against the graphic elements of the Jaguar grill; the car headlights echoing Byrd's own head in the photo. The red tone over the sleeve and the high contrast photograph make for a strong image. The Jaguar XK150 was a symbol of sophistication and smooth power, and the message of the sleeve is simple: Jazz equals class.

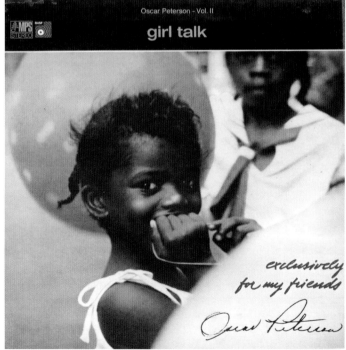

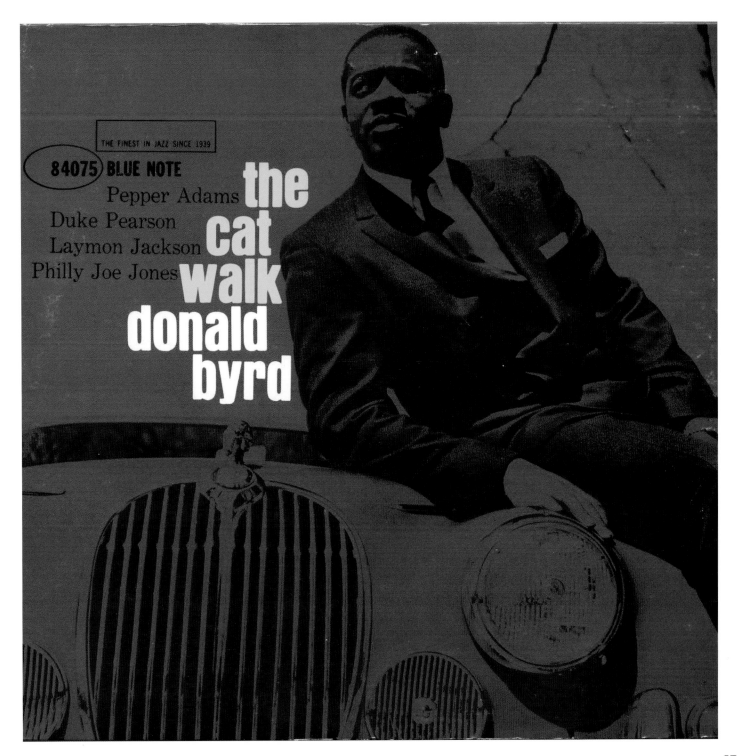

THE FINEST IN JAZZ SINCE 1939

84075 BLUE NOTE

Pepper Adams
Duke Pearson
Laymon Jackson
Philly Joe Jones

the cat walk

donald byrd

▶ **Oh Yeah / Charles Mingus**
RELEASED 1962 | ATLANTIC
RECORDS | USA | SLEEVE DESIGN
LORING EUTEMEY | ALBUM
PRODUCED BY NESUHI ERTEGUN
Loring Eutemey, co-director of design at Atlantic Records from the late 1950s until 1963, and after that head of design until the mid-1970s, has something of a cult following for his off-the-wall interpretations of song titles. Here he illustrates Oh Lord Don't Let Them Drop that Atomic Bomb on Me with an ordinary Portobello mushroom; Eat That Chicken provides an excuse for an old text book or catalogue illustration of a fine-looking hen; Passions of a Man is illustrated by a pink rectangle with an red heart superimposed. The whole thing is clean, funny, and years before the invention of Clip Art. Eutemey always maintained that his job was to provide Jazz and R 'n' B musicians with the "dignity and gravitas usually given to classical musicians". As well as being distinctive, this cover also gives Mingus's heavyweight subject matter a little levity.

▲ **Cannonball & Coltrane /**
Cannonball Adderley and
John Coltrane
RELEASED 1965 | MERCURY
INTERNATIONAL | UK | SLEEVE
DESIGNER UNKNOWN | ALBUM
PRODUCED BY JACK TRACY
A 1965 reissue of a 1959 album, showing how Jazz was being repackaged for a new generation. Gone are the clean Reid Miles compositions, in come a vaguely psychedelic design – presaging the overtly acid-influenced style two years later when LSD use became widespread. What is it? It looks like a flower or some natural object, but is more likely to be a solarized photo of the bell of a sax; Jazz sleeve designers usually stick close to their subject matter. The mysterious dark centre of the instrument is colour-switched into a glorious explosion of colour, just what was about to happen to the 1960s generation by the time the decade was over.

stereo SH-K 8007

MINGUS OH YEAH

LONDON ATLANTIC

OH LORD DON'T LET THEM DROP THAT ATOMIC BOMB ON ME

ECCLUSIASTICS

HOG CALLIN' BLUES   WHAM BAM THANK YOU MA'AM

PASSIONS OF A MAN   EAT THAT CHICKEN   DEVIL WOMAN

1960s The Beatles

In part because of their great fame, but also because their sleeves were genuinely innovative, the Beatles' cover art was hugely influential. There is not a Beatles sleeve that has not been copied, parodied or referenced in some way. Even The Beatles themselves did it, parodying their first album *Please, Please Me* on the sleeve of the "Blue album", *The Beatles 1967–1970*, by getting Iain Macmillan to reshoot their full 1969 hirsute selves in the same poses and positions. By the time EMI left Manchester Square the staircase the group had posed on had become so revered as a Rock artifact that they took it with them, reinstalling it at their new headquarters.

With The Beatles was already a marked departure from usual Pop sleeves, with the unsmiling quartet in monochrome, to the dismay of EMI's marketing folk. *Revolver* was even more of a departure: it dispensed with the usual glamour shot, replacing it with a collage and line-drawings by their Hamburg friend Klaus Voorman.

The *Sgt Pepper* album was supposed to provide fun for all the family, not just the hippies who understood the drug references. The album came complete with an inner sleeve of The Beatles beaming "good love vibes" at the listener and a card insert which included a false moustache and a cut-out drum front. *Sgt Pepper* was the first album to print the lyrics on the sleeve, enraging the sheet music publishers by depriving them of thousands of sales but truly providing something for everyone who bought it. The first band to parody it was the Mothers of Invention with *We're Only in It for the Money* but soon there were dozens, then hundreds.

The minimalist "white album" shocked everyone, with people muttering darkly about Yoko Ono's influence. "Most people, among them Yoko, think it was Yoko's idea," said Richard Hamilton. "But my contact with the project was only through Paul." *The Beatles* came full of goodies, including a large fold-out fine-art collage by Richard Hamilton and a set of four portrait shots by Richard Avedon (suitable for framing) for the people expecting to see the Fab Four on the sleeve. With the album you got everything: full colour and minimalism. It was hard to beat, but in terms of influence *Abbey Road* was the most copied of all – even more parodied than *Sgt Pepper*. The Beatles' sleeves haven't aged; true Rock icons, they are constantly referenced by each generation of designers returning to the source.

▶ **As The Beatles broke new ground with each new album, they also pushed the boundaries of album cover art**

JAMES HENKE, ROCK AND ROLL HALL OF FAME

▶ **With The Beatles / The Beatles**
RELEASED 1963 | PARLOPHONE | UK | SLEEVE DESIGNED BY ROBERT FREEMAN | ALBUM PRODUCED BY GEORGE MARTIN
Freeman shot the photo in the Palace Court Hotel, Bournemouth. The Beatles, fed up with their jolly "mop top" image, showed him pictures by the Hamburg photographer Astrid Kirchherr, saying they wanted something similar. They sat in front of dark maroon curtains in polo-necked sweaters, the windows letting in bright sunlight. "He got this very moody picture which people think he must have worked at for ever and ever in great technical detail, but it was an hour," McCartney recalled. An EMI executive later said: "Why are they looking so grim? We want happy Beatles for happy fans."

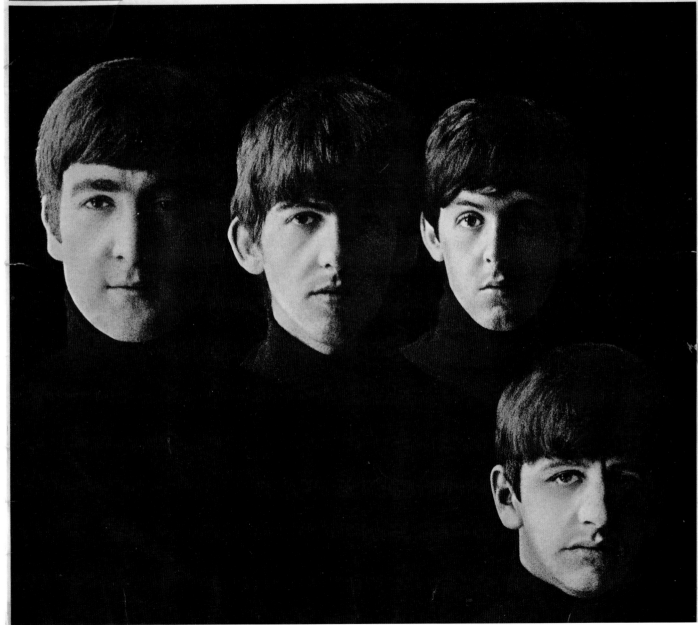

◄ Rubber Soul / The Beatles

RELEASED 1965 | PARLOPHONE | UK | PHOTOGRAPH BY ROBERT FREEMAN | ALBUM PRODUCED BY GEORGE MARTIN

The title was a typical Beatles pun. "That was Paul's title," said John Lennon. "It was like 'Yer Blues', I suppose, meaning English Soul. Just a pun." The photo was taken by Robert Freeman at Kenwood, Lennon's house in Weybridge. "The distorted effect in the photo was a reflection of the changing shape of their lives," said Freeman. The image, chosen by The Beatles from his contacts, was stretched by rephotographing a print at an angle. The lettering, an early U.K. example of blobby psychedelic, was influenced by the work of Alan Aldridge who later did *The Beatles Illustrated Lyrics*.

◄ Abbey Road / The Beatles

RELEASED 1969 | APPLE RECORDS | UK | SLEEVE DESIGNED BY PAUL MCCARTNEY | PHOTOGRAPH BY IAIN MACMILLAN | ALBUM PRODUCED BY GEORGE MARTIN

On August 8, 1969, Iain Macmillan took the famous photograph of the four Beatles strolling across the zebra crossing outside EMI's Abbey Road studios where virtually all of their recordings were made. Like *Sgt Pepper* it was based on a pencil sketch by Paul McCartney. The sleeve has been much parodied, including one sleeve by McCartney himself on *Paul Is Live* in 1993. Beatles fans and London tourists love to have their picture taken crossing Abbey Road and it has become one of the London sights, like Big Ben and Buckingham Palace.

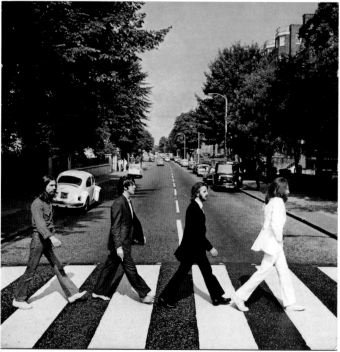

▶ The Beatles / The Beatles

RELEASED 1968 | APPLE RECORDS | UK | SLEEVE DESIGNED BY RICHARD HAMILTON | ALBUM PRODUCED BY GEORGE MARTIN

Paul McCartney worked with Richard Hamilton on the sleeve. "Since *Sgt Pepper* was so over the top," said Hamilton, "I explained: 'I would be inclined to do a very prissy thing, almost like a limited edition.' He [Paul] didn't discourage me so I went on to propose a plain white album." "So now he was saying, 'Let's call it "The Beatles" and have it white, really white,'" recalled McCartney, "and I was saying, 'Well, I dunno. It's a great concept, but we are releasing an album, here … Maybe if we emboss the word "Beatles" out of the white, that'll be good. We'll get a shadow from the embossing but it's white on white, it's still white.'" "But I still wanted something on the white," said Hamilton. "I suggested that they might number each copy, to create the ironic situation of a numbered edition of something like five million copies." "John got number one because he shouted loudest," remembered Paul. "He said: 'Baggsy number one!'"

The BEATLES

Nº 0538180

1960s Pop

After a couple of fairly bland years of Brill Building-produced hits, in 1964 Tin Pan Alley was delivered a blow by The Beatles from which it never recovered. The British Invasion of America brought everyone from Chad and Jeremy and Peter and Gordon to The Yardbirds, The Hollies, John Mayall, The Rolling Stones, Them, Jeff Beck, Manfred Mann, The Kinks, The Dave Clark Five, Herman's Hermits, Cat Stevens, The Searchers, The Zombies, Wayne Fontana and the Mindbenders, Spencer Davis, Gerry and the Pacemakers, Freddie and the Dreamers, Traffic, Tom Jones, The Who, Donovan, The Animals – and hundreds more – to the States, and to the American charts, transforming US Pop music for ever.

The Americans fought back with The Monkees and Sonny and Cher, but the British quickly took over the charts so that by 1965 almost half the records in the Top 20 were British. Of course there were some areas the Brits couldn't reach: Phil Spector's wall of sound was impenetrable and no Brit would even attempt a surfin' song, but as far as Pop went, any US band wanting to play the clubs on Sunset Strip had to grow their hair long and practise their English accent in order to get hired.

Album sleeves, meanwhile, had undergone a change. The Rolling Stones proved you didn't need the name of the band on the front, so big portraits or group shots were the norm. Until 1967 and The Beatles' *Sgt Pepper* sleeve, EMI still wouldn't spend more than £40 on album artwork, preferring a straightforward photograph of the artist. Decca was the same, but stumped up when The Rolling Stones wanted to go one better than The Beatles with their 3-D *Satanic Majesties* sleeve. Unfortunately they used the same photographer, Michael Cooper, so they were accused of copying The Beatles rather than outwitting them. The Scott Walker and Dusty Springfield sleeves here are rather better than most, and the Astrud Gilberto sleeve is a classic, but all typical examples of the time. The art departments didn't know whether they were aiming at the kids or a family audience.

Early in the decade, 1950s design ideas still dominated, but by the closing years rock had spawned psychedelia, which changed record sleeves as much as it did the minds of the bands. It could be said that album sleeves never recovered before CDs came along and made the big picture outdated.

▶ **I Haven't Got Anything Better To Do /
Astrud Gilberto**
RELEASED 1969 | VERVE | USA | ART DIRECTION BY DAVID E. KRIEGER | PHOTOGRAPH BY JOEL BRODSKY | ALBUM PRODUCED BY BROOKS ARTHUR

Brazilian Astrud Gilberto was famed as The Girl from Ipanema after adding vocals to the song written by her husband João Gilberto and she performed with Stan Getz in 1964. Yet in 1969 that was still her only big hit single and she was becoming better known as a Jazz singer. This is probably why she and Verve (a big Jazz label) felt comfortable releasing this album, with its stripped-down cover focusing only on Gilberto's beautiful face, lit by a single tear. Even the long title doesn't intrude on the bare beauty of the photograph, taken by Joel Brodsky. As bewitching as the cover, the music features bossa nova-tinged versions of Pop songs by great writers of the day, such as Harry Nilsson and Bacharach and David, as well as a moody version of In the Wee Small Hours of the Morning. The reverb-soaked title ballad with plucked guitar driven along by strings and a bossa nova rhythm is a perfect late 1960s Pop ballad, a mini opera in one act. [JM]

I Haven't Got Anything Better To Do/Astrud Gilberto

Verve

Metro-Goldwyn-Mayer Inc.

amen

J. LITTLETON CHANTE O. VERCRUYSSE

◀ Amen / John Littleton

RELEASED 1969 | EDITIONS STUDIO
SM | FRANCE | SLEEVE DESIGN
UNKNOWN | ALBUM PRODUCED
BY FRANCIS LE MAGUER

For this, the first of four such
themed albums, Louisiana-born
Littleton (who lived in France and
sang in French) recorded a series
of Spirituals written by a French
woman, Odette Vercruysse.
There's a female backing choir, a
small church organ and what
sounds like a three-piece band
featuring guitar, drums and bass.
Like the cover, everything is
perfectly placed. This is arguably
one of the greatest album sleeves
of all time. The three simple
ingredients are placed just so –
the title positioned in lower case
at bottom left, the singer in a
white suit next to a mike stand,
hands clasped as if in prayer as a
single spotlight shines out and
not on him. Littleton is not the
star of this album. God is. [JM]

▲ The Original / Ink Spots

RELEASED 1964 | ALLEGRO | UK |
SLEEVE DESIGN DAVID OR LAUREL |
ALBUM PRODUCED BY VARIOUS

By the time of this 1964 release
The Beatles had changed popular
music for ever and The Ink Spots
were pure nostalgia. The tracks
here are from various sessions
from the 1940s and early 1950s,
all enormous hits. In the mid-
1960s the vocal group was totally
out of fashion, one reason why
this sleeve is so remarkable.
While most of the hand-drawn
symbols are obvious, the noose
for You Always Hurt the One You
Love and the flower losing petals
for For Ever Now are pure
genius. Allegro, a cheap reissue
label, used generic sleeves with
the reverse listing other available
titles, which meant the track titles
had to be pasted on the front.
Despite this the cover artist (the
signature is not clear) succeeded
in creating a unique sleeve. [JM]

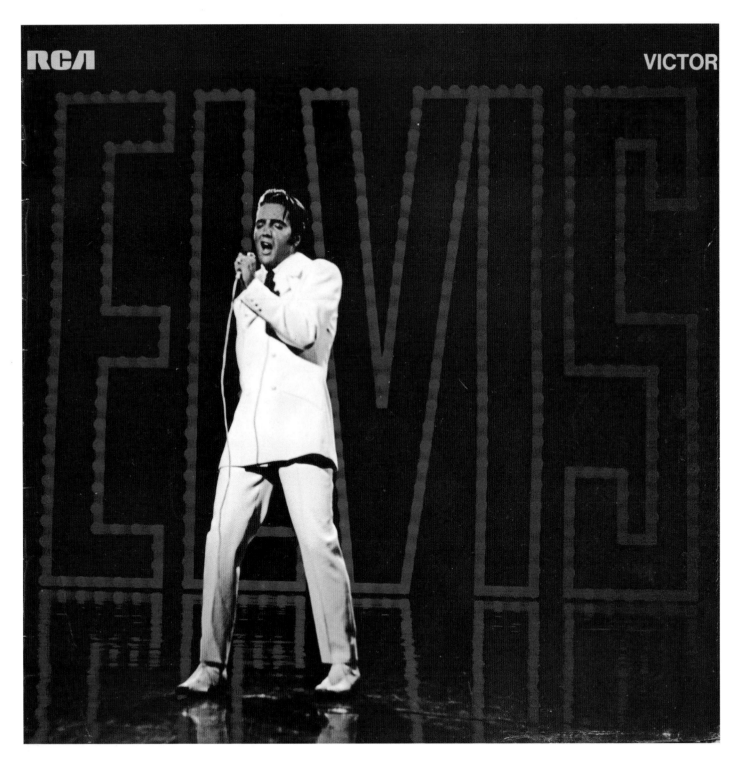

◀ Elvis NBC-TV Special / Elvis Presley

RELEASED 1968 | RCA VICTOR | US | ART DIRECTION GENE MCAVOY | ALBUM PRODUCED BY BONES HOWE

Elvis's 1968 *NBC-TV Special* brought the former King of Rock 'n' Roll a much needed credibility. For most of the 1960s he had released forgettable Pop hits and formulaic movies, but the "comeback" TV show was a huge success. For part of the show Elvis wore the white suit on this cover. With ELVIS spelled out in red bulbs ten feet high behind him, eyes closed, hair flopping, the Elvis on this cover could be the same age as the one on his debut release (see page 33). [JM]

▼ The Little Richard Story / Little Richard

RELEASED 1964 | JOY SPECIAL | UK | SLEEVE DESIGN BY BRIAN NICHOLLS | ALBUM PRODUCED BY LITTLE RICHARD

In 1964 Little Richard re-recorded all of his 1950s hits for the Vee-Jay label in the United States. He did so because he didn't own any of his original recordings, and after a four-year retirement from Rock 'n' Roll (1958–62), during which time he recorded only Gospel songs and became a preacher, he wanted to relive some of the glory days (and earn some money). The recordings (on which camp Little Richard emulator Esquerita played piano) were issued on various labels around the world, including five in the UK. The best-looking of the packages was definitely this one. Using photographs taken at a live TV performance, with Little Richard wearing a distinctly non-secular outfit twinned with more make-up than Mae West and hair just as high, the cover image is pure, unadulterated Little Richard – all sweat, swagger and sex. Twenty years later Prince would attempt the same look with almost as much effect, but until then even James Brown wouldn't dare to look so outrageous on an album sleeve. [JM]

▼ Reach Out / Burt Bacharach

RELEASED 1967 | A&M RECORDS | USA | SLEEVE DESIGN BY PETER WORF GRAPHICS | PHOTOGRAPHY BY JIM MCCRORY | ALBUM PRODUCED BY BURT BACHARACH

This Pop album looks more like a Jazz record with its elegant use of typography as a compositional element. It was necessary to include the track listing on the front cover, as Bert Bacharach was not yet well known, though the songs were. He wrote and arranged the music, conducted the orchestra, played piano, and even sang on one track. The collage of colour film frames is well done, making an altogether attractive package.

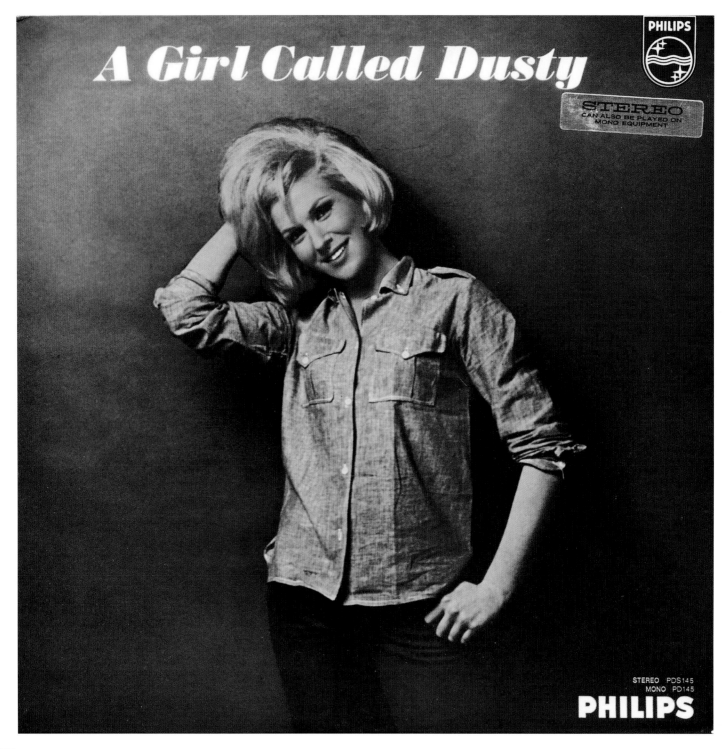

A Girl Called Dusty

PHILIPS

STEREO
CAN ALSO BE PLAYED ON
MONO EQUIPMENT

STEREO PDS145
MONO PD145

PHILIPS

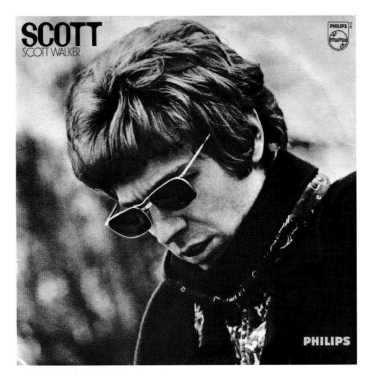

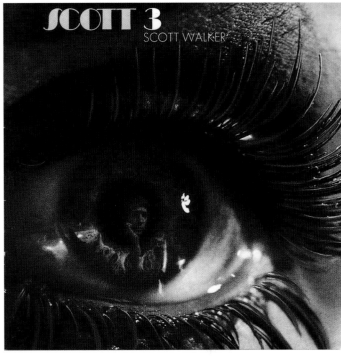

◄ A Girl Called Dusty / Dusty Springfield

RELEASED 1964 | PHILIPS | UK | SLEEVE DESIGN BY DUSTY SPRINGFIELD | PHOTOGRAPHY BY UNKNOWN | ALBUM PRODUCED BY IVOR RAYMONDE

Dusty's first solo album included songs that "run the whole gamut of 'Pop' music today", as the sleeve notes state. The image was more original, launching the much copied look of casual work shirt and jeans, combined with heavy eye-make-up, breaking the tradition of girl singers wearing frilly dresses. It was surprisingly modern for a time when the wearing of a trouser suit by a woman would cause shrieks of disbelief from passers-by.

▲ Scott / Scott Walker

RELEASED 1967 | PHILIPS | UK | SLEEVE DESIGN BY LINDA GLOVER | PHOTOGRAPHY BY CHRIS WALTER | ALBUM PRODUCED BY JOHN FRANZ

After considerable Pop success with the Walker Brothers in the UK, American Scott Engel decided to keep the Walker surname and launch a solo career in Britain. He chose to do so with this, his debut solo LP. Despite reaching Number Three in the UK charts, it was not what his legion of (mostly female) teenage fans expected. The cover, with its stark black-and-white photo of the singer wearing dark glasses yet wrapped up against a bleak English winter, is a fair reflection of the songs contained within. Alongside cover versions of his beloved Jacques Brel (including Amsterdam, later covered by Walker fan David Bowie) are similar string-laden hymns to heartache. The multi-coloured Pop of the mid-1960s was making way for music of an altogether darker hue.

▲ Scott 3 / Scott Walker

RELEASED 1969 | PHILIPS | UK | SLEEVE DESIGN BY LINDA GLOVER | PHOTOGRAPHY BY JOHN KELLY | ALBUM PRODUCED BY JOHN FRANZ

Neither of Scott's first two solo albums had shown any kind of eye contact, but this is all eye contact. Here we have Scott face-on, in colour, looking at the camera. However, he is reflected into the camera by a model's eye, so closely photographed that on looking at it for more than ten seconds the viewer loses all idea of what it is. It could be a fantastic insect or a creature from another planet. Much like the music, with nicely orchestrated ballads turning out to be dark, unsettling sound poems. [JM]

1960s **Rock**

Musicianship spread in the 1960s Rock scene, as speed of playing, knowledge of obscure chords, the ability to play complex time signatures and (in some cases at least) the ability to read music, all assumed an increasing importance. And with the use of mind-expanding drugs, the lyrics began to take a surrealistic turn, though Bob Dylan's amphetamine-inspired words are probably further out than anything LSD ever inspired. Not all bands took drugs, though: Frank Zappa's Mothers of Invention, for instance, did not. Freaky as he looked, he was straight as could be and insisted the band was too.

Zappa's lyrics and music were part of a carefully planned programme to subvert the youth of America and wise them up to the lies and hypocrisy of their government. His was definitely Rock music. The Doors, who used to back the Mothers on the Strip, had a more dramatic, theatrical approach, but one that still had a subversive political message.

But most of the bands playing Rock in this decade had one thing in common: they released few, if any, singles. The length of solos and the complex structure of much Rock music meant it could not be contained in the three to four minutes of a single and determined by the orders of commercial radio. You could put seven minutes on there but radio stations wouldn't play it. Bands such as Pink Floyd (after a couple of failed attempts at singles chart domination), and later Led Zeppelin, had a no-singles policy, which set them apart from many of their Pop contemporaries.

Out of 1960s Rock came an acceptance that at least one strand of Pop music was on its way to becoming an art form. Just as opera, photography and the cinema had begun life as popular entertainment, Rock was beginning to take itself seriously, studying its roots in Blues, R 'n' B, Gospel and Country music. Unearthing old Blues records and sometimes finding that the performers were still living, making a distinction between purely commercial Pop and music which it was hoped would put across a political message, or be an artistic expression in itself – "sculptures made out of air" as Zappa once described his guitar solos – or a Dionysian rebel call to arms: to sex, drugs, Rock 'n' Roll and fucking in the streets. Naturally the artwork chosen to adorn the albums of Rock musicians had to reflect the new-found seriousness, artistic intention and political message. Then again, the sleeves could also look like a joke.

▶ **Let It Bleed / The Rolling Stones**
RELEASED 1969 | DECCA | UK | SLEEVE DESIGN BY ROBERT BROWNJOHN | ALBUM PRODUCED BY JIMMY MILLER
This album was originally to be called *Automatic Changer*, which would have made the cover concept more intelligible since it is literally based on an auto-change record player. The famous cake was made by celebrity TV chef Delia Smith who was then working as a freelance food stylist for photographer Don McAllester. Her instructions from the album designer Robert Brownjohn were to produce a cake as gaudy and over the top as possible. Easy to do as the sleeve budget was £1,000. The last-minute name change was easily achieved by adding new lettering to the film can and the record. The same cake is smashed to pieces on the reverse of the sleeve. Regarded by many Stones fans as their best ever album.

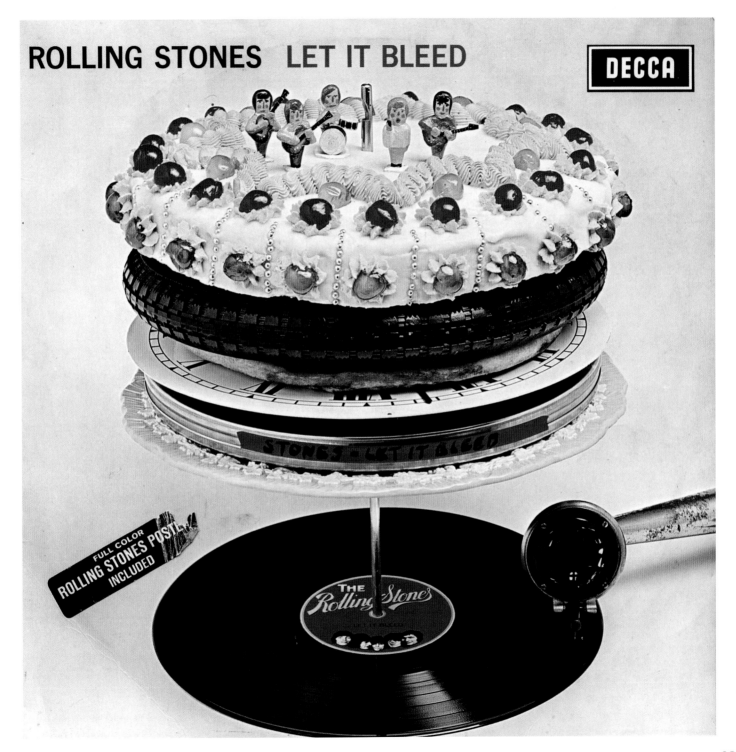

ROLLING STONES   LET IT BLEED

DECCA

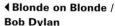
featuring I WANT YOU and RAINY DAY WOMEN Nos.12 & 35

◀ Blonde on Blonde / Bob Dylan

RELEASED 1966 | COLUMBIA | USA | PHOTOGRAPHY BY JERRY SCHATZBERG | ALBUM PRODUCED BY BOB JOHNSTON

The famous blurred photograph by Jerry Schatzberg sums up both the album and the image problem Dylan was having at the time. The record was made in Columbia's Nashville studios, but despite the presence of many well-known Country players on the record, *Blonde on Blonde* contains some of Dylan's most urban, drug-influenced songs. It was the double album that had one whole side of vinyl taken up by one song, Sad-Eyed Lady of the Lowlands, and contained the chart hit Rainy Day Woman Nos. 12 and 35 that proclaimed that "Everybody must get stoned". It had no title and no clue as to whose album it was, just the curious figure with long hair and an intense stare; and the image was turned ninety degrees and opened out to become a full-length portrait. The sleeve perfectly reflects Dylan's increasingly hazy blurring of musical boundaries, and the burgeoning hippie movement's psychedelic influences.

> ▶ One of the most imitated album covers of all time

GRANT SCOTT

THE JIMI HENDRIX EXPERIENCE ELECTRIC LADYLAND

◀ Electric Ladyland / The Jimi Hendrix Experience

RELEASED 1968 | TRACK RECORDS | UK | SLEEVE DESIGN BY DAVID KING | PHOTOGRAPHY BY DAVID MONTGOMERY | ALBUM PRODUCED BY JIMI HENDRIX

An idea of *Sunday Times* designer David King, it was anti-*Playboy*, showing nineteen girls as they really were, with no hairdressers, body make-up, no airbrushing. After they were recruited in London bars, the shoot at David Montgomery's studio took four hours, the girls receiving £5 each plus an extra £2 to take off their panties. The dark shot gives a rather seedy look to the sleeve. Jimi (who didn't show, hence the photo) hated it. American Christians banned it. It sold lots.

▶ Bringing It All Back Home / Bob Dylan

RELEASED 1965 | COLUMBIA | USA | PHOTOGRAPHY BY DANIEL KRAMER | ALBUM PRODUCED BY TOM WILSON

Dylan fanatics analyzed every detail of Kramer's photograph, even suggesting that Sally Grossman (wife of his manager Albert) was Bob in drag. As well as *Another Side of Bob Dylan*, albums by Lotte Lenya, Robert Johnson, The Impressions and Eric Von Schmidt are there, all Dylan influences. He has LBJ on the cover of *Time* and an ad for Louella Parsons' biography of Jean Harlow open on his lap. The mantelpiece displays *The Best of Lord Buckley* and *Gnaoua*, a Tangier avant-garde mag, and a harmonica denotes his folk roots.

Bob Dylan
Bringing It All Back Home

◀ **Cheap Thrills / Big Brother and the Holding Company**

RELEASED 1967 | COLUMBIA | USA | SLEEVE DESIGN BY ROBERT CRUMB | ALBUM PRODUCED BY FRED CATERO AND OTHERS

Columbia Records objected to the album's original title, "Sex, dope, and cheap thrills", and insisted on shortening it to *Cheap Thrills*. It was the group's drummer Dave Getz who suggested getting cartoonist Robert Crumb to do the sleeve artwork. His design was originally planned for the back cover, hence the song listing and naming the band personnel, but it was switched to the front after a pastiche high-school yearbook layout for the front didn't work.

▲ **The Who Sell Out / The Who**

RELEASED 1967 | TRACK | UK | SLEEVE DESIGNED BY DAVE KING AND ROGER LAW | PHOTOGRAPHY BY DAVID MONTGOMERY | ALBUM PRODUCED BY KIT LAMBERT

The sleeve was art directed by Dave King, assisted by Roger Law, whose wife, Deirdre Amsden, made the giant props. John Entwistle drew the lottery for the baked bean shoot but he contrived to show up late and Roger Daltrey, who had not yet been photographed, was drafted in his place. Unfortunately the beans were straight from the refrigerator and he immediately got cramp. John arrived late and got the girl.

▲ **A landmark album cover was the Andy Warhol-designed debut Velvet Underground release. The striking image of a yellow banana on a white sleeve that peeled back was truly scary in its simplicity**

ALAN EDWARDS MUSIC PR

▲ **The Velvet Underground & Nico / The Velvet Underground & Nico**

RELEASED 1967 | MGM | USA | SLEEVE DESIGN BY ANDY WARHOL | ALBUM PRODUCED BY ANDY WARHOL

MGM's Bob Wilson actually produced, and Andy sat and watched, having no idea of what to do in a recording studio. But the sleeve became a Rock 'n' Roll icon. It was designed during the few weeks in 1967 when hippies thought smoking dried banana peel would get you high. When you peeled the skin from the cover it revealed a phallic pink banana. In fact the phallic banana became a counterculture symbol in itself, particularly in Germany.

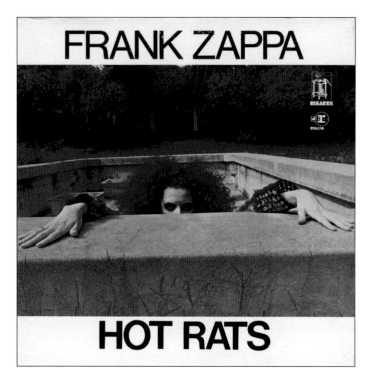

Hot Rats / Frank Zappa

RELEASED 1969 | BIZARRE RECORDS | USA | SLEEVE DESIGNED BY CAL SCHENKEL | PHOTOGRAPHY BY ED CARAEFF | ALBUM PRODUCED BY FRANK ZAPPA

Zappa chose the cover image after seeing 22-year old photographer Andee Cohen's (now Nathanson) shot of Miss Christine, singer with the GTOs, emerging from an empty lily pond in a deserted Beverly Hills house. The solarized image became one of Zappa's best-known sleeves and was Andee's first printed work. For many years it was incorrectly attributed to Ed Caraeff. The album did badly in the States but became probably his best-known release in Europe, where the Jazz-Rock fusion elements were more welcome.

Strange Days / The Doors

RELEASED 1967 | ELEKTRA RECORDS | USA | SLEEVE DESIGN BY WILLIAM S. HARVEY | PHOTOGRAPHY BY JOEL BRODSKY | ALBUM PRODUCED BY PAUL A. ROTHCHILD

Joel Brodsky's photographs appeared on four Doors' albums including this award-winning cover of *Strange Days*. Brodsky's famous photo of a bare-chested Morrison came from the same shoot. Given that Morrison was already a sex symbol, it was a daring move not to have the band on the sleeve. Instead Harvey and Brodsky hired circus performers and models to give a literal interpretation of the album title. Brodsky used the man who posed as the juggler as a dead clown on a later sleeve by Beacon Street Union.

▶ **The circus freaks on the cover of The Doors' Strange Days were an accurate measure of the mind of Jim Morrison**

MICK FARREN, MUSICIAN

Cruising with Ruben & The Jets / The Mothers of Invention

RELEASED 1968 | BIZARRE RECORDS| USA | SLEEVE DESIGN AND ILLUSTRATION BY CAL SCHENKEL | ALBUM PRODUCED BY FRANK ZAPPA

Cal Schenkel was closely involved in the development of Zappa's early albums which were all interrelated: "That came out of my love for comics and that style, the anthropomorphic animals, but also was part of a running storyline." Zappa was working on *Uncle Meat*, both an album and a movie, and parts were spun off into other projects. "I started working on the story of Ruben and the Jets that is connected with the Uncle Meat story," recalled Schenkel. "This old guy turns this teenage band into these dog snout people." The album featured loving pastiches of 1950s doo-wop with a sleeve designed to evoke that era.

So Far /
Crosby, Stills & Nash

RELEASED 1974 | ATLANTIC RECORDS | USA | SLEEVE DESIGN BY GARY BURDEN FOR R. TWERK | COVER ART BY JONI MITCHELL | ALBUM PRODUCED BY CROSBY, STILLS & NASH, AND CROSBY, STILLS, NASH & YOUNG.

Joni Mitchell's sleeve for her old friends is a lot cleverer than it looks; taking tiny details, usually outsides of a machine head, a guitar sound box, a skyline, she superimposes images of the band on a landscape. Despite the sketchy quality of the drawing there is considerable depth to the picture which recalls the work of Raoul Dufy and Jean Cocteau. The huge success of CSN&Y meant that they could go for a more relaxed, artistic image rather than try to express how laid-back and cool they were in yet more sepia or blurred photos.

▶ **We wrapped the first 1000 copies or so of the album like a block of hash and even had a special wax seal made for it**

TONY CALDER, IMMEDIATE RECORDS BOSS

Live Peace in Toronto
1969 / The Plastic Ono Band

RELEASED 1969 | APPLE RECORDS | UK | SLEEVE DESIGN BY YOKO ONO | ALBUM PRODUCED BY JOHN LENNON AND YOKO ONO FOR BAG PRODUCTIONS

One of Yoko's more beautiful sleeves. Many of the aphorisms in *Grapefruit* or her performance pieces concerned clouds: looking at them through small holes in pieces of paper, imagining them, meditating on them. Here we have a cloud, in a perfectly blue sky, and perfectly positioned – no doubt the photo was carefully cropped to achieve this exquisite balance. Today it would be a Photoshop job. Back then she just had to find the right picture, and here it is. Where else on the sleeve could it be positioned other than exactly where it is?

As Safe As Yesterday Is /
Humble Pie

RELEASED 1969 | IMMEDIATE | UK | SLEEVE DESIGN UNCREDITED | ALBUM PRODUCED BY HUMBLE PIE, A JOINT PRODUCTION FOR BEATRICE NOKES

1960s "supergroup" Humble Pie comprised the lead singer of The Herd (Peter Frampton), The Small Faces lead singer (Steve Marriott), the bassist from Spooky Tooth (Greg Ridley) and drummer Jerry Shirley. Immediate Records was formed by ex-Rolling Stones manager Andrew Loog Oldham and partner Tony Calder in the style of Phil Spector's Philles label. They'd scored big with The Small Faces, and had happily agreed to package *Ogden's Nut Gone Flake* (see page 75) to a more adult audience. It's done up as a parcel of hash. [JM]

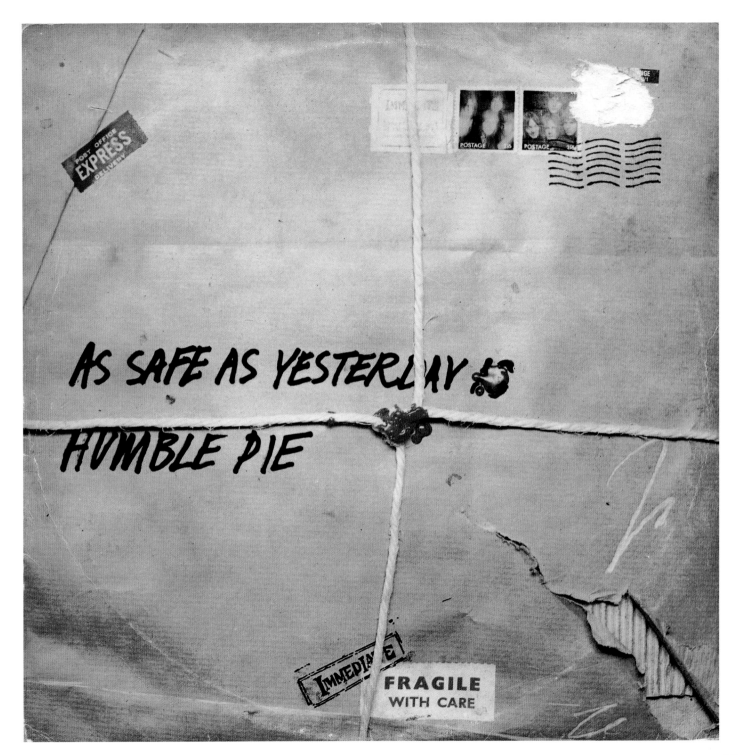

1960s **Psychedelia**

Sleeve designers have always tried to reflect something of the record they are packaging, but when it came to psychedelia, they were faced with the idea of representing "blown minds", something most of them were unfamiliar with. They did know that the underground hippie scene believed in free love, hence all the naked women on Hendrix's album sleeve. Had he shown up for the shoot he could have changed it but he was just too laid back.

Some bands attempted to reproduce the hallucinatory images they experienced on LSD – the cellular patterns of their own body, melting structures and flashes – but mostly an attempt was made to shift the consciousness of the viewer to give them some little jolt, or insight into the deeper meaning of things. The famous *Sgt Pepper* cover, hardly psychedelic in itself even though largely regarded as such, attempts to do this. The Doors' *Strange Days* offered a surrealistic tableau, designed to make the viewer curious. The Grateful Dead and Santana both produced well-known psychedelic sleeves, attempting to mirror the enhanced awareness experienced on acid, but most psychedelic design harked back to art nouveau, Aubrey Beardsley and Liberty's paisley patterns. Martin Sharp's two sleeves for Cream were perhaps the best UK examples of the genre, giving some insight into his private vision as well as that of the band by using collage and other elements, but most groups left it to the record company to sort out the sleeve.

The Small Faces' use of a real Victorian design was inspired. The Soft Machine were in the psychedelic tradition of excess: band members sitting round stoned would have wonderful ideas for album sleeves involving cut-outs, fold-outs, double gatefolds, pop-ups, huge posters, embossing and ultimately scratch 'n' sniff sleeves. (There were at least two of these: one by Melanie, meant to smell like flowers, and the other, a Punk-era collection from Akron, Ohio, which smelled like rubber tyres.) This Soft Machine sleeve was a success; the wheel actually turned to reveal glimpses of the band and obligatory naked women, and the construction was sturdy enough not to fall apart – which was a problem with the Small Faces sleeve which easily tore at the spine (as did the octagonal *Rolling Stones Greatest Hits*). The intention of a psychedelic sleeve was to get you high, or at least advertise that fact that the band within was, and proud of it.

▶ **The idea did get a bit metamorphosed when Peter was brought in**

PAUL MCCARTNEY

▶ **Sgt Peppers Lonely Hearts Club Band / The Beatles**
RELEASED 1967 | PARLOPHONE | UK | SLEEVE DESIGN BY PETER BLAKE AND JANN HAWORTH | ALBUM PRODUCED BY GEORGE MARTIN
This sleeve was based on a drawing by Paul of the band wearing long military band jackets, in front of a wall of photographs of their heroes, behind a municipal floral clock. Art dealer Robert Fraser suggested Peter Blake execute it. Waxwork models of the 1963 Beatles were borrowed from Madame Tussauds. Finding photographs of The Beatles' heroes was problematic, then EMI insisted on getting clearances from them all. EMI objected to Gandhi because of the Indian market, and John's choice of Hitler was pulled on the day of the shoot. The tableau was shot at Michael Cooper's studio in Flood Street, Chelsea.

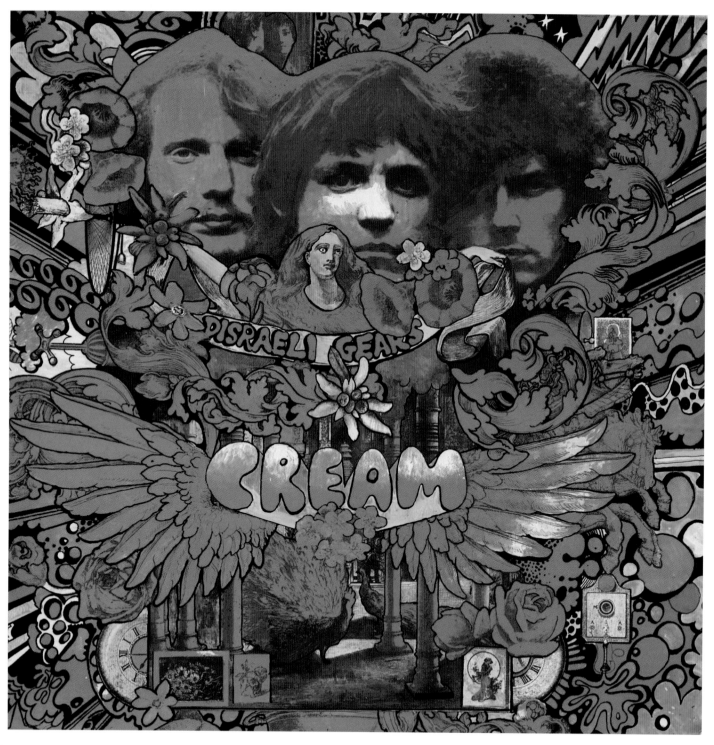

◀ Disraeli Gears / Cream

RELEASED 1969 | UK | SLEEVE DESIGN BY MARTIN SHARP | ALBUM PRODUCED BY FELIX PAPPALARDI

Australian Martin Sharp did two sleeves for Cream, the first being *Disraeli Gears*. "I commissioned my ex-studio mate, Bob Whitaker, to take some photos which were used in a collage on the back cover. I believe the photo used on the cover was a publicity shot that I got from Eric. I was using fluorescent paints at the time. It was the height of psychedelia. Some of the ingredients in the cover are made from Victorian engravings. It was done in black and white first, then painted with fluorescent colours."

▲ The Psychedelic Sounds of the 13th Floor Elevators / 13th Floor Elevators

RELEASED 1966 | INTERNATIONAL ARTIST | USA | SLEEVE DESIGNED BY JOHN CLEVELAND | ALBUM PRODUCED BY LELAN ROGERS

A wonderfully naive example of psychedelia. The 'Elevators of Austin, Texas, used local artist John Cleveland, who painted psychedelic designs, for their first album. The red and green creates a retinal clash around the lettering, then there is the eye within the eye, all of it derived from black light posters already being sold in the local head shop. One of the purest psychedelic albums: the band was seriously into LSD, and most of the songs were about it.

> **The art gave the extra data on the mood, and, back in the days of vinyl, was also a damned handy surface on which to roll a joint**
>
> MICK FARREN, MUSICIAN AND AUTHOR

▲ Ogdens' Nut Gone Flake / Small Faces

RELEASED 1968 | IMMEDIATE | UK | SLEEVE DESIGN CONCEPT BY TONY CALDER | ALBUM PRODUCED BY STEVE MARRIOTT AND RONNIE LANE

Ronnie Lane's idea was inspired by the tobacco tins that people kept marijuana in. When manager Andrew Loog Oldham contacted Ogdens, the company supplied various Victorian artwork. The band chose Ogdens' Nut Brown Flake, changing Brown to Gone. Oldham then went for broke, having the sleeve die-cut circular, and including psychedelic inside artwork and photographs to create a rival to *Sgt Pepper* for the greatest 1960s sleeve icon.

THE SOFT MACHINE

CPLP 4500 STEREO

abc RECORDS probe

> ▶ **Most of my favourite sleeves hark back to those times of stoned and ever creative graphic artists**
>
> ALAN EDWARDS, MUSIC PR

◀ The Soft Machine / The Soft Machine

RELEASED 1968 | COMMAND-PROBE | USA | SLEEVE DESIGN BY BYRON GOTO, ELI ALIMAN AND HENRY EPSTEIN | ALBUM PRODUCED BY CHAS CHANDLER AND TOM WILSON

The epitome of 1960s album graphics utilizing every trick in the book, but done well. A large circle is die cut from the front cover to reveal an insert disc that is in turn pierced by five holes corresponding to the cog-wheel designs. Through these holes – inevitably – we can see glimpses of a collage of naked women and the band. None can ever be viewed in their entirety, making the viewer turn the disc to see what is revealed. The justification for the naked women is, of course, that the band took its name from William Burroughs' novel *The Soft Machine*, referring to the human body, here confronted by the inhuman world of machinery. Human tenderness vs the state.

▲ Abraxas / Santana

RELEASED 1970 | COLUMBIA RECORDS | USA | ILLUSTRATION BY ABDUL MATI KLARWEIN | GRAPHICS BY ROBERT VENOSA | SLEEVE ART BY MATI | PHOTOGRAPH BY MARIAN SCHMIDT | ALBUM PRODUCED BY FRED CATERO AND SANTANA

Carlos Santana personally chose Abdul Mati Klarwein to design this, impressing the Columbia art department such that it hired him for Miles Davis sleeves, including *Bitches Brew*. A student of painter Fernand Leger, Klarwein's mature style combines psychedelia with Dali to come up with a unique vision. Other key influences include Hindu iconography and Renaissance altar pieces. (The drapery on *Abraxas* could almost be 14th century.) Klarwein was the greatest of all "psychedelic" painters. And his student Robert Venosa went on to become one of the greatest of the psychedelic visionary artists of the era.

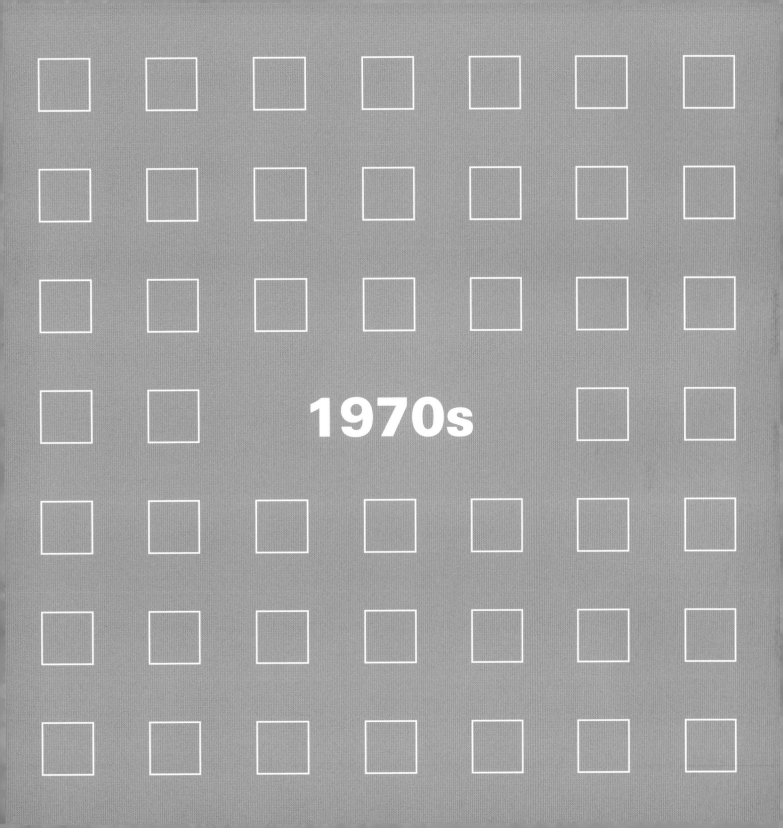

1970s

1970s Pop

This was the decade when the record business became an industry, outstripping Hollywood. What had previously been a relatively small community of musicians expanded into a massive enterprise with the advent of stadium Rock, and its attendant roadies, lighting crew, security, sound mixers, drivers and office staff – because 150 people on the road in a fleet of buses and trucks takes some managing.

The music industry had arrived. Annual business passed the billion-dollar mark early in the decade. Artists took more control of their presentation with bands such as Roxy Music art directing their own sleeves so that they presented almost a brand image to the public; in this case a series of half-naked young women. No one was ever going to remember the names of all the band members in Chicago, so they opted for a memorable logo – not dissimilar to Coca-Cola's – and made each successive album a variation on it.

Artists such as David Bowie now had much bigger budgets and could experiment with different images. Album sleeves became art directed. Previously the sleeves were all pretty much created in-house by the same art department that made the advertisements; now independent designers were being brought in by artists determined to control every aspect of their "product" as it was always known in the industry. The design group Hipgnosis was perhaps the epitome of this, with its memorable covers for Pink Floyd, but there was plenty of innovation elsewhere too. From Alice Cooper's *School's Out* and Jethro Tull's 12-page mock-up of an English local newspaper to The Who's collection of facsimile invoices, letters and a poster that accompanied the plain fold-out sleeve of *Live at Leeds*.

Big companies such as Columbia, responsible for the likes of Springsteen and Dylan, continued to produce their own sleeves but small outfits such as Virgin allowed their acts much greater leeway. This was the decade that began with the singer-songwriter movement that gave us Carole King, James Taylor, Carly Simon and hundreds more; that moved through Disco, Funk, Krautrock and Reggae (among other strands) and ended with Punk. It's impossible to generalize about such a diverse spread of activity but it did produce some remarkable music, from Abba to Zappa, and some clever, well-designed sleeves.

▶ **School's Out / Alice Cooper**
RELEASED 1972 | WARNER BROS | USA | SLEEVE CONCEPT SOUND PACKAGING CORP | DESIGN WILKES & BRAUN, INC | ALBUM PRODUCED BY BOB EZRIN FOR NIMBUS PRODUCTIONS
It wasn't the band's first album – it was their fifth – but it was their breakthrough. The title and design concept for the packaging came from the album's first track, a riotous, triumphant anthem of teenage rebellion. In the U.K. a generation of soon-to-be Punks came alive when they first saw Alice on the nation's only music TV show, *Top of the Pops*, adopting the attitude and in some cases the theatricality of Alice with his snake and messed-up hair. The album, a working facsimile of a school desk with fold-out legs, originally came with a pair of girl's panties made from paper stretched across it to prevent the vinyl slipping from under the hinged front cover. Few of the panties survived their removal, and one can't help but feel that was the idea. The front (or "top") of the desk had the carved initials of all the band members and the Warner Bros record company logo. Inside the sleeve was a photograph of a desk's contents, including catapult, flick knife and comic featuring Lovely Liberace. [JM]

◀ It was much
more fun to do
Roxy sleeves and
deal with these
iconic glamour
girls than it was
to have my picture
taken for my
own records

BRYAN FERRY

◀ Country Life / Roxy Music
RELEASED 1974 | ISLAND RECORDS |
UK | SLEEVE DESIGN BY NICHOLAS
DE VILLE | PHOTOGRAPHY BY ERIC
BOMAN | ALBUM PRODUCED BY
ROXY MUSIC AND JOHN PUNTER
A parody of *Country Life*
magazine, like all previous Roxy
sleeves this was conceived by
Bryan Ferry with designer
Nicholas de Ville and fashion
stylist Anthony Price. The shoot
was in Portugal where Roxy was
recording. The two German girls,
Eveline Grunwald and Constanze
Karoli, walked into a bar where
Ferry was drinking. The shoot
was at night, the flash illuminating
them against a hedgerow. Was
this the first sleeve to show pubic
hair? Possibly. Many U.S. chains
banned it, and the Canadians just
used a picture of the hedge.

**▲ Aladdin Sane /
David Bowie**
RELEASED 1972 | RCA | UK | SLEEVE
DESIGN BY DUFFY AND CELIA PHILO
FOR DUFFY DESIGN CONCEPTS |
ALBUM PRODUCED BY MAINMAN
PRODUCTIONS
With possible titles including "A
Land Insane" and "Love Aladdin
Vein", "Aladdin Sane" was a play
on "A Lad Insane", possibly
referencing Bowie's schizophrenic
brother. Bowie: "The flash on the
original Ziggy set was taken from
the 'High Voltage' sign that was
stuck on any box containing
dangerous amounts of electricity.
I was not a little peeved when
Kiss purloined it. Purloining, after
all, was my job." The flash and
astral sphere forehead were
applied by Pierre La Roche from
the House of Arden. Duffy's
sleeve used a seven-colour
process not possible in the U.K.,
so the sleeve had to be printed
in Switzerland.

WT. 1.05 OZS

◀ X / Chicago

RELEASED 1976 | COLUMBIA
RECORDS | USA | SLEEVE DESIGN
BY JOHN BERG | ART LOGO DESIGN
BY NICK FASCIANO | PHOTOGRAPHY
BY COLUMBIA RECORDS PHOTO
STUDIO | ALBUM PRODUCED BY
JAMES WILLIAM GUERCIO

It is very hard to find a group
image for an eight-man line-up;
too large for most people ever
to get to know the names of
individual members. Chicago got
round this by pushing their logo,
presenting it in all manner of
different situations and forms.
It was very effective. The tenth
Chicago album was the first to be
certified platinum and contained
their first Number One single, If
You Leave Me Now. The artwork
was stunning, using their
distinctive logo as the brand
name for a chocolate bar, loosely
designed to look like a Hershey
bar. The image is enormously
enlarged and looks authentic.

▶ Broken English / Marianne Faithfull

RELEASED 1979 | ISLAND RECORDS |
UK | PHOTOGRAPHY BY DENNIS
MORRIS | ALBUM PRODUCED BY
MARK MULLER MUNDY

Faithfull's breakthrough album
had a deceptively plain sleeve.
The deep blue tone over a high
contrast black-and-white photo
by Island Records' photographer
Dennis Morris made a striking
image. Cropping created a perfect
classical composition, as carefully
planned as any Renaissance
Madonna; the glowing cigarette
is almost unnecessary, but very
effective nonetheless. The choice
of pose captured the stressed,
edgy image of the survivor that
Marianne had at that time. Like
many successful designs it was
very simple and very strong.

▶ The B-52's / The B-52's

RELEASED 1979 | ISLAND RECORDS |
USA | SLEEVE DESIGN BY SUE AB
SURD | PHOTOGRAPHY BY GEORGE
DUBOSE | ALBUM PRODUCED BY
CHRIS BLACKWELL

The B-52s came from Athens,
Georgia, and B-52 is southern
slang for a beehive hairdo, in this
case nicely styled by La Verne.
"We never thought of it as being
camp," claimed Kate Pierson.
However, Fred Schneider did
have a thing about 1960s girl
groups. "They were always
mysterious," he said. "You could
hardly see their eyes because of
their hair. It seemed real exotic."
This was the image projected by
this cartoonish sleeve in bright,
modern colours. It was like
American Graffiti come to life,
only with slightly off-the-wall
post-Punk Pop music.

1970s The Rolling Stones

By the end of the tax year of April 1971, the Rolling Stones were tax exiles ensconced in and around Cannes in the south of France, and Rolling Stones Records was up and running. *Sticky Fingers* was their first release. On December 12, 1974, Mick Taylor left the group, to be replaced by Ron Wood. After the debacle of Altamont in 1969, the band made a conscious effort to switch their image from one of flirting with demonic imagery and black magic to one of sexual decadence: their 1975 tour featured a fifteen foot high inflatable penis on stage (unless *Goat's Head Soup* counts as devilish).

After numerous drug busts involving various members of the band and their entourage the band was routinely criticized in the press, but as Mick Jagger said: "It's not The Rolling Stones that destroy people. They destroy themselves." The fact is that many of the Stones albums from this period were marred by Keith Richards' ongoing heroin addiction. This caused them huge problems, and in 1977 cost them an enormous amount of money when Richards was arrested in Toronto trying to bring heroin into the country. The maximum sentence for trafficking in heroin was life. The trial was delayed by nearly two years while Keith supposedly took a cure. He was eventually given a one-year suspended sentence, to the outrage of much of the Canadian press and establishment.

"About one per cent of our songs glorify drugs," said Keith Richards, "and Mick wrote them anyway." It was a decade that produced a number of great Stones sleeves, even if the contents weren't always up to their usual standard: *Sticky Fingers*, *Exile on Main Street*, *Love You Live* (their second Andy Warhol cover), *Time Waits for No One* and *Some Girls* were all from the 1970s. (This string of great sleeves continued into the 1980s with *Emotional Rescue*, *Sucking in the Seventies* and *Under Cover*.)

By now the Stones had become an institution, they were big business, with merchandising and posters, and entire books devoted to the artifacts of their career, and yet, amazingly, they managed to keep their streetwise, rebellious image. They were multi-millionaires who hobnobbed with conservative politicians and New York-based Eurotrash, yet the fans still related to them. And on they go, into the 21st century, a British tradition like the slap of leather on willow, warm beer and the lengthening shadows across a county ground.

▶ **Sticky Fingers / The Rolling Stones**
RELEASED 1971 | ROLLING STONES RECORDS | USA | SLEEVE DESIGN BY CRAIG BRAUN | PHOTOGRAPHY AND COVER CONCEPT BY ANDY WARHOL | ALBUM PRODUCED BY JIMMY MILLER

Sticky Fingers moved the Stones from devil worship to the high camp sexuality of the early 1970s. The idea of the working zip was Andy Warhol's, probably suggested by a drawing Warhol made of Serendipity restaurateur Stephen Bruce's crotch. For the sleeve Warhol photographed *Interview* magazine staffer Glenn O'Brien; Jay Johnson, the twin brother of Warhol's boyfriend Jeb Johnson; and Jay's best friend Corey Tippin. Warhol never revealed which he used but it is generally thought that Jay appeared on the outer sleeve and Glenn O'Brien's jockey shorts appear when the zip is pulled down to reveal the first use of the lip and tongue logo designed by John Pasche. The Peter Webb group photograph on the inlay card was originally to have been the sleeve until Jagger got Warhol involved.

87

◄ Some Girls /
The Rolling Stones

RELEASED 1978 | ROLLING STONE
RECORDS | UK | SLEEVE DESIGN
BY STEVE CORRISTON | ALBUM
PRODUCED BY THE GLIMMER TWINS

This was to have been called
More Fast Numbers. The original
sleeve design featured members
of the band showing through
die-cut holes in the sleeve
alongside pictures of Hollywood
stars. However, Rolling Stones
Records had neglected to get
clearance for these images and
Lucille Ball, Farrah Fawcett and
Raquel Welch all threatened legal
action, feeling that they were
displayed in a not altogether
flattering light. The sleeve had to
be reshot and as an interim
measure the album continued
shipping with the celebrities
blanked out and the words
"Pardon Our Appearance" and
"Cover Under Reconstruction"
rapidly pasted in before a new
set of pictures could be
substituted. This is the interim
design but it is still striking,
reminiscent of the *Exile on Main
Street* sleeve with its multiplicity
of images making an overall
design statement.

▶ Exile on Main Street /
The Rolling Stones

RELEASED 1972 | ROLLING STONE
RECORDS | USA | SLEEVE DESIGN
BY JAN VAN HAMERSVELD AND
NORMAN SEEFF | PHOTOGRAPHY BY
ROBERT FRANK | ALBUM PRODUCED
BY JIMMY MILLER

Designer Jan Van Hamersveld
asked Robert Frank, who was
planning to film the Stones on
tour– the rarely shown
Cocksucker Blues – for a cover
shot. Frank offered a photo he'd
taken in 1950 somewhere on
Route 66, images of freaks, circus
performers, burlesque acts and
lynchings, tacked on the wall of
a tattoo parlour. Photographer
Norman Seeff used the format for
all the album, including back and
inner sleeves. It's classic Frank.
Who else would photograph the
walls of a tattoo parlour?

▶ Black and Blue /
The Rolling Stones

RELEASED 1976 | ROLLING STONE
RECORDS | UK | PHOTOGRAPHY BY
HIRO | ALBUM PRODUCED BY THE
GLIMMER TWINS

Ron Wood's first album with The
Stones, he enters stage left on
the back of a wraparound sleeve,
still separated from the other
Stones. Japanese photographer
Hiro posed the group like a mime
tableau, with Keith whispering
into Mick's ear as he stares into
the camera. The shoot was in
February 1976 in Florida. There
was much adverse publicity over
the poster campaign for the
album, featuring a woman tied in
bondage to a chair, the title hinting
that her man had beaten her up.
Predictably and rightly, the band
backed down, the ads being
replaced with group portraits.

1970s Rock

In Britain, the 1970s saw the rise of various independent record labels, as artists resisted being ripped off by the big corporations. The move was spearheaded by The Beatles with Apple Records, which continued into the 1970s, and was taken up by Rolling Stones Records, a very successful vehicle for the Stones ever since. Frank Zappa was tired of suing his record companies and started his own Bizarre label, followed by Straight, then by other corporate entities including Zappa Records and Barking Pumpkin Records.

Some of the new labels, such as David Geffen's Asylum, were absorbed back into the big corporate world, and others, like Paul McCartney's MPL, served merely as a way of controlling every aspect of his records which were then leased to EMI as a complete package, ready to go. By now Rock was well established as a serious art form, and Virgin had great success with bands such as Tangerine Dream, a German electronic trio, and radical improvisational group Henry Cow. Henry Cow's first three albums all featured a painting of a sock, the first one without the name of the band. Kraftwerk, Can and other German bands began to make an impact, as Rock continued to expand beyond Britain and America.

The small labels proliferated: Stiff Records, with its catchy corporate slogan "If it ain't stiff, it ain't worth a fuck", and Rough Trade, which kept all its obscure Punk singles in print year after year.

Punk was possibly the most significant cultural event of the decade, but before that artists such as Van Morrison, David Bowie, James Taylor, Lou Reed and Iggy Pop were all producing significant work. Rock began to break up into factions: the Frank Zappa/Captain Beefheart side was anathema to followers of Rick Wakeman and Yes. Steely Dan was not Steeleye Span. The laid-back stylings of Stephen Stills, David Crosby and Neil Young did little for Zeppelin fans. The one thing they all had in common was a respect for musicianship. Even Abba was recognized as making beautifully crafted songs, even if they didn't mean anything.

This trend got out of hand though, so we had fifteen-minute John Bonham solos, and even longer Jimmy Page solos. Even good-time bands with names featuring Brothers – the Allman Brothers, Doobie Brothers, Flying Burrito Brothers – held the stage for a while.

The sleeves in this section reflect the variety and humour of what seemed to be a very serious time in rock music, though.

▶ **Born to Run / Bruce Springsteen**

RELEASED 1975 | COLUMBIA RECORDS | USA | SLEEVE DESIGN BY JOHN BERG | PHOTOGRAPHY BY ERIC MEOLA | ALBUM PRODUCED BY BRUCE SPRINGSTEEN, JOHN LANDAU AND MIKE APPEL

Springsteen's manager Mike Appel hired photographer Eric Meola, a friend of sax player Clarence Clemons, to do a shoot for the album sleeve. Meola shot nine hundred frames over a three-hour session: outside in the shadows created by a fire escape, in his studio listening to a radio, playing the guitar. The key elements for Springsteen were the black leather jacket and his large Elvis badge – which is hardly visible in the chosen shot. He was nervous and the session began badly but after a while he plugged into an amp and began playing with Clarence. As Clarence bent over to blow his horn, Springsteen casually leaned on him. It was the magic shot that leapt from the contact sheet. The pose became a Rock icon. Columbia's art director wrapped the picture as a double spread, with Clemons mostly on the back, and Andy Engel used the ultra thin lettering he put on a lot of Columbia albums. The result, an all-time classic sleeve.

BRUCE
SPRINGSTEEN

BORN TO RUN

JETHRO TULL FEATURE ON PAGE 7

The St Cleve Chronicle
& Linwell Advertiser

Friday January 7th 1972 | No.1003 | Price 3p Weekly

THICK AS A BRICK

JUDGES DISQUALIFY "LITTLE MILTON" IN LAST MINUTE RUMPUS

ART DEMO FORCES CLOSURE

THREE poets and five painters were arrested yesterday afternoon outside Lady Parrit House after repeatedly causing disturbance and harrassing members of the public visiting the museum and gallery throughout the day. They were demonstrating against gallery policy of showing only resident exhibition works, and resident exhibition works, and led by heavily bearded Ahab Gross demanded that the Gal-

Ugly scenes as Constable Grimpoce tries to calm the protesters.

lery showed the "work of the people" and gave more attention to new and unknown local artists. Mr. Gross allegedly squirted a tube of Cadmium Yellow oil paint at a police constable and signed his name

THE SOCIETY FOR LITERARY ADVANCEMENT AND GESTATION, (SLAG), announced their decision late last night to disqualify eight year old prizewinner Gerald (Little Milton) Bostock following the hundreds of protests and threats received after the reading of his epic poem "Thick as a Brick" on B.B.C. Television last Monday night.

A hastily reconvened panel of Judges accepted the decision by four leading child psychiatrists that the boy's mind was seriously unbalanced and that his work was a product of an "extremely unwholesome attitude towards life, his God and Country". Bostock was recommended for psychiatric treatment following examination "without delay". The first prize will now be presented to runner up Mary Whiteyard (aged 12) for her essay on Christian ethics entitled, "He died to save the little Children".

The Literary Competition, which was for children aged from 7 to 16 years of age, was sponsored by leading national newspapers and received thousands of entries from schools all over Britain. Mr. Humphrey Martin, the Headmaster of Moordale Primary School said Gerald, nicknamed "Little Milton" by his English master because of his poetic ability, was mentally advanced for his age, although inclined on occasions to obscure and verbose assertions which led him to being somewhat unpopular with his schoolmates. He went on to say that without doubt the child had a great future academically and that his progress was unsurpassed in the history of Moordale Primary. Gerald and his parents moved to St. Cleve four years ago from Manchester when Mr. Bostock decided for health reasons to live away from the City. David Bostock now does occasional

Daphne is well known to the Congregation of St. Cleve Parish Church for her activities in social work and her wonderful buffet luncheon at the fete last Saturday. Well done, Daphne! Mr. Bostock said this morning of "Little Milton's" disqualification, "We are heartbroken at the way the Judges changed their minds, and the loss of the prize money and scholarship means we shall find difficulty in paying the instalments on Gerald's Encyclopaedia Britannica. I shall have to do Dr. Munson's roses next week after all." When he heard of the decision against him, Gerald went to his room and locked the door. "Mrs. Bostock and I are sorely vexed at the way this has turned out", said Mr. Bostock of No. 6 Pollitt Close, St. Cleve.

Many local residents are also annoyed and hurt by the news and as some consolation to Gerald and his parents the St. Cleve Chronicle prints the poem this week on page 7.

Many of the viewers who heard Gerald read his work on the "Young Arts" programme on B.B.C. 2 felt that it was not one poem but a series of separate ones designed to appear impressive. Many of the viewers' complaints were centred around "Little Milton's" use of a four-letter word during the interview which followed his reading. The Producer of "Young Arts" "We have come to expect that sort of language from adults on television these days, but to hear it from a child of eight is particularly depressing. When I was his age I did not even know what the word g——r

Flashback to last week's presentation dinner held in Gerald's honour by the Committee of the St. Cleve District Art and Literary Society at the Parrit Rooms. Left to right: Lord Clive 'Polly' Parritt, Mr. and Mrs. Bostock, Gerald Bostock, Lady Parrit, Julia, Gerald's chum with whom he writes poems.

◀ **Weasels Ripped My Flesh / Frank Zappa**

RELEASED 1970 | BIZARRE | USA | SLEEVE DESIGN BY NEON PARK | ALBUM PRODUCED BY FRANK ZAPPA

Frank Zappa saw drawings that Neon Park had done for a group called Dancing Food, and telephoned him in San Francisco where he was working with the Family Dog poster design group and asked him to come down to Los Angeles. He showed Park a men's magazine with a cover featuring a man, naked to the waist, in water swarming with weasels that were climbing over him and biting him. Zappa said: "This is it. What can you do that's worse than this?" He was paid $250. Zappa had to battle with Warner Bros to get it released and after that there were problems with the printer. "I was greatly amused by the cover," said Park, "and so was Frank. I mean, we giggled a lot."

▲ **Thick as a Brick / Jethro Tull**

RELEASED 1972 | CHRYSALIS | UK | SLEEVE CONCEPT BY IAN ANDERSON | NEWSPAPER WRITTEN BY IAN ANDERSON, JEFFREY HAMMOND, JOHN EVAN | ALBUM PRODUCED BY IAN ANDERSON AND TERRY ELLIS

Folk-Rock band Jethro Tull's move into progressive Rock came with the requisite "concept". In this case, a 12-page spoof of a regional newspaper, the St Cleve Chronicle. The album was ultra-prog, a continuous piece of music. And it seems the newspaper took longer to make than the album.

Written by band members Ian Anderson, John Evan and Jeffrey Hammond, it was an accurate pastiche, complete with children's competitions, local ads, and news of the minutiae of village life – even the typos found in such papers. It had been done before, but never twelve pages of it.

◀ **Its strong use of paint and oblique brush strokes are as much what Dylan is about as anything else he does**

GRANT SCOTT

▶ **Planet Waves / Bob Dylan**

RELEASED 1974 | ASYLUM | USA | SLEEVE DESIGN BY BOB DYLAN | SPECIAL ASSISTANCE ROBBIE ROBERTSON

More accomplished than his earlier work, this self-drawn album sleeve shows Dylan in the thrall of German Expressionism. The image contains references to Erich Heckel, Max Beckmann and Ernst Kirchner. There is even incorporated text: the songs are described as "Cast Iron Songs & Torch Ballads" but he has not yet mastered the peace sign which has four arms. Dylan also drew the back cover, which saved on typesetting. One wonders if it began life in colour, and was reduced to black and white. It would be entirely like Dylan to see the monochrome position print they would have made for the mock-up and preferred it to the colour original.

▲ **Self Portrait / Bob Dylan**

RELEASED 1970 | COLUMBIA | USA | SLEEVE PAINTED BY BOB DYLAN | ALBUM PRODUCED BY BOB JOHNSTON

After Dylan's painting on the sleeve of *Music from the Big Pink* by The Band in 1968 did so much to get the group known and sell the album, it seemed logical that he should illustrate one of his own albums. This album has a similar feel, probably because the portrait is pink with a centrefold of Dylan working with chickens and being a farmer. If you have an album called *Self Portrait*, then a self portrait makes the most obvious sleeve. This is Dylan in his Fauvist period: shockingly crude and powerful yet owing much to early Matisse. The curious lack of pupils in the eyes suggests that this is really a mask; devious Zimmerman has managed to avoid telling us anything about himself yet again.

▼ Live at Leeds / The Who

RELEASED 1970 | TRACK RECORDS | UK | SLEEVE DESIGN BY GRAPHREAKS | ALBUM PRODUCED BY THE WHO

The sleeve of *Live at Leeds* was designed to look like a bootleg. *Great White Wonder* by Bob Dylan had appeared earlier in the year in a plain white sleeve with the title roughly rubber stamped on the bottom right corner. This was quickly followed by Rolling Stones, Zappa, and more Dylan bootlegs. They all featured the title rubber stamped on to blank album sleeves. It was some time before printed bootleg sleeves appeared and even longer before pictures appeared on them. Most were illegal live recordings of concerts, thus the idea of using this format for a legitimate Who live record. The original came with a collection of invoices, clippings, gig lists and paperwork inside, like the mimeographed track-list accompanying some early bootlegs.

▼ Aja / Steely Dan

RELEASED 1977 | ABC RECORDS | USA | SLEEVE DESIGN BY PATRICIA MITSUI AND GEOFF WESTERN FOR OZ STUDIOS | PHOTOGRAPHY BY HIDEKI FUJII | ALBUM PRODUCED BY GARY KATZ

The impeccable surfaces, cool Jazz-oriented sounds and sheer perfectionism of Donald Fagen and Walter Becker are typified by this minimalist photograph of a Japanese girl. The four design elements on the square format give a strong, stark image. Steely Dan was always cited by UK Punk bands as an example of what they were opposed to, such as musical ability. This sleeve shows the same attention to detail as the band paid to their music.

▶ Candy-O / The Cars

RELEASED 1979 | ELEKTRA | USA | SLEEVE DESIGN BY RON CORO AND JOHNNY LEE | PAINTING BY ALBERTO VARGAS | ALBUM PRODUCED BY ROY THOMAS BAKER

It was drummer David Robinson's idea to bring 80-year-old Alberto Vargas out of retirement to paint a cover for them. Vargas, whose scantily clad ladies featured in *Esquire* magazine in the 1950s, needed a model for his painting, so Robinson set up a shoot in Beverly Hills. Candy Moore (her name was coincidental) was hired, and Robinson was so impressed by her that they had a brief affair. The public liked the sleeve too, with *Candy-O* going platinum.

THE **CARS**
CANDY - O

Vargas

1970s AOR

Album-Oriented-Rock (also known as Adult-Oriented Rock) grew from the ashes of the once progressive FM radio which in the 1960s was the cool alternative to the rigid format of AM Top 20 playlists.

The growth of the singer-songwriter coincided with the ageing of the baby boomers, who by now were less likely to spend the evening dancing to a Rock band than they were to have pleasant dinner parties with friends. Carole King's *Tapestry* caught the mood perfectly: not too slick, but beautifully played with words her generation could relate to.

A whole new market was soon identified as AOR. This was music where the words were important; the lyrics might concern themselves with romantic relationships or quirky, humorous, adult themes. Some examples include James Taylor, Boz Scaggs, Randy Newman, Harry Nilsson, Paul Simon, Linda Ronstadt, Jackson Browne, Carly Simon, Leonard Cohen and Robert Palmer. It was late-night FM radio listening exactly like that described on Donald Fagen's *The Nightfly*. Some of the same market liked The Eagles, Emmylou Harris and Gram Parsons if they were real music aficionados, so Country Rock crossed over into this territory.

It was also music to listen to in a bedsit, or a student dorm, or late at night on headphones. Male singers were no longer supposed to look rebellious or threatening; they were supposed to be sensitive and romantic, like the suave Bryan Ferry. A suggestion of sexual availability did not go amiss, though. Robert Palmer was usually accompanied by a half-naked or even naked woman who was clearly not his spouse.

As Carole King once pointed out, Carly Simon was always photographed with her legs apart, but this was the norm; female AOR singers were supposed to be sexy but not too sexy, unless they were Donna Summer which was a little different. By the early 1970s, FM had a large enough audience to no longer be "underground". Even though they were playing album cuts, FM stations quickly became as formulaic as the AM ones. AOR bands such as Foreigner, Styx and Kansas often incorporated high-harmony vocals derived from CSN&Y and the like. Unthreatening bands like Fleetwood Mac, REO Speedwagon, Journey and Toto all did well. Led Zeppelin's Stairway to Heaven became the FM radio anthem. As a genre, AOR was pretty much over by the end of the decade.

▶ **Slow Dancer / Boz Scaggs**
RELEASED 1974 | COLUMBIA | USA | SLEEVE DESIGN BY TONY LANE | PHOTOGRAPHY BY ETHAN RUSSELL | ALBUM PRODUCED BY JOHNNY BRISTOL
This is the 1976 reissue of *Slow Dancer* with a different cover. (The original had a portrait shot of Boz.) This sleeve, designed by Tony Lane around a photograph by famed Rock photographer Ethan A. Russell, is based on the poster used for the Boz Scaggs concert on March 8, 1974 presented by Bill Graham at the Paramount Theater, Oakland, CA. It is a very evocative image: a 1950s tango school in Rio perhaps, except the 1970s flares give it away. Russell is known for his unusual poses and concepts, this one suited Boz perfectly.

32760

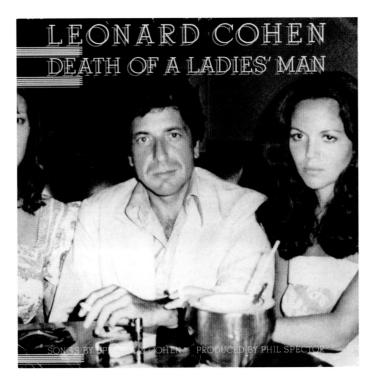

◀ Sneakin' Sally Through the Alley / Robert Palmer

RELEASED 1974 | ISLAND RECORDS | UK | SLEEVE CONCEPT AND PHOTOGRAPHY BY GRAHAM HUGHES | ALBUM PRODUCED BY STEVE SMITH

This looks more like a highway tunnel that Robert is sneaking down, and is someone coming up behind them in hot pursuit? Sally seems to have lost some of her clothes, perhaps in an event that triggered their hasty flight. They are frozen, like deer in the headlights, by the flash of a camera. The fluorescent green lettering was used by computer screens at the time – who are they running from? Irate parents? A government? The cover hints at a number of storylines. At least Sally hung on to her necklace. Let's hope they got away safely.

▲ Death of a Ladies' Man / Leonard Cohen

RELEASED 1977 | COLUMBIA RECORDS | USA | SLEEVE DESIGN BY RON CORO, BILL NAEGELS/GRIBBITTI | ALBUM PRODUCED BY PHIL SPECTOR

Images like this were common on the walls of eateries in the days when freelance photographers roamed restaurants snapping the diners. This picture was taken by an unknown roving lensman in a Polynesian establishment. On the left is Eve LaPierre and on the right is Cohen's muse Suzanne. The songs are all about love and affairs so the image is apposite. One of Cohen's strangest albums, it includes his memorable track Don't Go Home with Your Hard On with background vocals by Bob Dylan and Allen Ginsberg.

▲ Sail Away / Randy Newman

RELEASED 1972 | REPRISE RECORDS | USA | SLEEVE DESIGN AND PHOTOGRAPHY BY MIKE SALISBURY | ALBUM PRODUCED BY LENNY WARONKER AND RUSS TITELMAN

One of the almost reluctant stars of the 1970s singer-songwriter movement was Randy Newman. This sleeve gives the buyer a good indication of what to expect. It is a gatefold, but the image is shifted sideways. Like Dylan's *Blonde on Blonde*, the title therefore is printed sideways in what appears to be Warner-Reprise's standard in-house typeface (which was used for ads, press releases and so on). Nothing fancy or pretentious. Just an honest, albeit slightly wonky, portrait of a man playing the piano.

1970s Pink Floyd

Pink Floyd were only the second band (after The Beatles) that EMI let use an outside designer for their album sleeve, for *Saucerful of Secrets*. They chose Storm Thorgerson, and Aubrey "Po" Powell, asking them to "do something spacey and psychedelic". The pair called themselves Hipgnosis.

The designers superimposed thirteen images, including an almost invisible one of the band, to make Britain's first psychedelic sleeve. This was one of the few times that Pink Floyd appeared on their sleeves, after they opted for the anonymity of Hipgnosis's concepts. Most people had no idea what they looked like; when they performed live, they were always obscured by swirling light shows, and as they grew more successful, so increasingly surreal sleeves were created.

For *Ummagumma* they posed the band next to a picture of the band posing next to a picture of the band – and so on to infinity. That gave the fans something to look at when they were rolling joints on the sleeve. "My job, as I see it, is to invent an image related to the music," said Thorgerson. On *Wish You Were Here* he carefully studied Roger Waters' lyrics before proposing the celebrated series of images that finally accompanied the album.

Thorgerson described *Wish You Were Here*'s music as "very moody and atmospheric, and it has this sense of wide open spaces of the inner mind, or of some unknown terrain. Most of my pictures reflect that". He worked for Pink Floyd for eleven years when suddenly Roger Waters decided to drop him. His last work for them was with Dave Gilmour who got him to design their 1981 greatest hits package, *A Collection of Great Dance Songs*, which Waters had no interest in. Anyone who has seen the sleeves of Waters' solo albums must wonder at the reasoning behind the bassist's decision.

The two best-selling Pink Floyd albums were *Dark Side of the Moon*, with its striking sleeve image of the old physics lab experiment of creating a rainbow from a beam of light, and *Another Brick in the Wall*, which most listeners agreed was a pretty tough collection to listen to but which sold well on the popularity of the hit single of the same name. By then (1979) Pink Floyd were on their last legs, a band torn apart by seemingly irreconcilable differences, but as one of the greatest stadium acts of the progressive era they had certainly made their mark.

▶ **Atom Heart Mother / Pink Floyd**
RELEASED 1970 | EMI HARVEST | UK | SLEEVE DESIGN BY HIPGNOSIS | ALBUM PRODUCED BY PINK FLOYD
When you are trying to illustrate an album called *Atom Heart Mother*, which contains tracks with such titles as Breasty Milk and Funky Dung, it is obvious that a cow on the cover is the only answer. The animal on the front cover is a Holstein called Lullabell III but those on the back and inner sleeve remain anonymous. After the clutter of 1960s psychedelic covers, and the fold-outs and pop-ups, this was a refreshing and certainly memorable image and set the way for a whole series of disconcerting sleeves that the Hipgnosis team was to create for Pink Floyd.

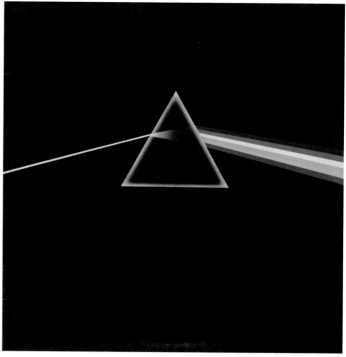

▲ Wish You Were Here / Pink Floyd

RELEASED 1975 | EMI HARVEST | UK | SLEEVE DESIGN BY HIPGNOSIS | PRODUCED BY PINK FLOYD

Hipgnosis designer Storm Thorgerson selected the title of the album and worked closely with the band on its packaging. He noticed that in America Roxy Music's *Country Life* had to be packaged in opaque green cellophane in case puritans objected to its photo of semi-naked women showing bare breasts and pubic hair. It inspired him to wrap *Wish You Were Here* in black plastic shrink wrap so that the sleeve would be "absent". The title and the artist would be identified only by a sticker (designed by George Hardie at Hipgnosis) showing two mechanical hands shaking. EMI in the UK and CBS in the US objected, but the band had shipped millions so they couldn't stop them. The sleeve was conceived as a series of "studies in absence". The cover image of a man in flames represented the "fear of getting burned" – a reluctance to reveal your true feelings when meeting someone. It also referred to the music biz, and possibly to the fact that the band was still "missing" founder Syd Barrett, to whom one of the best songs, Shine On, You Crazy Diamond was dedicated.

▲ Dark Side of the Moon / Pink Floyd

RELEASED 1973 | EMI HARVEST | UK | SLEEVE DESIGNED BY HIPGNOSIS | SLEEVE ART BY GEORGE HARDIE | PHOTOGRAPHY BY HIPGNOSIS | ALBUM PRODUCED BY PINK FLOYD

Storm Thorgerson, looking for an image relating to the Floyd's light show, came up with the prism transforming a thin white light into a rainbow. Roger Waters modified the design by making it continue through the inner sleeve, converting back to white light on the back, like the continuous rhythm of the music itself. It became an instant icon, suggesting Pink Floyd whenever you saw it.

▶ Animals / Pink Floyd

RELEASED 1977 | EMI HARVEST | UK | SLEEVE DESIGNED BY STORM THORGERSON AND AUBREY POWELL, HIPGNOSIS DESIGN | ALBUM PRODUCED BY PINK FLOYD

Roger Waters wanted a shot of a pig "for real" – not stripped in – floating above Battersea Power Station, London, so a forty-foot inflatable pig was floated into position to be shot by an eleven-man crew. Unfortunately, it broke free, landing in a field in Kent. The next day the pig flew again, but when the band saw the shots they preferred the sky from the first day's shoot. So Thorgerson had to strip in the pig from the second day after all.

1970s Prog Rock

One outcome of the experimentation of the 1960s bands was Progressive Rock, music where commercial considerations took second place to artistic ones, and where musicians stretched the boundaries of what is normally known as Rock.

The most extreme example was Lou Reed's *Metal Machine Music*, a double album of white noise feedback distortion. Brian Eno, who left Roxy Music because he was too avant garde for Bryan Ferry, made a series of solo albums of unusual musical textures and odd lyrics.

Miles Davis's breakthrough Jazz-Funk album *On the Corner* qualifies as Prog Rock because no one at the time knew what to call it. He had flown over the British cellist Paul Buckmaster for the sessions, and then immersed himself in Stockhausen. But the results, with amplified trumpet via wah-wah pedal appalled the critics, pleasing only Miles.

The core of prog were bands who saw Rock as an art form waiting to be taken seriously. Like Emerson Lake & Palmer, taking Rock in a classical (albeit pretentious), direction, the Electric Light Orchestra and Yes.

John Cale doubtless belongs to Prog Rock. While with The Velvet Underground, his classical training and experimentation with jarring sounds created by sawing at his viola or cello only hinted at what he would do solo. His unique version of Elvis's Heartbreak Hotel on 1975's *Slow Dazzle* sounds more like Nick Cave than Cave himself ten years later. As befits a true Prog Rocker, Cale's lyrics were intelligent if opaque, yet he attempted to set them in songs with a classic Pop structure. Similarly, Frank Zappa's old high-school chum Captain Beefheart was adored in Europe, pushing the boundaries of Rock with his Blues-style delivery over jagged, fragmented melodies.

Naturally all these artists wanted their album sleeves to reflect the seriousness of their intention, and so this category contains some of the most innovative covers of all, from the craziness of Cal Schenkel at Bizarre to Andy Warhol's design for John Cale's *The Academy in Peril*. ELP even hired H.R. Giger to make a sleeve (an idea repeated, with disastrous consequences, by Debbie Harry for her first solo album). You won't find any Roger Dean-designed sleeves in this book, by the way. While they were clearly distinct, Dean's sci-fi influenced paintings had little true artistic or graphic merit and were neither innovative nor influential.

▶ **We went to the farmer's market and got this actual fish head, a real fish**

CAL SCHENKEL, DESIGNER

▶ **Trout Mask Replica Captain Beefheart & His Magic Band**
RELEASED 1970 | USA | SLEEVE DESIGN BY CAL SCHENKEL | PHOTOGRAPHY BY ED CARAEFF | ALBUM PRODUCED BY FRANK ZAPPA
Cal Schenkel was Zappa's in-house designer for Bizarre and Straight Records. "Someone, I guess that was me, decided, 'Well, why don't we get a real fish head?'" said Schenkel. "We rigged it up for a prop, and it was just an amazing session." Don van Vliet (Captain Beefheart) wore the fish head himself. Somehow, it fitted perfectly. The sleeve suited the strangeness of the album and both have become an icon.

STRAIGHT STEREO
STS 1053

TROUT MASK REPLICA

CAPTAIN BEEFHEART
& HIS MAGIC BAND

FRIPP & ENO
(NO PUSSYFOOTING)

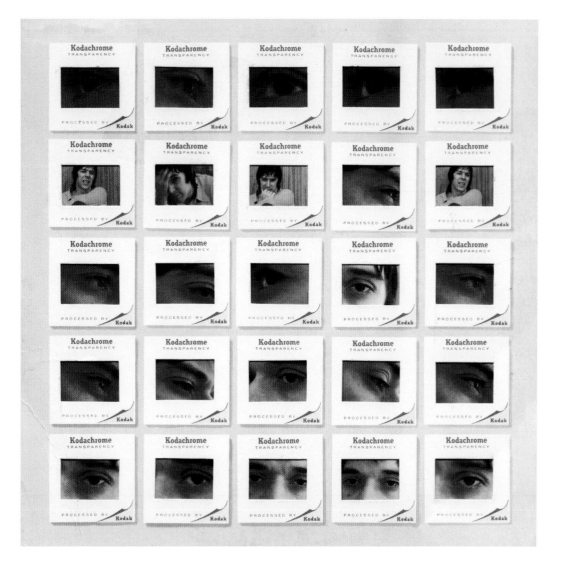

**◀ No Pussyfooting) /
Robert Fripp and Brian Eno**
RELEASED 1973 | ISLAND
RECORDS | UK | SLEEVE DESIGN
AND PHOTOGRAPHY BY WILLIE
CHRISTIE | ALBUM PRODUCED BY
ROBERT FRIPP AND BRIAN ENO
A memorable sleeve that
accurately reflects (no pun
intended) the contents of the
album, which consisted of two
long electronically modified
instrumentals, one on each
side. It was a forerunner of the
ambient sound genre. The sleeve
folds out with two more virtually
identical images on the inside
and the same room – this time
uninhabited – on the back. Eno
has brought along some of his
pornographic playing cards
which he studies while Fripp
times him. The sleeve bears
some serous scrutiny; where,
for instance, is the photographer?
This must have been fiendishly
difficult to shoot. The room
is a wonderful period piece,
complete with a tourist painting
on a slice of wood.

**▲ John Cale /
Academy in Peril**
RELEASED 1972 | REPRISE RECORDS |
USA | SLEEVE DESIGN BY ANDY
WARHOL | PHOTOGRAPHY BY ED
THRASHER | ALBUM PRODUCED
BY JOHN CALE
Cale knew Warhol from his days
in The Velvet Underground when
Warhol designed their first two
album sleeves. The artist was
not cheap, so Cale exchanged
the design for Warhol's right to
use his *Days of Steam* in the
movie soundtrack of *Heat*. This
is a lesser known Andy Warhol
sleeve but uses many of his
standard techniques, notably
repetition of an image. Like his
multiple Marilyns or soup cans,
he simply made a design with
transparency frames which were
then die-cut to show a series of
images of Cale on the gatefold
behind. Warhol clearly liked the
work – it has his rubber-stamped
studio signature on the back.

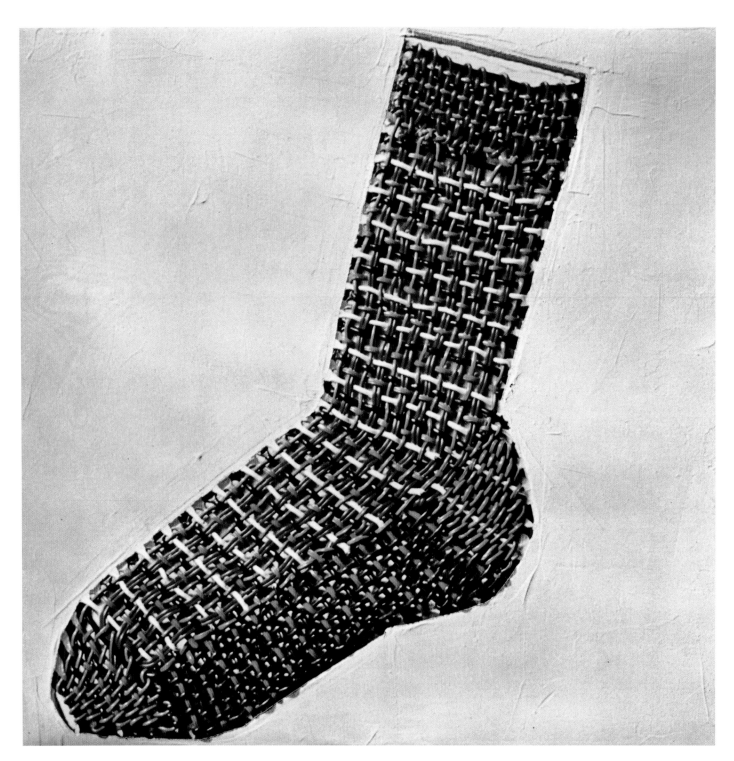

◀ In Praise of Learning / Henry Cow

RELEASED 1975 | VIRGIN RECORDS | UK | SLEEVE DESIGN BY GREGG SKERMAN | PAINTING BY RAY SMITH | ALBUM PRODUCED BY HENRY COW, SLAPP HAPPY AND PHIL BECQUE

When Henry Cow signed to Virgin they used one of artist Ray Smith's paint socks as the sleeve of their debut album, *Leg End*. They used one again on their second, this time featuring their name, and on this, their third and final album. The socks make a wonderful series, purer even than Chicago's series of numbered LPs. How did Smith make them? You would think it impossible to make paint behave that way.

▲ Brain Salad Surgery / Emerson, Lake & Palmer

RELEASED 1973 | MANTICORE/ ATLANTIC | UK| DESIGN AND ART DIRECTION BY FABIO NICOLI ASSOCIATES | COVER PAINTING BY H.R. GIGER BY ARRANGEMENT WITH THE HOUSE OF IDEAS, ZURICH | ALBUM PRODUCED BY GREG LAKE

For *Brain Salad Surgery*, ELP turned to Swiss surrealist painter H.R. Giger. Six years later Giger's fabulous paintings would be used as the basis for sets in Ridley Scott's *Alien,* but it was here that his unique style got its first mass-market airing. His cold, medical style was new for album cover design at the time, but has been much copied since. [JM]

▲ On the Corner / Miles Davis

RELEASED 1972 | COLUMBIA RECORDS | USA | SLEEVE ILLUSTRATION BY CORKY MCCOY | ALBUM PRODUCED BY TEO MACERO

"It was with Sly Stone and James Brown in mind that I went into the studio in June 1972 to record *On the Corner*," said Miles Davis. "During that time everyone was dressing kind of 'out on the street', you know, platform shoes that were yellow, and electric yellow at that, handkerchiefs around the neck, headbands, rawhide vests, and so on. Black women were wearing them real tight dresses that had their big butts sticking way out back." Davis wanted Columbia Records to market the album to young black people, and this cover by the trumpeter's former flatmate cartoonist Corky McCoy (who went on to illustrate *In Concert*, *Water Babies* and *Big Fun* for Miles) was designed to appeal to youth, rather than Davis's usual audience of Jazz aficionados. But the traditional jazz critics were appalled and the album failed to reach its intended audience. Davis was disappointed when it didn't achive the commercial success that he had hoped for, but it certainly widened his audience among the earnest, white, long-haired and often greatcoated Proggresive Rock fans, for whom *On the Corner* became a treasured addition to their library of albums.

1970s Euro Rock

By mid-decade, European Rock music was reaching the US as well as UK. Because of language, many European bands picked up on the instrumental side. Jazz fusion was big: Frank Zappa's work in particular was huge, though relatively unknown in the US.

Continental Europeans also embraced consciousness-expanding drugs, from which emerged post-psychedelic electro-Rock fusion combining bold experimentation and skilled playing. Amon Duul formed in 1968, and quickly split into two groups: Amon Duul I and II. The former split after one album; the latter made many, and their electronic experiments and doom-laden lyrics, made them the first German band known throughout Europe.

Another German band, heavily influenced by the 1960s art scene (they used a Bridget Riley work on their debut sleeve), was Faust, who mixed the sound of vacuum cleaners with chants and electronic strings to create a remarkable sound.

One of the most influential of German Rock-based Euro Rockers were Can. They would later even be claimed by some Punk bands as an influence. Can managed to sell decent numbers of albums in America, probably because they did employ guitar

solos on their records – although never fiddly ones. The fact that they had a multiracial line-up may have helped too. Can's image and album sleeves were both closely controlled by the band – their biggest-selling album, *Saw Delight*, with its motor saw blade illustration that featured a stained glass effect had no credit otherwise, so one can only assume that it is the work of the band themselves.

However, by far the most influential of all the Euro Rock acts of the decade was Kraftwerk, who are credited with single-handedly inspiring the 1980s electronica movement. Adopting a sparse, almost modernist approach to both their music (which was created completely electronically) and album artwork (see *Autobahn*) the four men from Düsseldorf created a mystique about themselves that still endures to the present day.

By the end of the 1970s, as Punk Rock was blazing its way through England and elsewhere, David Bowie had mutated into a Euro Rocker. (He cleverly never put a safety pin through his nose.) As with his earlier identities, through *Heroes* particularly and *Low* and *Lodger* less so, he set a new style standard with his album sleeves.

> ▶ **It's such a perfect example of beauty in the everyday, of realism and of subversion**
>
> PETER SAVILLE, DESIGNER

▶ **Autobahn / Kraftwerk**
RELEASED 1974 | VERTIGO | GERMANY | ALBUM PRODUCED BY RALF HUTTER AND FLORIAN SCHNEIDER
The first album by the German originators of synth-Pop came as a shock after the excesses of Prog Rock, the sleeve perfectly reflecting the clean sounds within. Kraftwerk had internalized the metronomic beat of the motorway. "We were on tour and it happened that we just came off the autobahn after a long ride," said Florian Schneider. "When we came in to play we had this speed in our music." What better image for the sleeve than the international highway sign for the autobahn itself? Designer Peter Saville acknowledged this unattributed sleeve as a major influence.

◄ Landed / Can

RELEASED 1975 | VIRGIN | UK |
SLEEVE DESIGN BY CHRISTINE |
ALBUM PRODUCED BY CAN

Can's seventh album continued their tradition of colourful and eye-catching sleeve designs. If you don't use a group photograph – and Can never did – one of the few ways you can deal with a group is to use the common design convention of multiple images, as in Andy Warhol's soup can paintings. For this collage, "Christine" (a friend of the band? Girlfriend?) takes one image of each member of the group and multiplies them, hand-colouring and annotating them to make each one into a portrait stereotype: pirate, clown, bandit, artist, and the curly moustache that Duchamp gave the Mona Lisa. The result is a vibrant image, the luminous colours set off by a black frame.

► Heroes / David Bowie

RELEASED 1977 | RCA | UK |
PHOTOGRAPHY BY MASAYOSHI
SUKITA | ALBUM PRODUCED BY
DAVID BOWIE AND TONY VISCONTI

This is Berlin period Bowie. The monochrome sleeve, short hair and black leather jacket counter the threat posed by newly arrived Punk, which was questioning the validity of Rock dinosaurs such as the Steely Dan, Led Zeppelin and even the Stones. David wanted to show he was still hip. This is the second of his Teutonic Trilogy (the others being *Low* and *Lodger*) and the image by Sukita, one of Bowie's favourite photographers, matches the music perfectly. Ziggy's red spiky hair came from a model shot by Sukita for Kansai Yamamoto's first London collection that David saw in *Honey* magazine in 1971.

► The Faust Tapes / Faust

RELEASED 1973 | VIRGIN |
UK | SLEEVE DESIGN BY UWE
NETTELBECK | PAINTING, "CREST",
BY BRIDGET RILEY | PHOTOGRAPH
BY ROBERT HORNER | ALBUM
PRODUCED BY UWE NETTELBECK

These were live and rehearsal tapes, not a studio album, and were offered to fans for the bargain price of 49 pence. Bridget Riley's *Crest* from 1964 made a perfect album sleeve for those not familiar with Faust's brand of electronic Kraut-Rock. Challenging work but attractive, not threatening. *Crest* was well chosen because it originated in a diamond format and didn't need to be cropped. (The white spaces on the sleeve are not part of the painting.) The original is eye-boggling, but even this reduced version is a powerful experience.

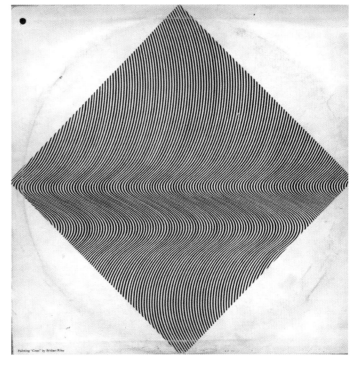

1970s **Funk**

Funk began, as much else did, with James Brown. The self-styled Godfather of Soul had found himself playing peacemaker between white authorities and black youth during the riots that had ripped the heart out of major US cities following the assassination of Martin Luther King Jr in 1968 – he had appeared on national TV to ask for calm. In 1970 he released *Funky Drummer* and the new beat had begun. Pretty soon the new decade found that there was a wealth of black acts making decidedly funky music and most of it had a political, that is to say black consciousness, message. Even acts who had been regarded as good-time Soul groups began singing about change. Like the O'Jays, who commissioned a cover image depicting the plight of African slaves being carried to America. 1950s group the Isley Brothers donned new, sparkling clothes and got political and funky, providing 1980s Rap act Public Enemy with the basis for their biggest hit Fight the Power. Former Stax A&R man Isaac Hayes wrote and performed the soundtrack for the hugely successful black movie *Shaft*, and went on to turn Bacharach and David hits into long, drawn-out Funk operas on a series of unique albums. One, *Black Moses*, boasted a cover that folded

out four ways to reveal Hayes standing on a beach as though on a crucifix, in aviator sunglasses and a coat of many colours.

The Pop charts soon filled up with Funk hits that carried a message, such as Syl Johnson's Am I Black Enough for You? and Stevie Wonder's Living for the City. Even the golden (but troubled) boy of Motown, Marvin Gaye, got funky and political, releasing first What's Going On with its heavy conservation message and then Let's Get It On, in which he really implored people to make love (that's LURVE), not war.

Because Funk bands were selling a message as well as music, packaging became important. There was a trend for a while for sleeves to be gatefold and to use all of the space for a single image, as with Donald Byrd's *Street Lady* (see page 118) and Ohio Players' sleeves (see opposite). There were also countless die-cut sleeves, such as Curtis Mayfield's *Superfly*, *Marvin Gaye Live* and Lonnie Liston's *The Mack*, which had to be handled and opened to be fully appreciated. They're not included here because we couldn't fold out the die-cut piece on the page, but find them if you can. This was the dawning of much innovation in black music and design.

▶ **Fire / The Ohio Players**
RELEASED 1974 | MERCURY | USA | ART DIRECTION BY JIM LADWIG | SLEEVE DESIGNED BY LEN WILLIS | PHOTOGRAPHY BY STAN MALINOWSKI | ALBUM PRODUCED BY THE OHIO PLAYERS
The Ohio Players' trademark was using erotic images on album sleeves. In 1971 they had put a skinny, shaven-headed woman in a leather bikini with a whip on the cover of *Pain* – when the sleeve folded out it revealed a man in leather trunks in the "crab" position. Their next three, *Pleasure*, *Ecstasy* and *Climax*, all bore similar sado-masochistic themes and used the same model. *Climax* had her stabbing a man in the back, but as it was released without the Players' permission, after they had left Westland for the larger Mercury, the cover was probably a "message" from the old label. Having signed to a major, in 1974 they released *Skin Tight*, its cover having only a mild S&M connotation in the studded leather belt worn by the model. It's this cover, though, that best displays the Players' classy objectification of women. Its message might be crude (a hose, geddit?) but the photography and the very idea of using this as an album cover are sublime.

The beginning
of "bling"?

LLOYD BRADLEY, AUTHOR
"BASS CULTURE: WHEN
REGGAE WAS KING"

▶ **The beginning
of "bling"?**

LLOYD BRADLEY, AUTHOR
"BASS CULTURE: WHEN
REGGAE WAS KING"

◀ **Street Lady | Donald Byrd**

RELEASED 1973 | BLUE NOTE |
USA | ART DIRECTION AND
PHOTOGRAPHY BY MIKE SALISBURY |
ALBUM PRODUCED BY LARRY MIZELL

By 1973 trumpeter Byrd had
been gaining a reputation in
clubs and discos as a purveyor
of cool Jazz-Funk fusion. But
that was a bit too cool and so
he released first *Black Byrd*, a
collection of "street"-themed
songs about junkies and funkin',
and followed it up with *Street
Lady*. Comparable to Curtis
Mayfield's *Superfly* and, later,
Short Eyes or Isaac Hayes' *Shaft*,
Street Lady is the soundtrack to
a movie that was never made.
It's also a "message" album.
Unlike The Ohio Players, about
whom the best that could be
said was that they were
promoting the beauty and sex
appeal of black women, the
sleeve for *Street Lady* might be
about sex, but it's more about
exploitation. The "prostitute" on
the cover – which folds out to
reveal her in full length, wearing
hotpants and platform shoes – is
not glamorous in any real sense,
although it would make a great
poster for a blaxploitation movie.

▲ **Rhapsody in White / The
Love Unlimited Orchestra**

RELEASED 1974 | USA | SLEEVE
DESIGN BY BARRY WHITE | ALBUM
PRODUCED BY BARRY WHITE

Arranged, conducted, and with
sleeve "art concept" all by Barry
White. Our hero stands three
quarter view, holding in his pot
belly, waistline further obscured
by his folded hands, his hair a
lacquered helmet, while a harem
of four lovely girls admire his rear
silhouette. His expression is one
of defiance, the arrogance of a
man flaunting his success at the
peak of his career. But at the same
time it's seductive: he knows his
music turns the ladies on. He
thrusts his lower lip forward in
a sexy pout. Who else would
dare to put a sleeve like this on
an album, with its confusion of
typefaces and the suggestion
that this somewhat municipal
looking building might actually
be where Barry lives? [BM]

◀ One Nation Under a Groove / Funkadelic

RELEASED 1978 | WARNER BROTHERS | USA | ART DIRECTION BY ED THRASHER | ILLUSTRATION BY PEDRO BELL | ALBUM PRODUCED BY GEORGE CLINTON FOR THANG, INC

In the early 1960s George Clinton had quit as producer for Motown to run a barber shop, disillusioned by the lack of success for his own Soul act, The Parliaments. In 1969, however, he released the first Funkadelic album and a year later launched Parliament (using much the last line-up of The Parliaments, but Motown had bought the band name). So began the life of an incredible, ever-changing, Funktastic, bombastic experiment in Funk. Both Parliament and Funkadelic scored hit singles and albums, as did bassist Bootsy Collins (who joined from James Brown's JBs in 1972), all under the aegis of the P-Funk family. All the various P-Funk release sleeves were drawn in a kind of doped-out futuristic cartoon style by four artists: Pedro Bell, Overton Loyd, Ronald P. Edwards, and Diem Jones. *One Nation*, with its nod to the Iwo Jima flag raisers' monument, is cleaner and more striking than many of Funkadelic's covers, despite listing the tracks on the front. The sleeve perfectly captures the strident, pioneering R 'n' B contained within – on a 12-inch LP and accompanying 7-inch EP that played at 33⅓ rpm.

▶ This Boot Is Made for Fonk-N / Bootsy's Rubber Band

RELEASED 1979 | WARNER BROTHERS | USA | SLEEVE DESIGN BY ARCHIE IVY, OVERTON LOYD | ALBUM PRODUCED BY DR FUNKENSTEIN

Dr Funkenstein is George Clinton, of course. Bassist Bootsy's music is far more Soul-oriented than Parliament's or Funkadelic's. This cover uses a P-Funk style comic drawing of Bootsy, with "Me" badge and lascivious tongue. The artwork seems crammed into too small a space, hinting at Bootsy's "stretchin'" music. Collins's sound is all up front, sliding, stretching Funk, falsetto choruses and bleeding edges, hence his head busting out of the side of the frame, the neck of his bass needing to fit in shot, the title curling back at the gaping mouth.

▶ Gloryhallastoopid (Or Pin the Tail on the Funky) / Parliament

RELEASED 1979 | WARNER BROTHERS | USA | ART DIRECTION BY ED THRASHER | ILLUSTRATION BY OVERTON LOYD | ALBUM PRODUCED BY GEORGE CLINTON

On the front, against a black background, is a bizarre space donkey in a fantastic costume. Inside are four pages of brilliantly drawn comics. Most packaging of album sleeves up to this point had some kind of relevance to the music – even Zappa's Weasels was obviously a satire on advertising. *Gloryhallastoopid* was unique in that it seemed to dare anyone to buy it. That thing on the cover is an ass. "Do you identify with an ass in ridiculous clothes? Then buy this record," seems to be the message.

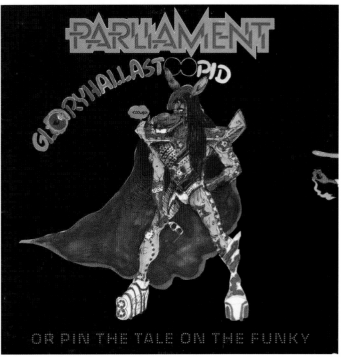

Sir Joe Quarterman
& Free Soul
A SUBSIDIARY OF G S F INC.
GSF
RECORDS
school bus
Sir Joe + Free Soul

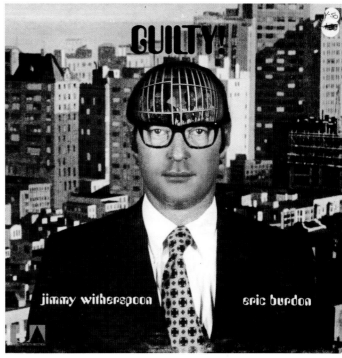

◀ Sir Joe Quarterman and Free Soul / Sir Joe Quarterman and Free Soul

RELEASED 1973 | GSF | USA | SLEEVE DESIGN BY BARNEY/VAN ARTWORK JOE QUARTERMAN | ALBUM PRODUCED BY COTTER WELLS, BILL TATE AND JOE QUARTERMAN FOR MANTIS RECORD CORP

The only Sir Joe/Free Soul album was a 1990s Deep Soul classic, so maybe a clue to their lack of success lies in the cover. Drawn by Joe, it's a naive tableau of scenes from the world of Free Soul, hinting that there was either no budget to have a professional designer (GSF was a small New York label) or that Joe's ego dictated they use his artwork.

▲ Ship Ahoy / The O'Jays

RELEASED 1973 | CBS | USA | ART DIRECTION BY ED LEE | ARTWORK BY JAMES BARKLEY | ALBUM PRODUCED BY GAMBLE AND HUFF

The O'Jays' *Ship Ahoy* is overtly political, a hymn to the millions of Africans shipped to America in the 18th century. The cover (painted by a minor artist whose best-known work was for a United States stamp and who illustrated children's books) puts the three O'Jays in the hold of a slave ship, along with the slaves. That a band best known as a Pop act should produce such a sleeve was enough to make even the most myopic of white music fans take note that something was about to change.

▲ Guilty! / Jimmy Witherspoon / Eric Burdon

RELEASED 1971 | UNITED ARTISTS RECORDS | UK | SLEEVE DESIGN BY ERIC BURDON | ART DIRECTION BY HOWARD MILLER AND PHOTOGRAPHY BY MICHEL STRAUSS | PRODUCED BY JERRY GOLDSTEIN AND ERIC BURDON

This was very much a product of the growing political awareness and radicalism in the United States, when the Black Panthers were being shot down in cold blood by the dozen and even white students were being gunned down during anti-Vietnam war protests. Ex-Animal Eric Burdon's inspired cover – black men trapped behind bars in the white jail of a complacent white middle-class male's head – has to be one of the most bizarre ever published on an album sleeve. The album includes the San Quentin Prison Band, recorded on location, as well as a poem by the editor of the *San Quentin News* on the back sleeve. [BM]

▼ Keep on Steppin' / The Fatback Band

RELEASED 1974 | ACE RECORDS | UK | SLEEVE DESIGNED BY TED PETTUS | ALBUM PRODUCED BY THE FATBACK BAND

Keep on Steppin' is packed with the smoothest grooves that the Fatback Band had recorded at the time. With its use of graffiti for the title, the cover predates the then nascent Hip-hop movement by at least three years, while the dancing girl adds a degree of innocence that was mirrored only by the other sleeve on this page, *Skin I'm In*. Simply because there were no brooding macho men on the cover, nor a blatantly sexist photo, *Keep on Steppin'* was as cool a cover as the band it sold.

▼ **Probably the greatest album cover ever, this typifies a trend in 1970s funk whereby the sleeve represents the music rather than the artists**

LLOYD BRADLEY, AUTHOR

▼ Skin I'm In / Chairmen of the Board

RELEASED 1974 | INVICTUS | USA | SLEEVE DESIGNED BY TERESA ALFIERI | HAND LETTERING BY VIRGINIA | TEAM PHOTOGRAPHY BY MIRELLA RICCIARDI | ALBUM PRODUCED BY JEFFREY BOWEN, HOLLAND-DOZIER-HOLLAND PRODUCTIONS INC

The image choice by label Invictus followed a trend for pro-black consciousness records. The photo was taken by a (white) British woman who had lived in Africa, published in her first book, *Vanishing Africa*. The stare of the girl in what looks like a rag dress is extremely powerful, and the hand lettering adds a further element of class.

▶ There's a Riot Goin' On / Sly & The Family Stone

RELEASED 1971 | EPIC RECORDS | USA | SLEEVE DESIGN BY JOHN BERG | ALBUM PRODUCED BY SYLVESTER STEWART AND SLY STONE

Released when Black Power and anti-US sentiment were at their highest, Sly put the American flag on the cover of what is undoubtedly his greatest album. There is an irony at work here that was probably lost on many fans. There is no sight of the star, nor any sign of the title (except for a small sticker that Epic clearly felt was needed). With such a cover the message was clear: you can be proud to be American and still protest about America.

1970s Reggae

Until the mid-1970s, Reggae was mainly single-driven. In keeping with the Jamaican Reggae industry, 7-inch singles were the lifeblood of even British-based Reggae acts. At the end of the 1960s Reggae and Ska had seen unprecedented sales and Top 40 success for both Rock Steady numbers by the likes of the Skatalites, Desmond Dekker, The Pioneers and Dandy. John Holt and Johnny Nash had also scored hit singles (even in the USA for Nash). But until Island Records signed Bob Marley, the only Reggae albums that sold significantly were the *Tighten Up* compilations on Trojan Records. These collections of Jamaican and UK hits were as notable for their covers – usually featuring scantily clad women – as they were for the great tunes therein.

Although *Tighten Up Volume 1*, released in 1968, depicted a Jamaican woman in a hat and dress, Volume 2 showed a (white) female torso with the title written in lipstick on her stomach, her arms crossed and almost covering her breast. From Volume 3 on (to Volume 8 and then 1975's *20 Tighten Ups*), black women were pictured in various states of undress. Volume 4 had a photo of a naked woman being buried in what look like chocolate Smarties (possibly a nod to The

Who's *Sell Out*). Reggae sleeves in Jamaica tended to be plain, the name of the producer, studio, or even the performer often missing.

The soundtrack to *The Harder They Come*, released in the same year as *Catch a Fire*, used the same artwork as the movie poster. It was also a compilation, despite being credited to the film's star Jimmy Cliff (who sang only half of the album's 12 tracks). So when Bob Marley's debut album for Island was released (see opposite) the packaging and the very fact of its existence were unusual in several ways. The first 20,000 copies were sold in a massive hinged, cardboard lighter, but after that the cover featured Marley smoking an enormous joint.

After 1976, much more Reggae was released on the UK market, artists often being championed by famous Punk groups. But this was not Pop-friendly Reggae (even Marley's debut could be considered Pop); this was Roots, Dub and Lovers' Rock Reggae, all performed by dreadlocked Rastafarians singing in patois, who didn't care whether the white man understood or not. The sleeves here are a mixture of British and Jamaican artists, but are all examples of how the first real wave of Reggae albums were sold to a growing white audience.

▶ **Catch a Fire /
Bob Marley & the Wailers**
RELEASED 1973 | ISLAND | UK |
SLEEVE DESIGN BY ROD DYER, BOB
WEINER | ART DIRECTION JOHN
HOERNLE | ALBUM PRODUCED BY
BOB MARLEY AND CHRIS BLACKWELL
Bob Marley's Island debut was intended to launch the career of the world's first Reggae superstar. So his UK-based label, run by an expat white Jamaican, decided to make a statement with the sleeve. Taking the title almost literally they created a Zippo lighter, complete with hinged lid, fake wick and striking stone. The disc slipped out of the top of the lighter. Released the same year as Alice Cooper's *School's Out* (shaped as a school desk with lifting lid, see page 81) and a year after The Rolling Stones' *Sticky Fingers* (with Warhol's zipper fly, see page 87), *Catch a Fire* represents the epitome of inventive album packaging. Possibly because there was a limit on square-shaped ideas that could be employed, but more likely to do with the cost, future inventive packaging was limited to PiL's *Metal Box* (page 139) and *Return of the Durutti Column* (page 147). The album did establish Marley as a star in the making, and the packaging played no small part in that. [BM]

▼ Two Sevens Clash / Culture

RELEASED 1978 | LIGHTNING RECORDS | UK | SLEEVE DESIGN BY LIGHTNING | ALBUM PRODUCED BY JOE GIBBS AND ERROL T

In the immediate aftermath of the British Punk explosion, Jamaican Reggae was enjoying an upswing in popularity. Johnny Rotten of The Sex Pistols and Paul Simonon of The Clash both championed the music in a way that no white musician of any note had before, and a generation of British youth was listening to Reggae for the first time. Punk bands would play records by such Roots Reggae Rasta superstars as Augustus Pablo, Red Uhuru and, possibly more than any other record during the summer of 1977, this. DJ Don Letts had played *Two Sevens Clash* at the Roxy every night. His copy was a Jamaican release. British Reggae label Lightning licensed the LP and got it out in early 1978. The cover points to Punk graphics (the yellow echoing the Pistols' album) while the photograph makes gods of the band.

▼ Forces of Victory / Linton Kwesi Johnson

RELEASED 1979 | ISLAND RECORDS | UK | SLEEVE DESIGN BY ZEBULON DESIGN | PHOTOGRAPHY BY DENNIS MORRIS | ALBUM PRODUCED BY LINTON KWESI JOHNSON

Poet Linton Kwesi Johnson was of the first generation of British West Indians, often experiencing almost institutionalized racism. On this debut LP, LKJ fought back. The title, combined with the stark image of a WWII-era microphone by Island Records photographer Dennis Morris, evokes the wartime radio broadcasts by former Prime Minister Winston Churchill that kept up the fighting spirit of the British public.

▶ Bush Doctor / Peter Tosh

RELEASED 1978 | ROLLING STONE RECORDS | UK | PHOTOGRAPH BY ARA GALLANT | ALBUM PRODUCED BY PETER TOSH, ROBBIE SHAKESPEARE AND THE GLIMMER TWINS

Former Wailer Peter Tosh was an inspiration, certainly to other Jamaican musicians, and clearly had something in common with Stones Jagger and Richards. All three were stoned rebels. Bob Marley had enjoyed only limited success in the US when *Bush Doctor* was released, its sleeve designed to distance Tosh from Marley's almost martial, khaki image. Here is a man of fire and energy – a mystical man, a Bush Doctor with magical powers.

▲ **Hulet / Aswad**
RELEASED 1979 | GROVE-ISLAND RECORDS | UK | ASWAD LOGO BY EARL | ALBUM PRODUCED BY ASWAD AND MICKEY CAMPBELL
Earl's cover owes something to the original Rastafarian banner made in Notting Hill in 1965. On the banner, the image of the Lion of the Tribe of Judah was taken by designer Larry Lewis from the Egg Marketing Board's lion logo, which was stamped on each egg. Though the lion is a common design element on Reggae records, this particular logo is a very satisfactory combination of elements, including the golden coronation crown of the Ethiopian emperor Haile Selassie, the Jamaican national colours and a clever use of the band's name to make up the body of the lion. [BM]

▶ **Best Dressed Chicken in Town / Dr Alimantado**
RELEASED 1978 | GREENSLEEVES | UK| SLEEVE PHOTOGRAPHY BY D.K. JAMES | ALBUM PRODUCED BY W. THOMPSON, AN ISDA PRODUCTION
Dr Alimantado had become known in the UK for the title track of this album, a compilation of recordings made between 1973 and 1976. His single Born for a Purpose – written after the Doctor had only just survived being run down by a bus in Kingston – had been adopted by The Sex Pistols' Johnny Rotten in 1977 as a kind of personal anthem. Punk made the Doctor a minor star in the UK, as it did various other Jamaican Reggae artists. None was quite as original or odd as the former James Winston Thompson, though. *Best Dressed Chicken* was described by Greensleeves as "three minutes of musical madness" and the cover image it chose to sell his UK debut album reflected this. That's Kingston the Doctor's "posing" in, and yes, his fly is open and yes, that's a bus in the background. It is a wholly accurate snapshot of Jamaica in the late 1970s and it's a wholly arresting album cover too.

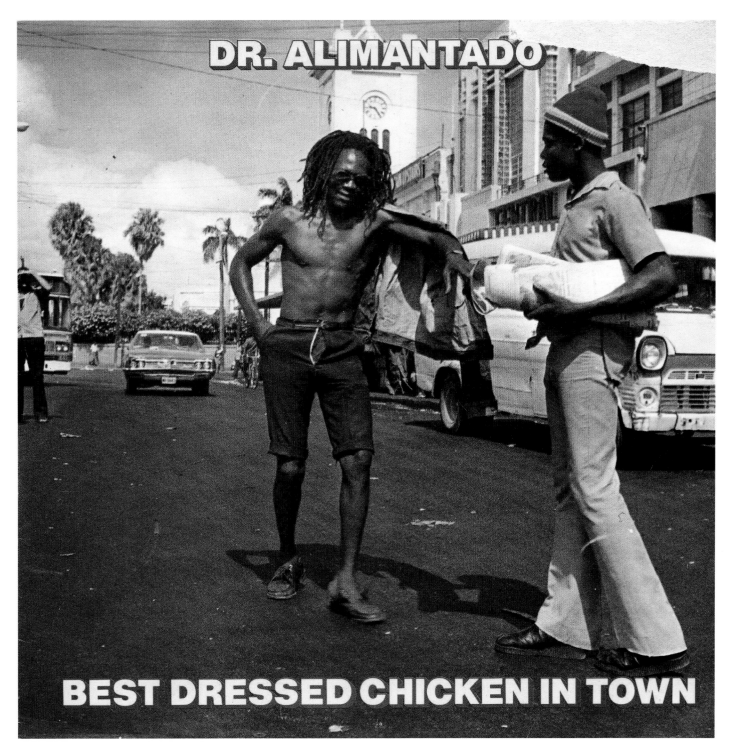

1970s Punk

Just as Dave King's visual trademarks characterized mid-1960s design – torn paper edges to images, screen prints enlarged to make the dots very large, images blown up out of all proportion – so Jamie Reid's devices sum up British Punk design: photos reduced to line-shots, stark black and white with no middle ground. Type was cut from newspapers like a ransom note, with a mix of typefaces so that none of the words matched (or in the case of The Sex Pistols logo, individual letters were cut to provide a mixture of faces). Typography is usually arranged within an organizational grid which this method negates. The same applies to the whole word, which no longer has the shape that normal typography would give it. Because no regular typefaces were used, Reid was able to use out-of-date faces without anyone noticing. These often jarred with each other, providing some of the visual dynamic he was seeking. He also introduced other design conventions: the Union Jack, last used by the Mods; t-shirts with slogans stencilled on them; torn clothing with rips mended with safety pins. His image of the Queen with a safety pin through her cheek at the time of the Silver Jubilee is the most iconic of the whole period. Reid's work, with

its purposefully amateurish feel, was quickly appropriated by most other Punk designers in the UK, who added new devices such as using worn-out typewriters with broken typefaces and lettering produced on a Dynotape machine, more usually used for labelling shelves in shops.

In the States the Punk movement began earlier. Iggy Pop, New York Dolls and other groups from the early 1970s provided a set of monochrome images, usually in full contrast with little middle ground, based around torn jeans and moody back alleys. This was copied to a degree in Britain: The Clash's first album cover was very much modelled on The Ramones' debut sleeve.

In Britain, much of the excitement of Punk was confined to singles – most Punk bands couldn't sustain a full album. The rise of small indie labels meant that many wildly experimental sleeves were released, Barney Bubbles's work for Stiff among the best.

Punk design was not confined to albums. Just as 1960s psychedelia is best found in poster art, Punk design was informed very much by Punk fashion; the Pistols did, after all, begin in a King's Road dress shop. As a design style it remains remarkably popular, and still informs CD design today. [BM]

> **The ultra simple album design was a powerful image which left you in no doubt that something entirely awesome and different was about to land on your turntable**
>
> ALAN EDWARDS, MUSIC PR

▶ **Never Mind the Bollocks Here's The Sex Pistols / The Sex Pistols**
RELEASED 1977 | VIRGIN RECORDS | UK | SLEEVE DESIGN BY JAMIE REID | ALBUM PRODUCED BY CHRIS THOMAS
Designer Jamie Reid's Sex Pistols graphics defined the look of Punk. "I saw Punk as part of an art movement that's gone over the past hundred years, with roots in Russian agitprop, Dada, surrealism and Situationism" Reid said. His Pistols sleeve was purposely crude: he chose ugly typography and intentionally clashing colours, and could not have been stronger or better matched to the band. [BM]

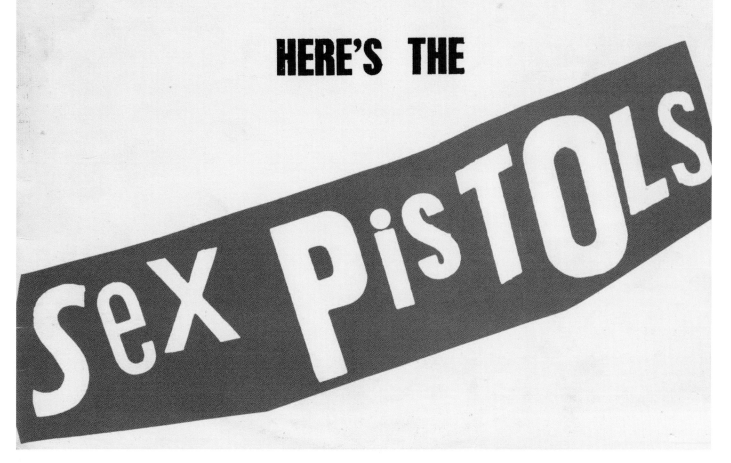

NEVER MIND THE BOLLOCKS

HERE'S THE **SeX PiSTOLS**

▲ New York Dolls / New York Dolls

RELEASED 1973 | MERCURY | USA | SLEEVE DESIGN BY ALBUM GRAPHICS, INC | PHOTOGRAPHY BY TOSHI ASAKA | ALBUM PRODUCED BY TODD RUNDGREN

The Dolls credited all the people who contributed to their good looks on the sleeve: hair by Shin, make-up by Dave O'Grady and photo by Toshi Asaka. The overall effect was that they looked like a bunch of drag queens who had been up all night – except David Johansen, checking his pancake. The high camp look was a spin-off of the Glam Rock introduced to the US by David Bowie, a daring trend when anyone with long hair risked the wrath of rednecks. [BM]

▶ Because as a teenager I was the worst wallflower weirdo, I knew what it felt like to be an outsider

PATTI SMITH

▲ The Idiot / Iggy Pop

RELEASED 1977 | RCA | UK | COVER PHOTOGRAPHY BY UNKNOWN | ALBUM RECORDED BY DAVID BOWIE | MIXED BY TONY VISCONTI

An album of songs co-written with David Bowie, far removed from Iggy's work with the Stooges, and recorded at the Hansa Studios by the wall which then divided the city. The sleeve is by an unknown photographer but it fits the mood of the album perfectly. Iggy stands in the rain in an ill-fitting too-tight jacket, in a grey landscape. It is similar to Bowie's *Heroes* sleeve, down to the mime gestures: is he doing his slithery snake gesture from his stage act or just feeling to see if it's raining? [BM]

▶ Horses / Patti Smith

RELEASED 1975 | ARISTA | US | COVER PHOTOGRAPHY BY ROBERT MAPPLETHORPE | ALBUM PRODUCED BY JOHN CALE

Patti had total control over her sleeve and chose ex-boyfriend Robert Mapplethorpe to take the photo. He shot it at his boyfriend Sam Wagstaff's place, where the sun cast a perfect light at a certain time of day, making an almost invisible diagonal across the picture. Patti bought a white shirt and black suit, and threw the jacket over her shoulder. With her hair uncombed, it was a daringly dishevelled image. Arista boss Clive Davis hated it, but it became an icon, many people buying the LP just for the sleeve. [BM]

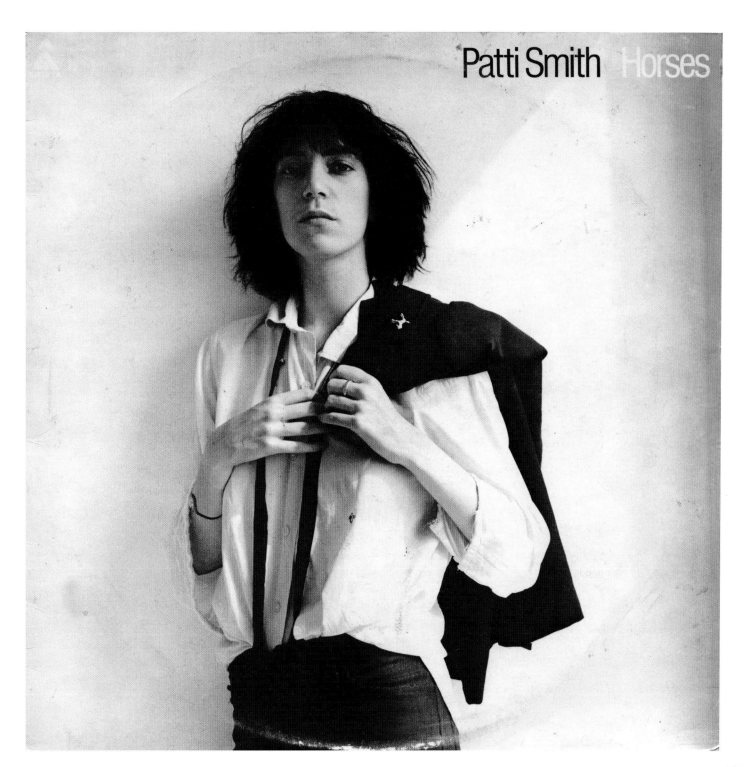

Patti Smith Horses

Ramones / The Ramones

RELEASED 1976 | SIRE | USA | SLEEVE DESIGN BY ARTURO VEGA | PHOTOGRAPHY BY ROBERTA BAYLEY | ALBUM PRODUCED BY CRAIG LEON

The photograph is by Roberta Bayley, doorkeeper at CBGB and house snapper for *Punk* fanzine. Her image of the group as a boy gang sums up what New York Punk was about, with the look of the CBGB's crowd – leather jacket and jeans torn at the knee – which The Ramones made their own. It didn't matter what you sounded like, the look was all important. The Ramones' lighting man Arturo Vega was in charge of all their design; their American eagle logo was his. They used to hang out at his Lower East Side loft, just around the corner from CBGB, on what is now Johnny Ramone Place. [BM]

Live at the Vortex / Various

RELEASED 1978 | NEMS | UK | SLEEVE DESIGN BY HOTHOUSE | PRODUCED BY ROBIN TURNER | LIVE RECORDING BY NICK SYKES

A blend of Punk graphics with the hard-edged typography of the Italian Futurists and the Bauhaus. The stark black red and white graphics owe a lot to David King's designs, including his books on the Comintern, Trotsky and Muhammad Ali. His huge letters are imposed like a rubber stamp over a collage of images from the Vortex. Only part of the word has been masked: mistake or meant? Very Punk. A lot of work has gone into the collage which was then made into a line shot to reduce it to stark black and white. The clean, direct design must have helped to sell this compilation of relatively obscure UK bands. [BM]

New Boots and Panties!! / Ian Dury

RELEASED 1978 | STIFF | UK | SLEEVE DESIGN BY IAN DURY AND BARNEY BUBBLES | PHOTOGRAPHY BY CHRIS GABRIN | ALBUM PRODUCED BY CHAS JANKEL

A memorable, original image conceived by Ian Dury who came across the old-fashioned shopfront while waiting for a bus. The shot was taken outside Axford's at 306 Vauxhall Bridge Road in Victoria, and the six-year-old boy in the picture is Dury's son, Baxter, who was staying with him that week. Gabrin took a whole roll of 24 shots, but he and Dury instantly agreed on which to use. Then Barney Bubbles, Stiff's in-house designer, took over and he and Dury cropped the picture square and added the marker-pen lettering. The title in combination with the picture suggests an unexplained story: are the panties Ian's or those of some unknown woman? [BM]

▼ Do It Yourself /
Ian Dury & the Blockheads

RELEASED 1979 | STIFF RECORDS | UK | SLEEVE DESIGN BY BARNEY BUBBLES | ALBUM PRODUCED BY CHAZ JANKEL

As befitted the new angular sound of the music, Barney Bubbles – who committed suicide in 1983 – put parallel lines, bright colours and blocks of shape on to Stiff albums by The Damned, Elvis Costello and Nick Lowe. There were at least three different versions of suburban wallpaper on the cover of this Blockheads album. All had the title, band name and track-listing on the front, and the little "Tommy the talking tool box" icon. Bubbles also created the Blockhead logo.

▼ **Speaking as someone who'd spent half his life at art colleges, Barney was easily the most incredible designer I'd ever come across. His vision was fantastic**

IAN DURY

▼ Three Imaginary Boys /
The Cure

RELEASED 1979 | FICTION RECORDS | UK | SLEEVE DESIGN BILL SMITH | PHOTOGRAPHY BY MARTYN GODDARD | ALBUM PRODUCED BY CHRIS PARRY

The Cure's debut album was produced by the A&R man who signed them, with a sleeve that the band apparently hated. Given that frontman Robert Smith is still wearing black eyeshadow and back-combing his hair as he nears 50, no wonder he didn't go for this witty sleeve. Maybe he thought that Parry, who claims responsibility for choosing Bill Smith's design and Goddard's photo, was suggesting that Smith was the fridge.

▶ Metal Box / PiL

RELEASED 1979 | VIRGIN | UK | SLEEVE DESIGN BY DENNIS MORRIS | ALBUM PRODUCED BY PUBLIC IMAGE LIMITED

A metal film can embossed with the band's logo, containing three 12-inch singles of album tracks and a scrap of paper with the track list on it. This was a high-design artifact that appeared as the public was discovering designers: designer colours, designer toothbrushes – now, a designer record container. Their slick commercial-looking logo was designed by Dennis Morris, who also worked on the metal box itself. But, did they name the album before or after they had the idea for the packaging? [BM]

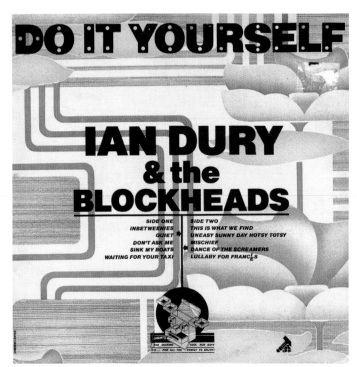

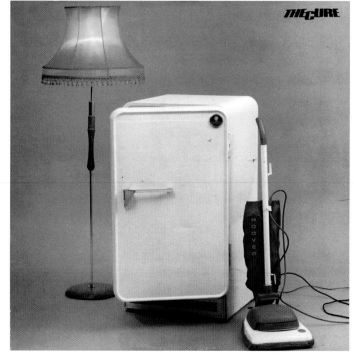

This is a RECORD COVER. This writing is the DESIGN upon the record cover. The DESIGN is to help SELL the record. We hope to draw your attention to it and encourage you to pick it up. When you have done that maybe you'll be persuaded to listen to the music - in this case XTC's Go 2 album. Then we want you to BUY it. The idea being that the more of you that buy this record the more money Virgin Records, the manager Ian Reid and XTC themselves will make. To the aforementioned this is known as PLEASURE. A good cover DESIGN is one that attracts more buyers and gives more pleasure. This writing is trying to pull you in much like an eye-catching picture. It is designed to get you to READ IT. This is called luring the VICTIM, and you are the VICTIM. But if you have a free mind you should STOP READING NOW! because all we are attempting to do is to get you to read on. Yet this is a DOUBLE BIND because if you indeed stop you'll be doing what we tell you, and if you read on you'll be doing what we've wanted all along. And the more you read on the more you're falling for this simple device of telling you exactly how a good commercial design works. They're TRICKS and this is the worst TRICK of all since it's describing the TRICK whilst trying to TRICK you, and if you've read this far then you're TRICKED but you wouldn't have known this unless you'd read this far. At least we're telling you directly instead of seducing you with a beautiful or haunting visual that may never tell you. We're letting you know that you ought to buy this record because in essence it's a PRODUCT and PRODUCTS are to be consumed and you are a consumer and this is a good PRODUCT. We could have written the band's name in special lettering so that it stood out and you'd see it before you'd read any of this writing and possibly have bought it anyway. What we are really suggesting is that you are FOOLISH to buy or not buy an album merely as a consequence of the design on its cover. This is a con because if you agree then you'll probably like this writing - which is the cover design - and hence the album inside. But we've just warned you against that. The con is a con. A good cover design could be considered as one that gets you to buy the record, but that never actually happens to YOU because YOU know it's just a design for the cover. And this is the RECORD COVER.

◀ Go 2 / XTC

RELEASED 1978 | VIRGIN | UK | SLEEVE DESIGN BY HIPGNOSIS | ALBUM PRODUCED BY JOHN LECKIE

Another late 1970s high-design concept, in which the elements of the design are all deconstructed by labelling them: "this is the inner sleeve bag", "this is the front cover" etc. It made for an eye-catching gimmick and attracted attention. The really clever bit of the (un)design was to make it appear as if there had been a printing error and part of the back sleeve was masked out. The missing information was to be found on the insert card where it is printed, as if in error, across colour photos of the band. But the concept is spoilt by a map of Swindon where the band mark their birthplaces and where they lost their virginity. [BM]

◀ Y / The Pop Group

RELEASED 1979 | RADAR RECORDS-WEA | UK | SLEEVE DESIGN BY RICH BEALE AND MALCOLM GARRETT | PHOTOGRAPHY BY DONALD MCCULLIN/SUNDAY TIMES | ALBUM PRODUCED BY DENNIS BOVELL

Along with Crass, Bristol's Pop Group were the anti-Pop group of the late 1970s. The vocals were screamed, the guitars hit and the drums thrashed. Dennis Bovell would also produce the Slits' debut album the same year, the cover featuring the three women topless and covered in mud. The Pop Group, however, chose to use a picture of real mud people for their debut album release. Taken in Papua New Guinea. the image is the least likely for an album of Western pop music imaginable.

▶ Unknown Pleasures / Joy Division

RELEASED 1979 | FACTORY | UK | SLEEVE DESIGN BY PETER SAVILLE | ALBUM PRODUCED BY MARTIN HANNETT

The black embossed sleeve shows a transcription of a signal showing a star going nova. "I remember that I took the artwork for *Unknown Pleasures* around to their manager's house about a week before I left Manchester," said Peter Saville. "Rob (their manager) said: 'Oh, I've got a test pressing. Do you want to hear it?' And I thought: 'Shit, can I handle 40 minutes of Joy Division?' But I'd just delivered the artwork, so I had to pretend like I was interested. Anyway, I listened, and in about 10 or 15 seconds I knew that I'd done the cover for something very important. The artwork was sitting on Rob's table, and I was thinking: 'Wow, this is really spooky.'"

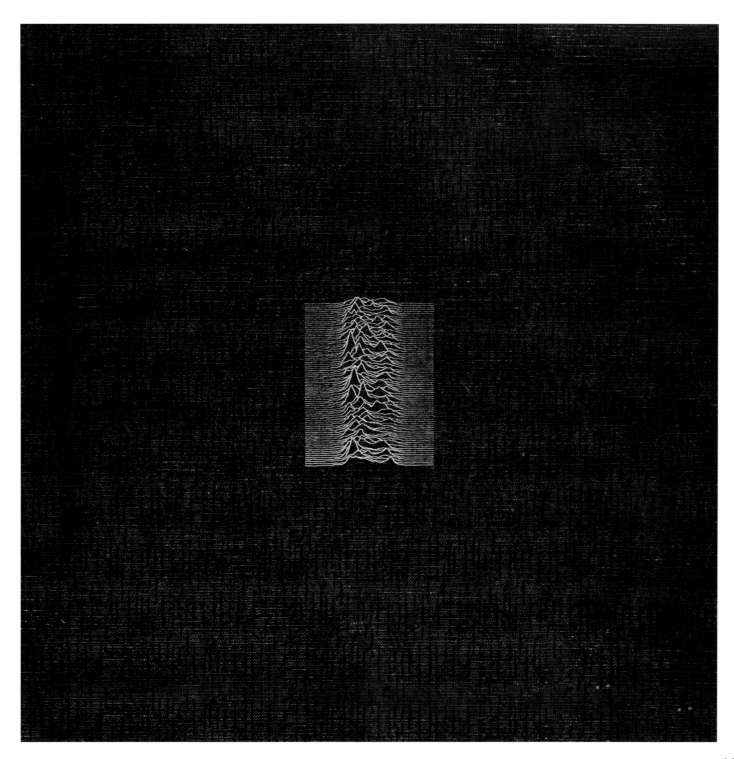

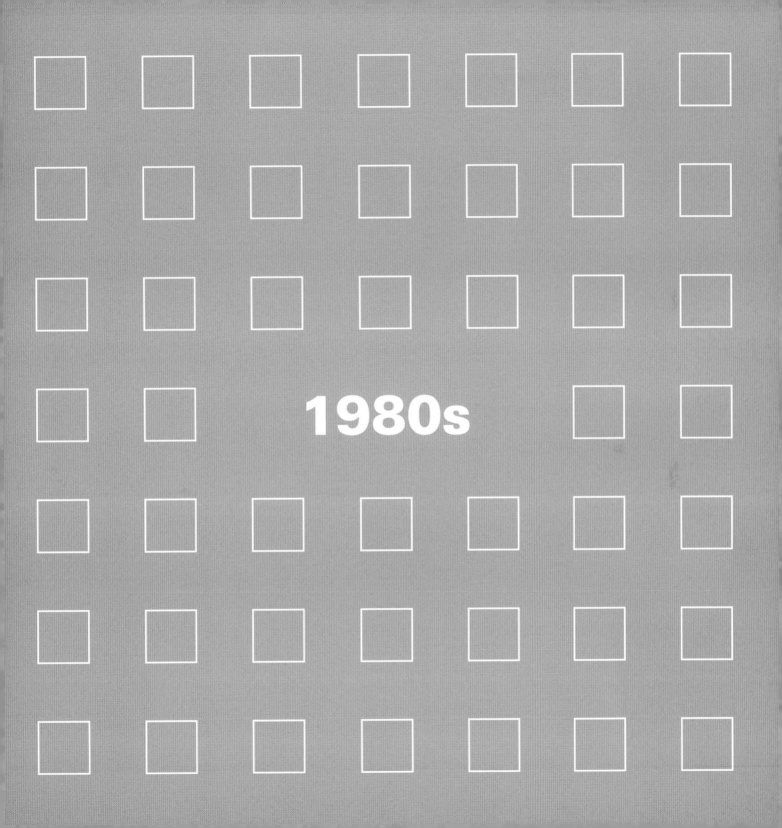

1980s

1980s Factory

The British Punk movement spawned a generation of do-it-yourself record labels across the country in the late 1970s. The Cortinas from Bristol signed to Step Forward, the label founded by *Sniffin' Glue* creator Mark P; in Coventry, a bunch of retro-Mods were founding 2 Tone Records; and a number of small independent record shops across the country released Punk singles, from Small Wonder and Rough Trade in London to Backs in Norwich. And in Manchester The Buzzcocks, released their debut EP *Orgasm Addict* on their own label, New Hormones. The cover of that EP set a new standard in both Punk music and its design ethos. *Orgasm Addict* used a black-and-white montage by Linder (using a naked female torso with zips for nipples and a steam iron for a head) and a bright yellow background with clinically disorganized type. It had been created by Malcolm Garrett, a design student at Manchester Polytechnic. He formed one of the most influential post-Punk design companies of the 1980s, Assorted Images, which created sleeves for Duran Duran, Culture Club and Magazine, among others. Garrett was at the Polytechnic at the same time as Peter Saville, who was commissioned to work on sleeves for a bunch of doom-laden post-Punks named Joy Division by a local TV producer/presenter, Anthony Wilson.

Factory Records became a kind of shining Northern light of musical and design invention. New Order, the band that grew out of Joy Division's collapse when the latter's lead singer, Ian Curtis, committed suicide in 1980, were a worldwide success. The design ethos of Saville was as instrumental in breaking the band and keeping them at the cutting edge as the faintly monotonous, dance-based Indie Rock they created. Saville's work for other Factory acts, such as Durutti Column and A Certain Ratio, cemented his reputation for originality and impeccable design knowledge. He also helped to create the identity of Factory-owned Manchester nightclub The Hacienda, where the Ecstasy-fuelled "Madchester" scene developed as various clothes- and football-obsessed kids including The Stone Roses and Happy Mondays danced into the early mornings.

Wilson never got to sign either of the other two big Manchester acts, The Smiths and The Stone Roses, but without Factory, the history of modern music and its graphic design would have been very different.

▶ **Low-Life / New Order**
RELEASED 1985 | FACTORY RECORDS | UK | SLEEVE DESIGN BY PETER SAVILLE ASSOCIATES | PHOTOGRAPHY BY TREVOR KEY | ALBUM PRODUCED BY NEW ORDER
Possibly the coolest cover in the New Order catalogue, despite featuring photographs of "the other two" in the band (drummer Stephen Morris and keyboard player Gillian Gilbert), and not singer Bernard Sumner or bassist Peter Hook. There is a translucent sleeve covering the actual jacket, on which the band name is printed – on either side of the tracing paper-like outer sleeve – and the track-listing. Inside the front sleeve, on the edge of the tracing paper are details of the designer and photographer. It's minimal, clean, and an intriguing cover. Neither Morris nor Gibert were well known (though briefly enjoying a Pop career as The Other Two), and so apart from the band name, there's no recognition point to the sleeve. The second "proper" New Order album, it got rave reviews and helped launch the Rock-Dance whole "Madchester" movement (epitomized by The Stone Roses and The Happy Mondays). No other album would look quite like *Low-Life*, even if many tried to sound like it.

◀ Power Corruption and Lies / New Order

RELEASED 1983 | FACTORY | UK | SLEEVE DESIGN BY PETER SAVILLE | ALBUM PRODUCED BY NEW ORDER

For New Order's second album release, designer Peter Saville merged classicism with contemporary technological colour coding and created a kind of New Order Code. The painting of roses by Fantin-Latour (1890) is offset by a row of coloured squares that represents an alphabet. On the reverse of the sleeve there is a coloured wheel that offers the decoding to the colour code on the front. The code on the front was used not only for the title of this album but also for the 12-inch single Blue Monday and Confusion. It was a brilliant combination of past and future, bringing together opposing artistic devices to create something new. In the same way New Order expanded the idea of a rock band by combining synthesizers and drum machines with a standard drums, bass and guitar line-up to create a new Rock-Dance music.

▶ Movement / New Order

RELEASED 1981 | FACTORY RECORDS | UK | SLEEVE DESIGN BY PETER SAVILLE AND GRAFICA INDUSTRIA | ALBUM PRODUCED BY MARTIN HANNETT

In an era of leather blousons, Peter Saville's graphic work for Joy Division was the sturdy overcoat favoured by their fans. Having established a sombre elegance with Joy Division, Saville designed *Movement* (New Order's debut after the death of Ian Curtis and the name change) as a statement of intent. With its matt, uncoated stock and slab typography it was a marker for 1980s Futurist typography. But its choice of muted colors avoids pastiche and takes an iconic graphic style and transports it from Communist Russia to the grey industrial North. [GS]

▶ Return of the Durutti Column / Durutti Column

RELEASED 1980 | FACTORY | UK | SLEEVE DESIGNED BY DAVE ROWBOTHAM | ALBUM PRODUCED BY MARTIN HANNETT

Durutti Column took their name from a Spanish Civil War anarchist championed by the Situationists. A sandpaper cover was used by Situationist Guy Debord on one of his books, designed to damage other books on the shelf. Factory Records spent so much on four thousand sheets of sandpaper, they had to bring in Joy Division to glue them down. Though the album was extremely dangerous to other records in the vicinity, its contents were the opposite. The other members departed after a row, leaving leader Vini Reilly to record an album of classically inspired guitar solos. [BM]

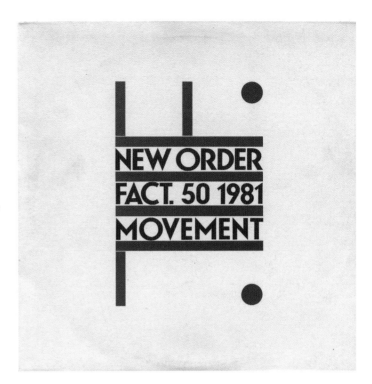

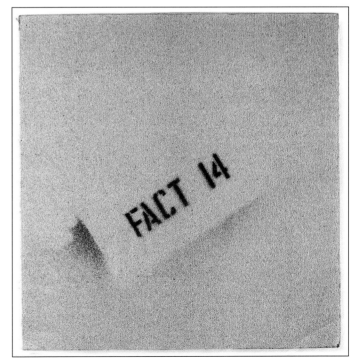

1980s Pop

In the 1980s the baby boomers who had first kicked off teenage culture were now used to buying albums as well as singles, so Pop acts were expected to deliver at least 40 minutes of wholly enjoyable music on an album. And by the middle of the decade they were expected to extend beyond that when CDs were introduced and marketed by the music business. For the industry the CD format was cheaper to manufacture but they could set the price that they wanted, which meant an enormous increase in profits. The higher price of manufacturing vinyl meant that its days were numbered.

As, of course, were the days of the LP sleeve. Not only would all new releases be pushed in the smaller format, but also the whole back catalogue of record companies would be shrunk down into the CD format – including the original artwork. The chance to sell the same records in a different format at a higher retail price was irresistible, and towards the end of the 1980s the major labels went into full re-issue mode, possibly at the expense of developing new talent.

Although 12-inch vinyl LPs were still being pressed until the end of the 1980s – and even into the 1990s at the request of certain bands – the new, smaller format meant the end of the large canvas for designers to work on in record company art departments. As the industry grew in terms of profit and units sold, so too the music changed. Pop music in the 1980s was dominated by a few major artists, three of whom had been inspired by and grown out of the Disco movement. Prince, Madonna and George Michael all made Disco-flavoured Pop of varying degrees and all three harboured dreams of a new kind of superstardom – one that for some involved entering the realm of movie stardom just like Elvis. Michael Jackson ruled the Pop world, and his sales seemed so assured that he didn't need any help with selling them by having decent sleeve design. Prince, who controlled every aspect of his career as far as he could, clearly didn't have a graphic sensibility – only *Lovesexy* stands out in the memory, and then more for its embarrassing image of a naked singer and positioning of a phallic flower than for any artistic merit. Bruce Springsteen made the transition from solid rocker to Pop superstar, using iconic imagery to do it. From Ireland, U2 had almost overnight Pop success despite an original ambition to be just a good albums band. And then came MTV and Adam Ant.

▶ **Born in the U.S.A. / Bruce Springsteen**
RELEASED 1984 | COLUMBIA RECORDS | USA | SLEEVE DESIGN BY ANDREA KLEIN | PHOTOGRAPHY BY ANNIE LEIBOVITZ | ALBUM PRODUCED BY BRUCE SPRINGSTEEN, JON LANDAU, CHUCK PLOTKIN AND STEVE VAN ZANDT
The sleeve literally takes its concept from the title: a piece of all-American chauvinism featuring worn Levi's jeans, complete with the all-important red tag, a faded baseball cap and the red and white bars from Old Glory. The choice of working-class symbols (jeans, baseball cap and the slightly flashy cowboy belt) rather than the symbols of corporate America (Coca-Cola, huge Detroit cars, skyscrapers) reveal Springsteen's leftward leaning, pro-working man stance and stops the image from being just another piece of American jingoism. The songs show the same mixture of American pride and blue-collar sympathy and the album did much to cement Springsteen's role as the conscience of the music industry. [BM]

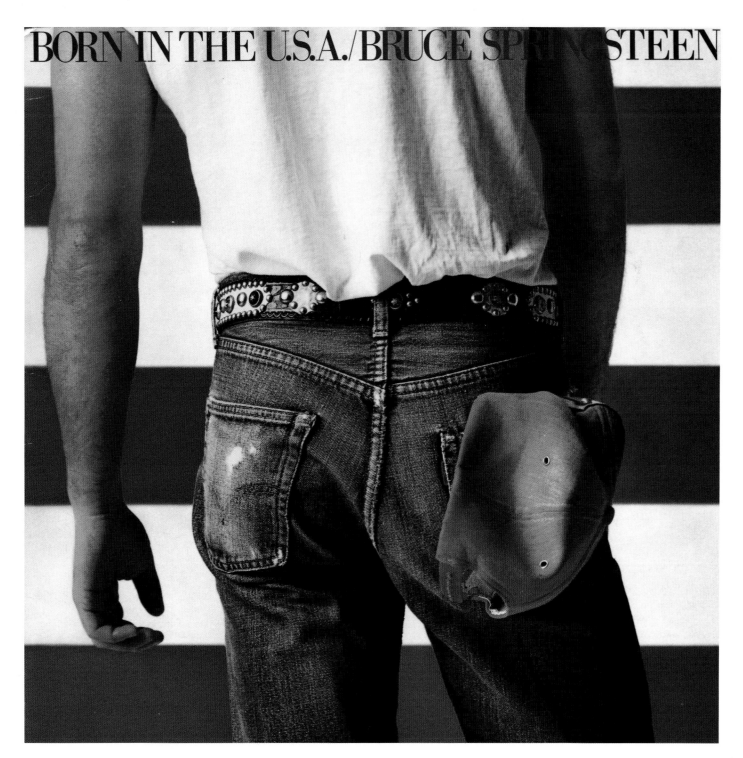

BORN IN THE U.S.A./BRUCE SPRINGSTEEN

149

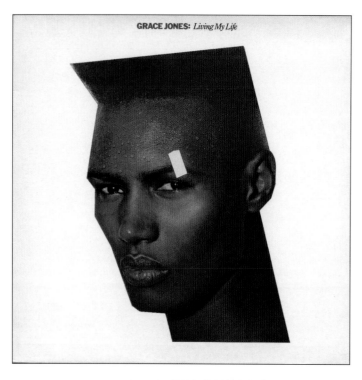

GRACE JONES: *Living My Life*

◀ **Living My Life / Grace Jones**

◀ **Living My Life / Grace Jones**
RELEASED 1982 | ISLAND RECORDS | UK | SLEEVE DESIGN BY JEAN-PAUL GOUDE AND ROB O'CONNOR | PHOTOGRAPHY BY JEAN-PAUL GOUDE | ALBUM PRODUCED BY CHRIS BLACKWELL AND ALEX SADKIN

Grace Jones joined French avant garde artist Jean-Paul Goude in 1978. He created her public image with extraordinary videos and album sleeves. He used cut-up photographs and collages to satirize the usual primitivist images of black females, playing with stereotypes. This cover uses one of his more straightforward pictures. The photograph has been doctored, hence the piece of sticking tape. By giving Grace a crew cut, a traditional male style, he further upsets the viewer's expectations. Together they were a powerful team. [BM]

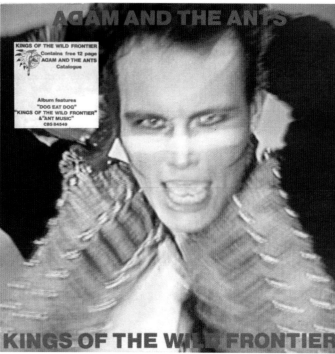

◀ **Kings of the Wild Frontier / Adam and the Ants**
RELEASED 1980 | CBS | UK | SLEEVE DESIGNED BY JULES AND ADAM ANT | ALBUM PRODUCED BY CHRIS HUGHES

Former art student and proto-Punk Stuart Goddard became Adam Ant in 1976, the night his band Bazooka Joe headlined on The Sex Pistols' very first gig. As Adam the Punk he wore black leather and cracked a whip. As Adam the Popstar he wore a white stripe on his face and made glorious, full-colour videos which had a story (all self-written), helping make MTV what it is today. On this, the band's second album, Adam's choice of image was inspired. Rather than the usual photo he opted for a video still, capturing the energy and sex appeal of Adam in full swing.

◀ **I knew that the video image was powerful and crude, that it would register immediately from billboards and buses, that it would have a great visual impact**

ADAM ANT

▶ True Blue / Madonna

RELEASED 1986 | SIRE RECORDS | USA | SLEEVE DESIGN BY JERI MCMANUS | PHOTOGRAPHY BY HERB RITTS | ALBUM PRODUCED BY MADONNA, PATRICK LEONARD AND STEPHEN BRAY

True Blue confirmed Madonna a superstar, featuring her at her most image conscious. From the start she carefully controlled her public persona, playing with different roles and aspects of her character. This is a very carefully calculated album, mixing serious songs with dynamic dance tracks, yet still managing to cohere. Herb Ritts's picture sets the tone for the whole thing; beautifully conceived, carefully framed, artificially colour corrected, a beautifully balanced composition by one of the great masters of portrait photography [BM]

▶ Faith / George Michael

RELEASED 1987 | EPIC | UK | SLEEVE DESIGN BY GEORGE MICHAEL AND STYLOROUGE | PHOTOGRAPHY BY RUSSELL YOUNG | ALBUM PRODUCED BY GEORGE MICHAEL

An album sleeve (and videos) perfect for the MTV age. This carefully composed photograph is raunchy and clearly spoke different things to different folks. On the face of it we have a Tom-of-Finland influenced leatherbar biker-type sniffing his armpit, but to millions of ladies he was as heterosexual as they came, and the image gave off powerful pheromones. After four years in the shallow end of Pop with Wham!, George Michael came up with a stunning debut solo album. *Faith* remained in the charts for more than a year, selling more than seven million copies. [BM]

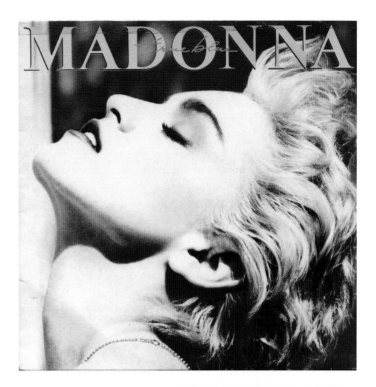

◀ Boy / U2

RELEASED 1980 | ISLAND RECORDS | UK | SLEEVE DESIGN BY STEVE AVERILL | PHOTOGRAPHY BY HUGO MCGUINNESS | ALBUM PRODUCED BY STEVE LILLYWHITE

The young boy naked to the waist on U2's first album was six-year-old Peter Rowan. He made such a striking image that they used him again, this time wearing an American army helmet, on *War*. He became a skateboard champ, and is now a photographer. "It's true to say that I am more famous for those U2 pictures than anything I have done since," he admitted. The photograph, of course, makes a reference to famous the picture of Jim Morrison in a similar pose. [BM]

▲ Murmur / R.E.M.

RELEASED 1983 | INTERNATIONAL RECORDS SYNDICATE (IRS) A&M | USA | ALBUM PRODUCED BY MITCH EASTER AND DON DIXON

Southern Post-Punk, Art Rock from Athens, Georgia. *Murmur* was R.E.M.'s first album and stands out from their later work because it was a novel for them all: everything they had experienced in their lives to that date was pumped into it. It was rumoured that subliminal cricket chirps were used throughout the album. It has a very southern feel enhanced by the sleeve image of kudzu-covered undergrowth: is it an overgrown graveyard, a ruined shack or just weed-clogged woodland? [BM]

> ▲ Those covers were very carefully positioned – they were "pitched" at a perceived audience
>
> PETER SAVILLE, DESIGNER

▲ Dazzle Ships / OMD

RELEASED 1983 | VIRGIN RECORDS | UK | SLEEVE DESIGN BY PETER SAVILLE ASSOCIATES: M. GARRETT, K. KENNEDY, P. PENNINGTON, P. SAVILLE AND B. WICKENS | ALBUM PRODUCED BY RHETT DAVIES AND ORCHESTRAL MANOEUVRES IN THE DARK

For this, Orchestral Manouvres In The Dark's fourth album, Peter Saville perfectly represented a band becoming slightly distanced from their previous synthesized Pop. *Dazzle Ships* (the title and artwork was inspired by Saville's appreciation of *Dazzle Ships In Drydock At Liverpool 1919*, by the painter Edward Wadsworth) includes a gatefold sleeve, cut-outs, and moving bits.

1980s Rock

By the 1980s many of the former Rock Gods had died or retired. Led Zeppelin were soon to be no more; Eric Clapton was snoozing somewhere in England and Punk had seen off the careers of many of the more preposterous Progressive Rock dinosaurs. Bruce Springsteen, the one-time Future of Rock 'n' Roll, moved into the Pop arena in search of sales, as did first Genesis and then their drummer, Phil Collins. The lines between what was once considered Rock music and Pop music had become blurred to the point of non-existence, it seemed. So it was that a whole new generation of Rock bands came to the fore.

In America most of them became known as College Rock because they were played on college radio and performed at universities across the country. By the end of the decade these same bands would become the denizens of Alt Rock (as in Alternative, although to what was unclear). Some of the bands lumped into this spurious genre were a genuine alternative to the plodding, formulaic sounds of what Rock music had become. R.E.M., at least until they left their independent label for the massive major label WEA, played an intriguing, opaque version of Country Rock.

Talking Heads, who became one of the most revered live acts in the world, mixed funky rhythms, South American beats and bizarre lyrics into a classic Rock format. The Smiths seemed intent on returning the world to the sound of The Beatles and The Byrds. Bands from the scuzzy underbelly of American Rock (and who were lazily termed Goth in the UK) such as The Cramps and Gun Club were old-fashioned Rock 'n' Roll bands, more Gene Vincent than Bruce Springsteen. In the 1990s there would barely be a Rock genre at all, with more acts choosing to be considered Alt and in doing so creating a norm, but in the 1980s the bands displayed here were truly Rock 'n' Roll.

▶ **Rain Dogs / Tom Waits**
RELEASED 1985 | ISLAND RECORDS | UK | SLEEVE PHOTOGRAPHY BY ANDERS PETERSEN | ALBUM PRODUCED BY TOM WAITS
The figure cuddling up to the laughing woman on the sleeve looks very like the young Tom Waits, and the photograph was surely chosen because of this. But it is not him. The title of the picture is *Lily and Rose*, and it was taken by the Swedish photographer Anders Petersen at a bar in Hamburg called Café Lehmitz, some time between 1967 and 1970. Waits no doubt came across it in Petersen's book Café Lehmitz, published in Germany by Schirmer/Mosel, and was struck by the strong resemblance. The image perfectly complements the edgy, streetwise songs that Waits made so much his own. [BM]

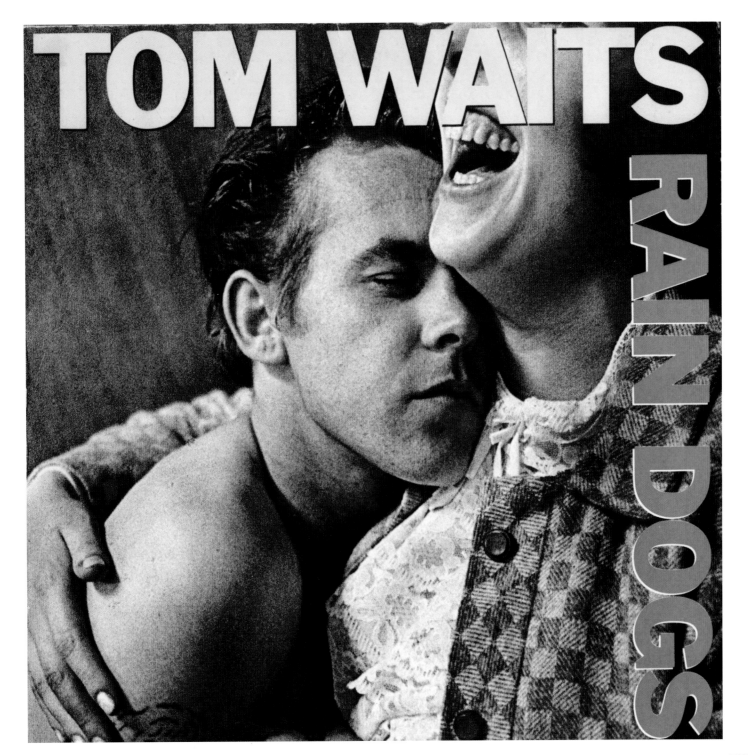

TOM WAITS

RAIN DOGS

THE NAME OF THIS BAND IS TALKING HEADS

NEW FEELING   A CLEAN BREAK
DON'T WORRY ABOUT THE GOVERNMENT   PULLED UP   PSYCHO KILLER

LIVE 2 LP SET (1977-1979)

ARTISTS ONLY   STAY HUNGRY
AIR   BUILDING ON FIRE   MEMORIES (CAN'T WAIT)

◀ **The Name of this Band Is Talking Heads / Talking Heads**

RELEASED 1982 | SIRE | USA |ART DIRECTION BY GARY SCOVIL AND JEFF JONES | ALBUM PRODUCED BY TALKING HEADS

A double live album, one disc of the original quartet recorded between 1977 and 1979, the second featuring tracks by the nine-piece extended line-up of 1980–81 including their hit Take Me to the River. The sleeve shows their transition from what appears to be a very early performance in a suburban living room – with both band and what can be seen of the audience looking fairly preppy – to concert footage of a full tilt boogie from the 1980s. [BM]

▼ **Remain in Light / Talking Heads**

RELEASED 1980 / SIRE / USA | SLEEVE DESIGN BY TINA WEYMOUTH AND CHRIS FRANTZ | TYPOGRAPHY BY M & CO. NEW YORK | ALBUM PRODUCED BY BRIAN ENO

Talking Heads Chris Frantz and Tina Weymouth created one of the first computer-generated sleeves. Tina, using the cursor, scratched out most of each face, leaving a block of colour like a mask. But lead singer David Byrne had hired an outside artist, Tibor Kalman, to work on it. After a typical Talking Heads row, Kalman's people finished up doing the lettering, Kalman having had the idea of inverting the "A"s in Talking Heads. [BM]

▼ **Meat Is Murder / The Smiths**

RELEASED 1985 | ROUGH TRADE | UK | SLEEVE DESIGN BY MORRISSEY | ALBUM PRODUCED BY THE SMITHS

A powerful vegetarian message from The Smiths. And though the title was Morrissey's, the entire band was in agreement with it. Morrissey said: "I don't really think that you can write a song about animal slaughter without it being quite strong. So it really had to be." The image of the soldier was taken from Emile de Antonio's 1968 film *In the Year of the Pig*. The original words painted on the child-soldier's helmet were "Make War Not Love", changed by the miracle that is Photoshop.

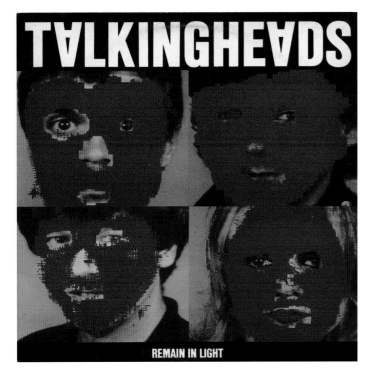

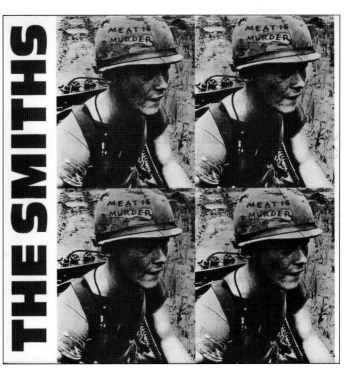

► The Sky's Gone Out / Bauhaus

RELEASED 1982 | BEGGARS BANQUET | UK | SLEEVE DESIGN BY DANIEL ASH | PHOTOGRAPHY BY FIN COSTELLO | ALBUM PRODUCED BY BAUHAUS

Named after the influential 1920s German art school and Modernist movement, on stage Bauhaus dressed only in black and projected videos on to a screen with rapid white strobe light. The cover for their second album perfectly encapsulates their onstage persona in its black-and-white starkness with a blinding white centre – it's like looking straight into a strobe at full speed – and presents a striking and powerful image for a band often criticized for their over-posturing and failure to achieve their own high ideals. [GS]

◄ Off the Bone / The Cramps

RELEASED 1983 | ILLEGAL RECORDS | UK | SLEEVE DESIGN BY DEAD JAW | ALBUM PRODUCED BY THE CRAMPS

Founding Cramps Lux Interior and Poison Ivy created not only a band in the spring of 1976 but a complete lifestyle. Their sound delves into Southern Rockabilly, crazed instrumental Rock, deranged psychedelia and 1960s Punk. A surprising amount of commercial success allowed them to create a completely 3-D cover front and back with *Off the Bone* (a compilation of early singles) with a free pair of 3-D glasses inside every copy. It is the ultimate expression of their love for 1950s American trash B-movie culture, featuring skulls, tombstones and gruesome caricatures of the band. [GS]

► Miami / The Gun Club

RELEASED 1982 | ANIMAL RECORDS (CHRYSALIS) | USA | SLEEVE DESIGN BY CHRIS D | ALBUM PRODUCED BY CHRIS STEIN

A side trip by Chris Stein of Blondie, it also features Walter Steding on fiddle, giving the LP a strong Warhol connection in that Debbie Harry was painted by Warhol, and Steding lived in one of Warhol's studios and was managed by him. Debbie appears as "D. H. Lawrence Jr." Gun Club leader Jeffrey Lee Pierce was president of Blondie's American fanclub. The solarized image of the band standing on the beach at Santa Monica (there were only three left when the sleeve was shot) is not a new idea – Zappa did it on *Freak Out* in 1966 – but it is made more eye-catching by intensifying the colours. [BM]

1980s Agit Rock

After the brief incendiary days of Punk – from the summer of 1976 until January 1978 when The Sex Pistols collapsed – there was a period of post-Punk invention which gave birth to scores of politically motivated bands. The Pop Group (see page 140), Gang of Four and Crass all sang overtly political lyrics set against loud, discordant guitars, the style of which would be aped twenty years later by bands such as Franz Ferdinand, Bloc Party and The Futureheads. In America the UK version of Punk had taken longer to make any in-roads, with The Sex Pistols' album taking 20 years to sell a million. It wasn't until The Clash released *London Calling* in 1980 that any kind of success was achieved by a British Punk act.

By the dawning of the 1980s, when both America and the UK were politically ruled by conservative governments headed by Ronald Reagan and Margaret Thatcher, the post-Punk movement had become known in the UK and Europe as Agit Rock (for Agitate) with bands actively promoting political activism and civil disorder in song and action. Crass were often seen (and filmed) at anti-capitalism and anti-globalization demonstrations in London, not performing but agitating. They never made much of a

sales impact in either the UK or America but their influence was immense. Here was a group of people who lived outside the law and preached open rebellion in a responsible way – they were not mindless anarchists but socialism-inspired idealists. They also made a fantastic and massive musical noise. In America the Dead Kennedys were the most visible of the West Coast bands who had been inspired by the Pistols, but acts such as Black Flag, X and Hüsker Dü were all making loud, furious noises and decrying the traditional way of American life. In the UK the protests of bands such as The Fall were not just anti-establishment but also anti-personal. Mark E. Smith seemed intent on creating a Northern English Republic which would mutate into the Fiefdom of Mark E. Smith. There were certainly enough members of The Fall over the band's 25-year existence to populate a small country. Throughout the decade, anti-American and anti-corporate globalization riots occurred in Germany, Great Britain and Holland, and all were played out to a soundtrack of Agit Rock. The artwork for Agit Rock was usually as uncompromising as the music that they made. Here are some of the very best examples.

▶ **Killing Joke / Killing Joke**
RELEASED 1980 | EG RECORDS | UK | SLEEVE DESIGN BY UNKNOWN | ALBUM PRODUCED BY KILLING JOKE
Beginning the band's tradition of using provocative images, this sleeve appears to show crowds of people climbing over a wall; perhaps a reference to the Berlin Wall? Are they escaping? Are they just Killing Joke fans breaking into a scrap metal yard? It's so black and white we can't really see what's happening. It does, however, capture the mood of this doom-laden group (Lemmy has a lot to answer for), though it was good that the end of the world didn't come when they thought it would, isn't it? [BM]

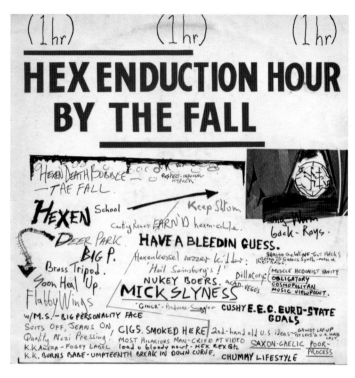

◄ Hex Enduction Hour / The Fall

RELEASED 1982 | KAMERA RECORDS | UK | SLEEVE DESIGN BY MARK E. SMITH, ALAN SKINNER | ALBUM PRODUCED BY RICHARD MAZDA, MARK E SMITH

Hex Enduction Hour is generally thought to be the album with the best Fall line-up, the strongest songs and the finest cover. As with the artwork of Smiths releases, this is a cover which comes at you from every angle with no consideration for conventional structure. It makes no sense, covered with abstract handwritten thoughts in cheap ink, commands heavily scratched and stated like a doodle by a deranged dictator. Its homemade aesthetic is confirmed by a badly set Letraset title, and a torn piece of unrecognizable painting. [GS]

► In God We Trust, Inc. / Dead Kennedys

RELEASED 1981 | STATIK RECORDS | USA | SLEEVE DESIGN BY WINSTON SMITH/FALLOUT PRODUCTIONS, JELLO BIAFRA | ALBUM PRODUCED BY NORM

Leader Jello Biafra always makes politics the core of the Dead Kennedys music; both his and the band's name were meant not just to offend but to make people think. The black humour of their lyrics relieved the relentless drive of music, but with *In God We Trust, Inc.* the songs became brutal. The cover image of Christ crucified on the dollar sums it up. Biafra directs his attention to the Ku Klux Klan and Ronald Reagan, the police state, poisoning in chemical factories, and his bête noire, organized religion and the so-called Moral Majority. [BM]

◄ As with the music, the parts of the sleeve come together almost despite themselves to form a strong, original and dynamic whole

GRANT SCOTT

◄ Thaw / Foetus Interruptus

RELEASED 1988 | SELF IMMOLATION/SOME BIZZARE | USA | SLEEVE DESIGN BY J. G. THIRWELL | EXECUTION BY MX.AI | ALBUM PRODUCED BY FOETUS INTERRUPTUS, CLINT RUIN, J. G. THIRLWELL

This sleeve features an end-on view of a handgun, presumably from a gangster comic as it has previously been used as a painting by Roy Lichtenstein and by various anarchist groups in New York in the early 1970s. There are also elements taken from popular Japanese manga comics and a large-screen image of a snarling German shepherd guard dog. The whole makes a successful statement of anarchic intent and features such catchy numbers as English Faggo/ Nothin Man, Asbestos and The Dipsomaniac Kiss. [BM]

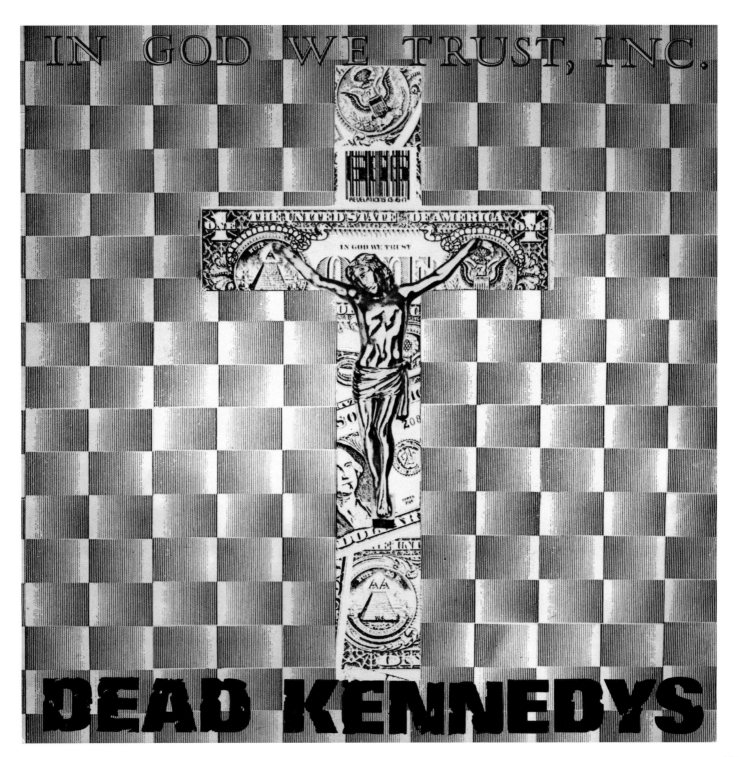

1980s Metal

Although the term Heavy Metal had been used since the early 1970s, the genre didn't really come into its own until the 1980s. Numerous Heavy Rock acts such as Humble Pie, Grand Funk Railroad, Deep Purple, Rainbow, Blue Öyster Cult and Kiss had been producing loud, bombastic Rock music since the end of the 1960s. But it wasn't really until the end of the 1970s (with acts such as Boston in the US and Iron Maiden, Samson and Judas Priest from the UK) that a new kind of Heavy Rock emerged.

Most of the new Heavy bands took aspects of earlier models – like the guitar style of Deep Purple's Ritchie Blackmore, the bass playing of The Who's John Entwistle, and the singing of Led Zeppelin's Robert Plant – and made them their own, though not always successfully of course. It often resulted in a plodding, dense sound with a strangled half-scream on top, and a permanently soloing guitar. It was clear that the more anthemic the songs were, the better they succeeded, though – as with Kiss and their All American Male.

So Heavy Rock bands of the 1980s rebranded it Heavy Metal, stomping out anthemic ballads with choruses you could sing along to – and lots of guitar solos.

They also began to create a new kind of graphic language. The Heavy Metal market seemed to be split into two distinct camps and has remained so. There are the power balladeers with their high hair and flowing scarves – as worn originally by Rolling Stone Keith Richards and his doppelgängers in Aerosmith – which is sometimes known as Poodle Rock; and then there are the death and devil-obsessed permanent adolescents who would be into Goth if the lyrics were not too clever for them.

Quite where that puts AC/DC is hard to say, but since they originally came from Australia it's safe to say "somewhere a bit different". The sleeve artwork for most Metal sleeves, to be brutally honest, was appalling. They either depicted the preening poodle rockers in all their finest make-up and wigs, or displayed an "illustration" that showed scenes of the futuristic destruction of planet Earth. Which is why the sleeves shown here are not at all typical of the genre – except the Iron Maiden one which was among the first and betrayed a certain sense of humour. The AC/DC and ZZ Top sleeves also have the added benefit of being witty, but only if you're inclined to see them that way.

▶ **Back in Black / AC/DC**
RELEASED 1980 | WEA | AUSTRALIA | SLEEVE DESIGN BY BOB DEFRIN | ALBUM PRODUCED BY MUTT LANGE
By the time AC/DC recorded *Back in Black* they had been touring the world for three years. The first album sessions in England in February 1980 had ended with lead singer Bon Scott dead in a car, after he'd been left asleep in the motor after a heavy night out. The coroner's verdict was that Scott had drunk himself to death. After recruiting Brian Johnson they retired to the Bahamas to record this, their first UK Number One album. (It reached Number Four in the US) AC/DC's image was strange. Guitarist Angus Young wore a schoolboy outfit on stage, including a pair of shorts, a satchel and a cap perched precariously on his unruly hair. The others wore too-tight jeans and t-shirts. So, with no image to sell the album – they'd already used Angus in his get-up – and perhaps in deference to the late Scott, the album was titled *Back in Black* and the cover was just that: black. Spinal Tap would later do the same thing with *Smell the Glove*, and Megadeth would also use an all-black sleeve (but for a black snake), but AC/DC were there first.

◀ The Number of the Beast / Iron Maiden

RELEASED 1982 | EMI | UK | SLEEVE DESIGN BY CREAM | ARTWORK BY DEREK RIGGS | ALBUM PRODUCED BY MARTIN BIRCH

Iron Maiden's third album, an early example of Metal's use of a devil image presented with humour. The devil looks like a Victorian villain, and not only has chubby thighs beneath his poorly-cut jeans but is also wearing a cardigan. Between his feet, in the burning pit background, a figure can be seen doing the Mexican hat dance, while on the back sleeve the band look very young and innocent, contentedly sitting in hell. An arresting and much imitated cover.

▼ MCMLXXXIV / Van Halen

RELEASED 1983 | WARNER BROS RECORDS | USA | ART DIRECTORS: RICHARD SEIREENI, DAVID JELLISON | ILLUSTRATION BY MARGO ZAFER NAHAS | PHOTOGRAPHY BY RAUL VEGA | ALBUM PRODUCED BY TED TEMPLEMAN

This was a very clever sleeve image. Could this be how Van Halen saw themselves: cute guys with a touch of naughtiness? The cupid, or baby angel, who is sneaking a cigarette appears posed by child model Carter Helm. He looks set for a good long nicotine session with two packs and an old-time jailbird smoker's grip between pinkie and middle finger but he is not old enough to have developed brand loyalty; there are two different brands there. The album was a monster, generating the band's only Number One single, Jump. It reached Number Two on the Billboard album charts, behind Michael Jackson's *Thriller*, which contained the hit song Beat It, featuring Eddie Van Halen on lead guitar. [BM]

▼ Eliminator / ZZ Top

RELEASED 1983 | WEA | USA | ART DIRECTION BOB ALFORD | ALBUM PRODUCED BY BILL HAM

After four albums and nine years, former Texas boogie band ZZ Top reinvented themselves, growing very long beards, donning shades and playing feedback-tinged Rock 'n' Roll that didn't vary much but proved popular. Previous albums made it to the US Top 20 if they were lucky, *Eliminator* made Number Nine, spawning a trio of hits around the world – Gimme All Your Lovin', Best Dressed Man and Legs. The cover featured ZZ Top's beloved customized car. It was so successful as their co-star in the videos that it almost won a Hollywood career.

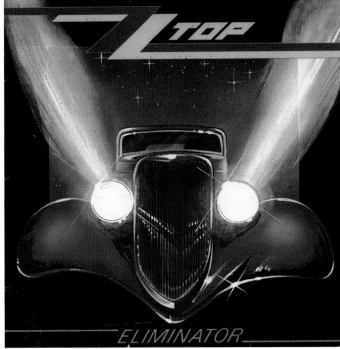

1980s Rap

Some time during the summer of 1973, a South Bronx DJ by the name of Kool Herc introduced Jamaican-style "toasting" (playing records and talking over the music via microphone) to the New York scene. Six years later, Grandmaster Flash, in his Isley Brothers-style Disco-inspired outfits, spun his way to Number Four on the R 'n' B charts with Rapper's Delight, powered by a Disco bassline taken from Chic's Good Times. Kurtis Blow and the Sugarhill Gang followed up the same year (1979) with a novelty hit, Christmas Rappin', and the scene was set for a new kind of music to rule the airwaves and inner-city streets.

In 1980, The Clash, British rockers and former Punks who had promoted Reggae heavily in the UK (and who had toured with Joe Ely, Mikey Dread and Bo Diddley in the UK during the late 1970s), undertook a tour of the U.S. with Grandmaster Flash as support. They then released Rap-mixed versions of songs such as Magnificent Seven and This Is Radio Clash. The Rock and Pop crowd began to listen to the new music as it developed – Talking Heads off-shoot Tom Tom Club helped the process of enlightenment too, when they released Wordy Rapping Hood. Once Run-DMC (with Aerosmith) had sold millions of copies of Walk This Way, the Rap scene was well and truly under way. Of course it was a white Rap act who reached the Number One slot in the album charts first (The Beastie Boys' *Licensed To Ill*, see page 171). But pretty soon black American Rap stars were emerging who were not just about having a good time, all the time. Boogie Down Productions drew on the legacy of black rights activists for visual and lyrical inspiration (see opposite). Public Enemy were by far the loudest and most threatening Rap act to emerge in the 1980s, with numerous acts following in their footsteps, benefitting from the gains that they made by getting radio and TV airtime and even live gigs. Unfortunately, their album sleeves were pretty dour affairs and are not included here. L.L. Cool J., on the other hand, created an iconic cover with *Radio* (page 170) and then *Mama Said Knock You Out* (page 207) as he established himself as half-lover, half-fighter, eventually building a career in movies as well as music. By the end of the decade Rap had almost overtaken Metal as the music of choice for disaffected white teenagers in Middle America, a long way from its origins in the South Bronx.

▶ **By All Means Necessary / Boogie Down Productions**
RELEASED 1988 | ZOMBA RECORDS | BMG RECORDS | USA | SLEEVE PHOTOGRAPHY BY DOUG ROWELL | ALBUM PRODUCED BY KRS-ONE FOR BOOGIE DOWN PRODUCTIONS
More of a fashion shoot than album sleeve shoot, the sleeve credits Kofi Tuda for Tumutu for grooming and wardrobe consultant Ms Melodie but no sleeve designer. The title is a quote from Malcolm X's famous speech: "We want freedom by any means necessary. We want justice by any means necessary. We want equality by any means necessary." The cover pose is a direct copy of the famous image of Malcolm X brandishing an M15, peering through the curtains. The angle of the head and the arms is extremely accurate – of course Malcolm was wearing a tie and tie-clip and had no baseball cap but the glasses are the same weight. [BM]

BOOGIE DOWN PRODUCTIONS

BY ALL MEANS NECESSARY

◀ **This and Boogie Down Productions' By All Means Necessary are up there in my top five all-time favourite Rap album covers**

CHRIS MORROW, PREMIERE RADIO, NEW YORK

▶ **Licenced To III / Beastie Boys**
RELEASED 1986 | DEF JAM RECORDS | CBS RECORDS | USA | SLEEVE DESIGN BY STEVE BYRAM | ILLUSTRATION BY DAVID GAMBOLI [AS WORLD B OMS] | ALBUM PRODUCED BY RICK RUBIN
The front sleeve shows a jet airliner with the Beastie Boys logo on the tail, with "Eat Me" set back-to-front as its registration. On the gatefold the image is deconstructed as the plane has crashed into a mountain, though there is not too much damage. The sleeve was pre-computer brush and ink over a photo collage. "We kind of carefully assembled the plane from photographs," said Steve Byram, "a bit like the way air accident investigators reassemble a crashed plane." [BM]

▲ **Radio / L.L. Cool J**
RELEASED 1985 | DEF JAM | USA | SLEEVE DESIGN UNKNOWN | ALBUM PRODUCED BY RICK RUBIN
James Todd Smith, AKA L.L. Cool J (or Ladies Love Cool James) was just 17 years old when he recorded this debut album, the first release on Rick Rubin and Russell Simmons's Def Jam label. He left school the same year to pursue a career in music and went on to sell in excess of 20 million albums. The success of the Radio single put him in the movies when he performed in *Krush Groove* (1986), and he's since made several other films. He's remained credible to his fanbase, a testament to both his music and the presentation of it. For his debut album there could have been no simpler image than this boombox, a massive "portable" radio-cassette player that was a must-have item for any self-respecting b-boy in America.

1980s Soul

Where once Soul music had been defined by what studio a song was recorded in as much as the person performing it, by the end of the 1970s Soul music was once more fragmented and homogeneous. Funk, Disco and even Rap had been born out of Soul, but Soul itself had almost ceased to exist as a recognized genre, having been replaced by the all-embracing soubriquet of R 'n' B (a music industry moniker for solely black music back in the 1950s). The 1980s were marked by many of the original Soul artists turning out new albums in what was to become a classic period. Alongside the remaining 1960s Soul artists still recording, including Aretha Franklin, Stevie Wonder and Al Green, there was a new band of young men who dressed in large-shouldered suits and sang about making love to a sexy lady all night. Keith Sweat, Will Downing, James Ingram, Freddie Jackson and Luther Vandross had all proved their worth as singers with bigger acts in the 1970s and early 1980s and then launched solo careers as Soul singers. Barry White and Teddy Pendergrass were undoubtedly the kings of smoochy Soul, and they ruled the singles and album charts from the mid 1970s to the early 1980s.

During the 1980s Soul music seemed to be all about sex – not the crude, semi-porn that rappers in the 1990s would chant about, but adult sex, always prefaced by love. There was no bad language either, but plenty of bump and grind. The songs dealt with adult relationships, the male singers expressing a degree of romance that sounds positively archaic in the light of twenty-first-century R 'n' B, Rap, Hip-Hop and Urban songs. Female Soul stars such as Anita Baker and Randy Crawford were similarly styled on the great female singers of the 1960s and 1970s, but with songs about adult relationships, not teenage daydreams.

There was also a lot of Pop in 1980s Soul. New Edition, who would give Bobby Brown his first break, Whitney Houston and, later, Boyz II Men were huge, their sound then not too dissimilar to that of platinum-selling acts like Destiny's Child and Beyoncé fifteen years later. But the music industry has decided that "Soul" is a redundant term, opting for something more "street" in order to sell it to a teenage audience obsessed with credibility. So Usher, who would have worn big-shouldered suits in 1987, is photographed in low-hanging prison jeans and t-shirt and sold as being an "Urban" star.

▶ **Give Me the Night / George Benson**

RELEASED 1980 | WARNER BROS RECORDS | USA | SLEEVE DESIGN BY RICHARD SEIREENI | PHOTOGRAPHY BY NORMAN SEEFF | ALBUM PRODUCED BY BRUCE SWEDIEN

George Benson's bid for the Soul/R 'n' B late-night market. This was a brilliant pairing with producer Quincy Jones who brought along his whole crew. Considering how successful the album was – it reached Number Three on the Billboard album charts and shipped platinum within four months – it is strange that they did not work together again. In keeping with the smooth arrangements and superb playing George presents a casual, relaxed image of himself in society photographer Norman Seeff's hand-coloured sleeve, wearing a loose-weave preppy sweater and an understated gold chain. Not for George the excesses of Bootsy or the gangster look. This is someone you'd like to have at your dinner party. [BM]

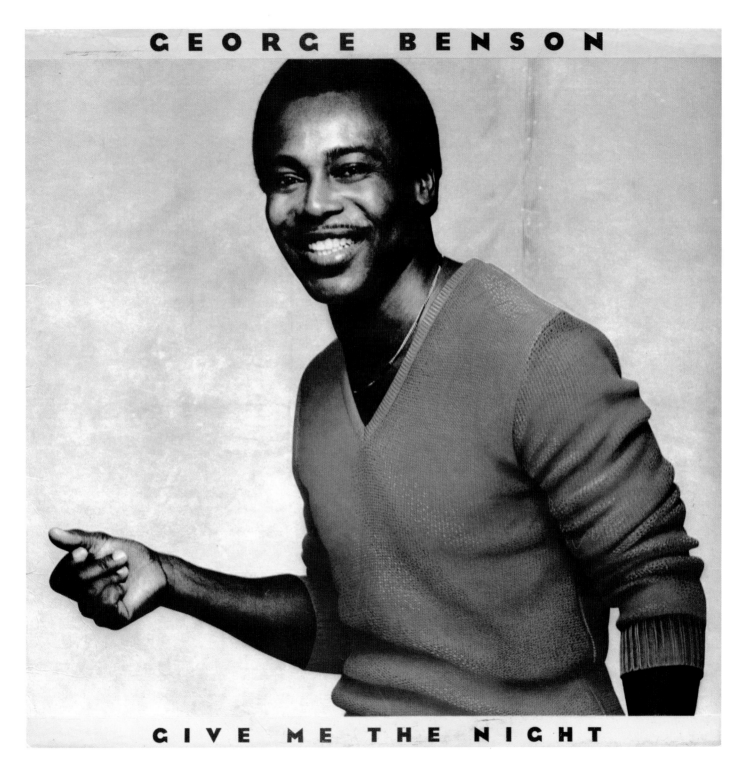

GEORGE BENSON

GIVE ME THE NIGHT

◀ Club Classics Vol. One / Soul II Soul

RELEASED 1989 | 10 RECORDS | UK | SLEEVE DESIGN BY DAVID JAMES | PHOTOGRAPHY BY JAMIE MORGAN | ALBUM PRODUCED BY JAZZIE B AND NELLEE HOOPER

British Soul II Soul founder Jazzie B started a Soul II Soul sound system in the early 1980s, but it was as a producer that he really hit pay dirt. This, the debut SIIS release, proved that there was a thriving Soul scene in London. It also proved the worth of designer David James, whose work for this sleeve clearly went on to "inspire" the poster and print ad marketing for Apple's iPod in 2004. Check out the in-profile silhouette shot of the funki dred (another of Jazzie's inventions) on the inside sleeve and then see the iPod ads.

◀ Don't Be Cruel / Bobby Brown

RELEASED 1988 | MCA RECORDS | USA | SLEEVE DESIGNED BY JULIE MOSS | ALBUM PRODUCED BY L.A. & BABYFACE AND MANY OTHERS

Although his first solo LP flopped, the former New Edition lead vocalist hit the spot with *Don't Be Cruel*, making Number One in the album charts and spawning a string of Top Ten singles. On the sleeve he looks every inch the superstar with his understated suit, white handkerchief in top pocket, white poloneck, and just a little bling in the gold bracelet peeking from his trouser pocket. Unsure of what image to put across, the designers opted to make the sleeve into a balance of textures pulled together by the gratuitous white tick at the bottom right. [BM]

▶ Ready for Teddy / Teddy Pendergrass

RELEASED 1981 | PHILADELPHIA INTERNATIONAL | USA | SLEEVE DESIGN BY ROSLAV SZAYBO | ALBUM PRODUCED BY GAMBLE AND HUFF AND VARIOUS

Teddy had been the voice of Harold Melvin and the Bluenotes in the 1970s, singing both The Love I Lost and If You Don't Know Me By Now. He went solo in 1977 feeling that he was being held back by Melvin. He could have been right. His first solo album sold more than a million copies that year, as did the next two in the following two years. He also scored numerous hit singles, all of them smoochy hymns to lurve and sex. As much as Barry White (who later seemed to get all of the credit), Teddy made the big macho Soul singer who could get a woman in bed simply by looking at them a cliché. Sadly, he was partially paralyzed when he crashed his Rolls-Royce in 1982, although he carried on recording. Released a year before that, this compilation has a perfect Theodore D. Pendergrass cover; with the red sofa and red background, and Teddy with his shoes off, laughing naturally, what woman could resist him?

READY FOR... *Teddy* PENDERGRASS

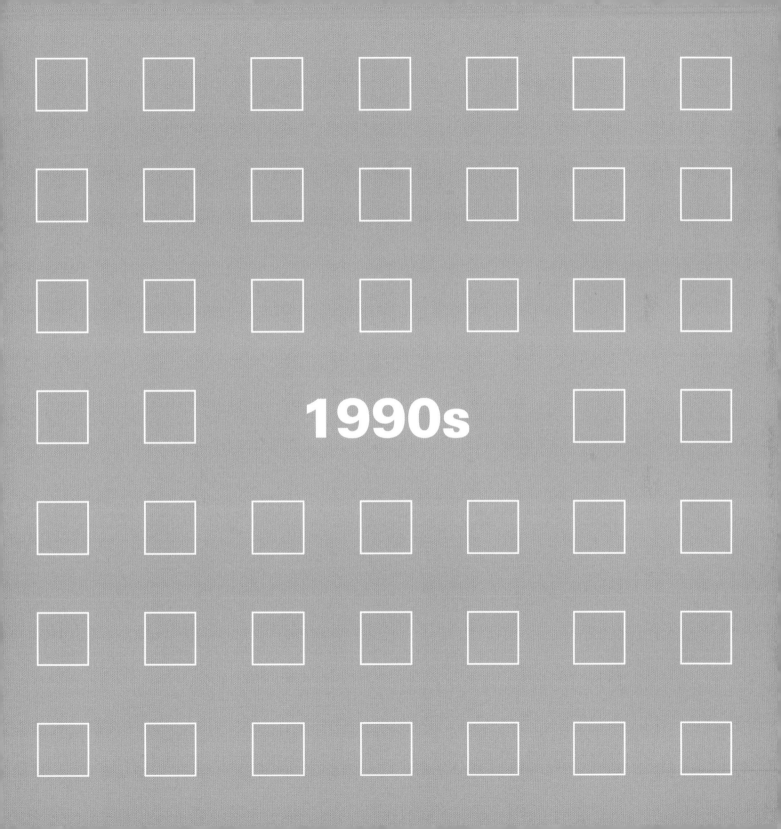

1990s

1990s Pop

The audience for Pop music slowly died away in the 1990s, with stars of the previous decade selling less with each release. Madonna attempted as many reinventions as Bowie had in the 1970s but with nowhere near the same success. Michael Jackson told the world that he was bad and somehow got away with it. George Michael had a spat with his record company, demanded his master tapes back, and went home to sulk. And Prince changed his name to Artist Formerly Known As [weird squiggle thing] in a run-in with his label. Bruce Springsteen seemed to get bored. U2 went from strength to yawning strength, selling out stadiums around the world.

Meanwhile a host of boy bands and girl singers rose to take their place. Manufactured by record company marketing men, the inane, superficial pap of New Kids on the Block "inspired" Take That, Westlife and a bunch of like-sounding acts too dull to recall. But this Pop sold singles, not albums, to teenagers distracted by new forms of entertainment including video games, the internet and, by the end of the decade, mobile telephones.

So a new kind of Pop developed, played by students of classic 1960s Pop and adopting its interesting choruses and charming melodic hooks. Acoustic guitars and "real" instruments were played again by new names and the occasional seasoned veteran, creating a fresh form of Pop music that wasn't actually as popular as it should have been. In the United States, Rickie Lee Jones recorded several albums of sheer perfection, some of it covers of American songbook standards, a lot of it wholly original. The enigmatic kd lang, meanwhile, became bored with trying to upset the Nashville hierarchy and put her magnificent voice to soaring tunes.

And a few odd acts arose from the British musical underground of the 1980s to become popstars, most deserving of which was Jarvis Cocker with Pulp, who found themselves an "overnight" sensation some dozen years after they first emerged.

As singles sales declined across the board, so the number of sales needed to get into the charts decreased. Musical tastes changed: the world moved on and no one bought albums, or rather CDs, by Pop acts any more. One good thing about the 1990s, though, was that artists and designers began to make the CD format work in terms of cover design.

▶ **Vingt à Trente Mille Jours / Françoiz Breut**
RELEASED 2000 | VIRGIN | FRANCE | SLEEVE DESIGN BY FRANK LORIOU | PHOTOGRAPHY BY LUC RAMBO | ALBUM PRODUCED BY FLORENCE BEAUVILLE, CHARLES BENSMAINE AND SANDRINE DELAUNE
Born and raised in Cherbourg, France, Françoiz's early musical influences were gleaned from her sister's record collection and late nights listening to Radio 1 DJ John Peel. After leaving school, she sang in a covers band and met and fell in love with Dominique A (a huge star in France). She accompanied him on stage for three years before, towards the end of 1996, realizing she wanted to do something for herself. There's a subtle feminine edge to her songs, with the swish of cool drum brushes, a Hammond organ, and slide guitar evoking a 1950s Jazz feel, with her velvety vocals breathing through. The photograph of Breut on the cover could just as easily been of Gainsbourg or Hardy, with its timeless quality and strong duotone printing. Yet when combined with the heavy blocked hand-printed font used for the typography, within such a confined form it has a strength and modernity which lift it above the run-of-the-mill cover. [GS]

françoiz
breut

VINGT À
TRENTE MILLE JOURS

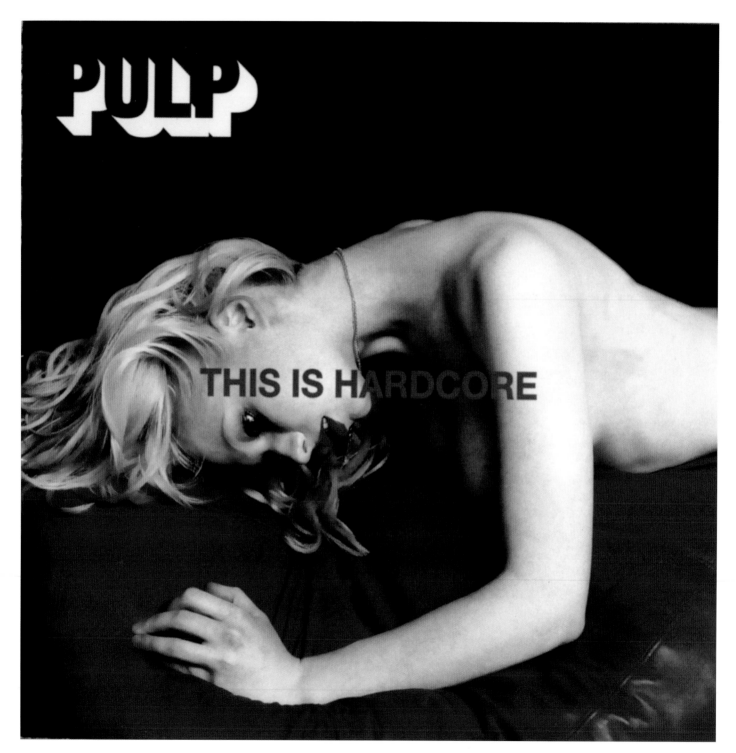

◀ This Is Hardcore / Pulp

RELEASED 1998 | ISLAND | UK |
SLEEVE DESIGN BY JOHN CURRIN
AND PETER SAVILLE | PHOTOGRAPHY
BY HORST DIEKGERDES | ALBUM
PRODUCED BY CHRIS THOMAS

Pulp first came into existence
as band in Sheffield in 1978.
They played their first Radio 1
session for DJ John Peel in 1981
and came to fame in 1995. That's
a long time to have to consider
fame and failure, but in the 18
years that singer and songwriter
Jarvis Cocker was fronting the
band, he didn't seem ever to
have become discouraged.
After garnering good critical
reviews for the 1994 album *His
'n' Hers*, the band finally made
the big time with the single
Common People, included on
the 1995 album *Different Class*.
Suddenly Jarvis, the tall, gangly,
bespectacled singer, was a sex
symbol. Ever the ironist, Jarvis
took sex as the theme for the
next Pulp album, *This Is
Hardcore*. The sleeve, as with
much of Peter Saville's work, is
striking and more memorable
than the music. Saville claims
that he was merely the facilitator
for the sleeve, however; that
Jarvis and New York artist John
Currin knew what they wanted,
and he helped them to achieve it.

▶ Ole 315-2 Philophobia / Arab Strap

RELEASED 1998 | MATADOR
RECORDS | USA | SLEEVE DESIGN
BY ADAM PIGGOTT | PAINTING BY
MARIANNE GREATED | ALBUM
PRODUCED BY GEOFF ALLAN AND
PAUL SAVAGE

A curiosity, including a booklet
in rhyming verse describing the
protagonist's sex life. The sleeve
art by Marianne Greated reminds
one of Paul Gauguin's South Sea
paintings in its colour but has a
curiously small head, presumably
because of the perspective of the
pose. We are not told who this
sitter is but the direct eye contact
suggests familiarity and trust. The
white background is unsettling.
Because we can't see the original
edges of the painting the model
appears to float or, even worse,
be engaged in levitation. [BM]

▶ Star / Belly

RELEASED 1993 | 4AD RECORDS |
USA | SLEEVE DESIGN BY CHRIS
BIGG AT V23 | PRODUCED BY TRACY
CHISHOLM AND BELLY

The surprise hit of 1993, with a
sleeve that is both attractive and
slightly disconcerting. The ballet
dancers are each attached to a
stand so they are models, like toy
soldiers, not real dancers. A nice
reversal, a positive rather than
negative image, although the
colours probably are negative.
The combination of clashing
orange and green, purple and
crimson is just right. The
composition hangs in delicate
balance, jarring yet luscious,
rather like the music. Presumably
there is some play on words at
work here between belly and
ballet that probably works better
in an American accent. [BM]

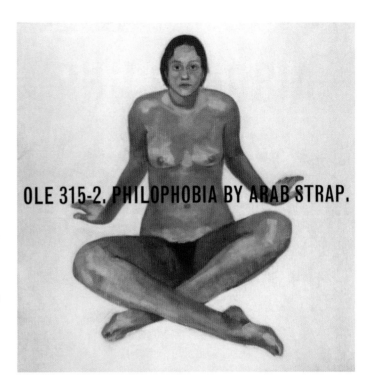

182

◄ Pop Pop / Rickie Lee Jones

RELEASED 1991 | GEFFEN | USA |
SLEEVE DESIGN BY KEVIN REAGAN |
ALBUM PRODUCED BY RICKIE LEE
JONES AND DAVID WAS

This was Rickie Lee Jones's
sixth album and she was as
difficult to categorize as she
had been when she released
her hugely influential debut,
eponymous LP in 1979. Is she
a Pop singer? Or is she a Jazz
singer? Sometimes she doesn't
seem to know either, and so
released albums such as this, a
beautifully crafted set of Jazz
standards only a couple of years
after her most successful Pop
album, *Flying Cowboys*. And
she called this album *Pop Pop* –
although it looks as if the title
was the idea of the sleeve
designer, Kevin Reagan, who
would go on to be creative
director of Madonna's label,
Maverick, and win a Grammy
for his work on her *Ray of Light*
album. In the early 1990s, faux
Japanese naive advertising art
was cool but not many major
labels used this crass but sweet
style to sell records.

▶ Am I Not Your Girl? / Sinéad O'Connor

RELEASED 1992 | ENSIGN
RECORDS | UK | PHOTOGRAPHY BY
KATE GARNER | PRODUCED BY PHIL
RAMONE AND SINÉAD O'CONNOR

A very sinister sleeve. Kate
Garner's black and white photo
uses the shadow to balance a
beautiful composition. The first
impression is of an attractive,
gamine young woman, but then
her feet become apparent. The
giant platform shoes, as worn in
early 1990s porn movies, make
the picture less obvious. The
pose shows cleavage but Sinead
is looking away, lost in thought.
It's not a picture of a whore,
but the title hints at several
meanings, including ownership,
with sleeve notes about the
destruction of self-esteem, rape
and sexual submission. [BM]

▶ All You Can Eat / kd lang

RELEASED 1995 | WARNER BROS |
USA | SLEEVE DESIGN BY KD LANG
AND JOHN HEIDEN FOR S.M.O.G. |
PHOTOGRAPHY BY GUZMAN |
ALBUM PRODUCED BY KD LANG
AND BEN MINK

Coming three years after kd's
Ingenue success and move to
LA (which she hated), this cover
reflects alienation and enhances
her oddness. The Japanese
writing, Communist hero-style
pose and glaring yellow and
green colour palette are
unsettling. The jaunty angles
and colours are in contrast to
the slow and medium paced
songs of loss, love and sexuality.
The title – like the later *Drag*, an
album of pro-smoking songs – is
visible only on the album spine.
Inside the booklet there's a photo
of kd dressed as a hotdog. [BM]

1990s Rock

Rock music in the 1990s continued to change, mutate, split and diversify, more than it had in the previous decade. Maybe it was the fact that sales of new albums began to slow down, while re-released "classic" Rock was issued on CD and sold to the original Rock fans who had discarded, in the main, their vinyl collections. What was once considered mainstream Rock almost ceased to exist – there was no new Doobie Brothers, Zeppelin, Yes, Kiss, Eagles or Floyd bubbling up in the 1990s. Only U2 and REM would grow into stadium fillers, albeit ones with half-decent designers working for them. It seemed that the era of multi-million selling Rock acts was now past.

The single biggest-selling American artist of the 1990s was Country singer Garth Brooks, swiftly followed by another Country artist, Shania Twain – and both owed a lot to Rock music. Heavy Metal saw a fall in popularity as first Rap, and then Alt Rock (later "Nu Metal") in the shape of the Red Hot Chilli Peppers, Offspring, Linkin Park, and others bands bit hard into the US disaffected teen market. And a grittier version of Alt Rock began to emerge, its leader a bizarrely attired, genderless shock-rocker called Marilyn Manson.

At the end of the 1980s a new Rock music movement had begun to emerge from Seattle which, while paying lip service to classic Rock, took more from the British Punk scene than just attitude, and married it to a wholly American look – lumberjack shirts, ripped jeans, biker boots, long hair and scuffed sneakers. Grunge would briefly light up the record charts in America and the rest of the world, and in doing so create a new teen identity.

In the UK, Rock music had ceased to be about Led Zeppelin at the end of the 1970s, and in its place a wave of new, usually Northern bands were emerging who married classic guitar riffs with Funk and Disco-derived dance rhythms. First the Stone Roses in 1989 and then Primal Scream and Happy Mondays struck gold sales with their hybrid Rock-Dance music. And there was a brief period in the UK when guitar-based, Beatles-obsessed bands Oasis and Blur created the storm in a British teacup with Britpop – but although some fans claimed that the album sleeves for both bands were great, they were as derivative and backward-looking as the music itself. It was the dance-influenced, more original Rock acts that created the interesting sleeves.

▶ **This is a beautiful cover, a really strong image. Bjork looks gorgeous, like a mysterious angel. Or an alien**

ADAM ANT

▶ **Debut / Björk**
RELEASED 1995 | ONE LITTLE INDIAN | UK | SLEEVE DESIGN BY ME COMPANY | PHOTOGRAPHY BY STÉPHANE SEDNAOUI | ALBUM PRODUCED BY NELLEE HOOPER, GRAHAM MASSEY AND BJÖRK
For her debut solo release Björk chose a photo of herself by Stéphane Sednaoui that did much to establish her image. The wide-eyed stare, highlighted by diamonds beneath each pupil, was a master touch. As was the plain, grey sweater. Björk is even better than Madonna at playing with her image. This is the debut of a young woman, thus the tousled hair, the little-girl sleeves on her sweater pulled down over the wrists. Her hands at her mouth is another great touch, intriguing and beguiling at the same time. Is she suppressing a smile? Praying? Smelling her finger tips? [BM]

▲ Homogenic / Björk

RELEASED 1997 | ONE LITTLE INDIAN | UK | SLEEVE DESIGN BY ME COMPANY | FRONT COVER ART DIRECTION BY ALEXANDER MCQUEEN | PHOTOGRAPHY BY NICK KNIGHT | ALBUM PRODUCED BY BJÖRK AND MARK BELL

Until signing the Sugarcubes and then Björk, British Punk label One Little Indian had never sold many records. They soon learned how to deal with massive orders, however, especially after Björk launched her solo career. Only four years into that career, Iceland's most famous singing daughter had a reputation for creating otherworldly music, and with this cover it's as if she set out to prove that she's from another world. It's Björk at her most playful, toying with the costumes of classical Japanese Kabuki theatre. The image was art directed by UK fashion designer Alexander McQueen, styled by his fashion journalist pal Katy England and photographed by fashion photographer Nick Knight. The image has been tinkered with so much that one wonders if she actually wore the clothes at all. It's an amazing composition: every element balances; every line leads where it should, all framing an enigmatic face, staring into your eyes through artificially wide pupils.

▶ Stick Around for Joy / Sugarcubes

RELEASED 1992 | ONE LITTLE INDIAN | UK | SLEEVE DESIGN BY ME COMPANY | ALBUM PRODUCED BY PAUL FOX

Paul White, the founder of the computer graphics design group Me Company, was involved with the setting up of the One Little Indian Record Company, so he worked with the Sugarcubes and Björk from the beginning. Me Company is now a major design group, but for the first 12 years they dealt with nothing but music. This sleeve celebrates the male sperm reaching the egg, but should be seen as part of a four-panel whole, culminating in the inner sleeve. The Sugarcubes' roots were in hippie culture; their name taken from a popular method of taking LSD. Me Company made it into an instantly identifiable logo for the band, with distinctive lettering inspired by the Beatles logo on Ringo's bass drum. Rendered in a very understated way, the sleeve is a far cry from their later work, such as Björk's *Homogenic* album, but it shows a cutting edge computer design group making a bold entrance into a then unknown field. [BM]

The Sugarcubes

Stick Around For Joy

SUGARCUBES

Stick Around For Joy ● One Little Indian Pleasures

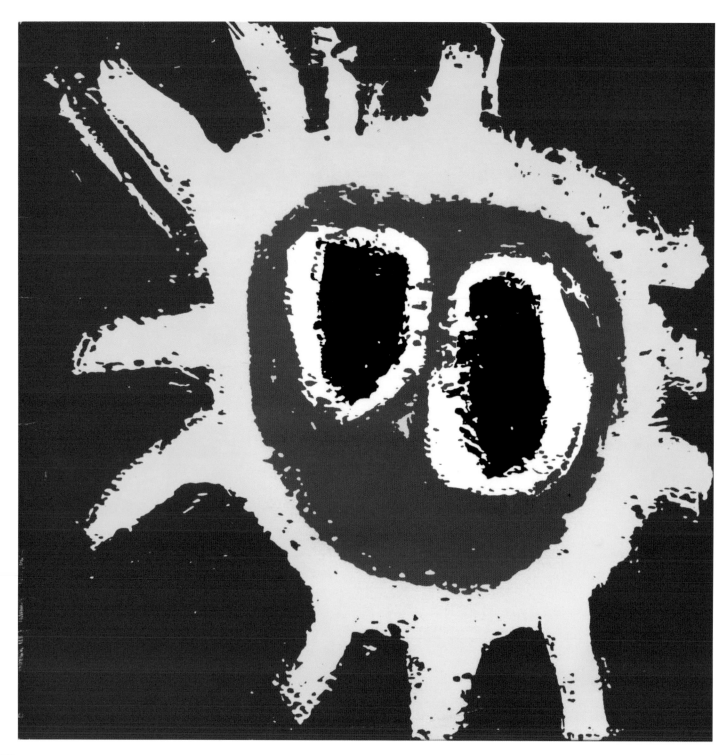

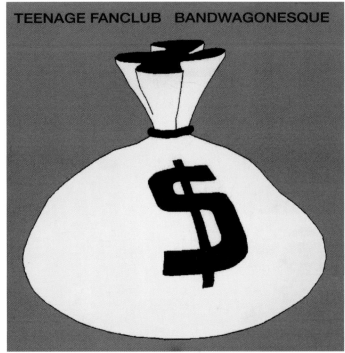

◀ Screamadelica / Primal Scream

RELEASED 1991 | CREATION | UK | SLEEVE IMAGE BY PAUL CANNELL | SLEEVE DESIGN BY ES(P) | ALBUM PRODUCED BY ANDREW WEATHERALL AND OTHERS

Primal Scream's acid and ecstasy influences are apparent in their third album's artwork. A yellow smiley face was on every t-shirt that summer, the symbol most associated with the emergence of E culture. The similarly vivid free-form graphic of the album was an image club-goers instantly recognized. No typography on the front, just a freaky figure with no mouth, which is as distinctive and contemporary today as it was then. [GS]

▲ It's Great When You're Straight Yeah / Black Grape

RELEASED 1995 | RADIOACTIVE RECORDS | UK | COVER DESIGN BY GRAND CENTRAL STATION | PHOTOGRAPHY BY PAT AND MATT CARROLL | ALBUM PRODUCED BY GARY KURFIRST

Ex-Happy Mondays Shaun Ryder formed Black Grape when the Mondays split, and used the same design company for this cover. The image is based on the only known photograph of the international hitman Carlos the Jackal, the irony of the title being a little heavy perhaps, but inside is a similar artwork based on the young Michael Jackson, in which his face is presented in several different colours.

▲ Bandwagonesque / Teenage Fanclub

RELEASED 1991 | CREATION | UK | SLEEVE DESIGN BY SHARON FITZGERALD | ALBUM PRODUCED BY DON FLEMING, PAUL CHISHOLM AND TEENAGE FANCLUB

Of all the album sleeves in this section, this one adorned what sounds most like a Rock album. From Scotland, Teenage Fanclub are huge fans of classic Rock music, not only citing their influences in interviews, but also covering songs by Big Star, Phil Ochs, The Flying Burrito Brothers, Neil Young and many others. Their debut album was released in 1990 to rave reviews which carried over to this, their second album. Unlike most of the bands who were emerging at the time, Teenage Fanclub showed no visible or audible sign of ever having gone to a dance club, their music being full of feedback, classic Pop hooks and droning bass and cymbals. The brash, bright, colourful image (drawn by a friend of the band) is as obvious as the big, brash guitar sound of the album. It's a bag of dollars and they want it. The title might suggest they're willing to jump on any bandwagon to get it – but they didn't. They stuck to their Rock roots.

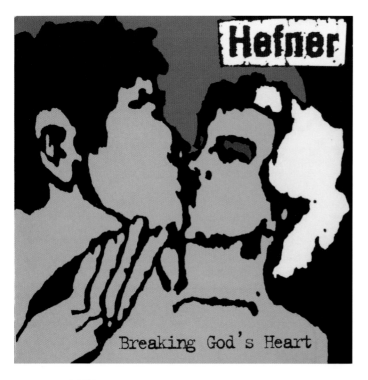

◀ Breaking God's Heart / Hefner

RELEASED 1998 | TOO PURE RECORDS | UK | SLEEVE DESIGN BY FLIRT/HAYMAN | ALBUM PRODUCED BY JOHN MORRISON AND HEFNER

Another Scottish band, romantics like Teenage Fanclub, who like cartoon imagery. Hefner's debut album continued a sequence of hand-drawn covers begun a few years earlier with independently released singles and EPs. There's a bittersweetness about this sleeve with its crude, Courier font title and stark fleshtones offset by the woman's yellow hair and purple eye make-up. The album made a lot of "Best of the Year" lists in music mags on both sides of the Atlantic, but Hefner founder Darren Hayman thought it was the band's worst.

◀ Sounds of the Satellites / Laika

RELEASED 1997 | TOO PURE RECORDS | UK | SLEEVE DESIGN BY LAIKA | PHOTOGRAPHY BY JOHN SUMMERHAYES | ALBUM PRODUCED BY LAIKA | SNOWSTORM CREATED BY GLOBAL SHAKEUP FROM ORIGINAL ARTWORK BY RACHEL FUSEN

Named after the first dog in space, for this their second album the British band had snowglobes made with Laika inside, next to a rocket ship, apparently both sitting on the Moon. Inside the CD booklet you will find instructions on how to order your own Laika snowglobe, which must be a first in music merchandising. Released on the same label as Hefner, this sleeve too has a childlike quality which is far from childish.

▶ Flashpoint / The Rolling Stones

RELEASED 1991 | VIRGIN | UK | SLEEVE DESIGN BY GARRY MOUAT AND DAVID CROW | ALBUM PRODUCED BY THE GLIMMER TWINS

A striking – no pun intended – sleeve for a rather poorly received Greatest Hits Live album, controversial only for the fact that the lyrics to the track Highwire were seen in Britain as opposing UK support for the first Gulf War conflict. Attempts were made to stop the release of that track as a single, and presumably the image of the open flame, used on the cover, was itself seen as incitement. The sleeve's great strength comes from its utter simplicity and familiarity. Anyone who has ever owned a gas heater will recognize the flame as the sign for the pilot light, and the thick outlines of the image come from road signs, such as the freeway sign used by Kraftwerk on *Autobahn*. It is also, of course, the sort of image that Andy Warhol would have painted if someone had suggested it to him. Such a simple image but with a number of associations. [BM]

RollingStones**Flashpoint**

Greatest Hits Live

Includes the single
Highwire

468135-1

191

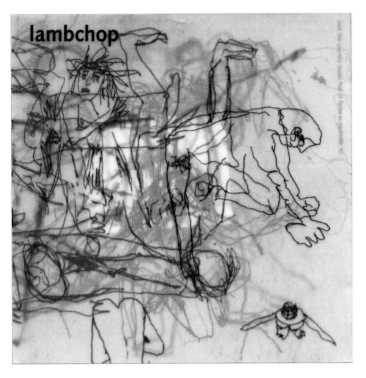

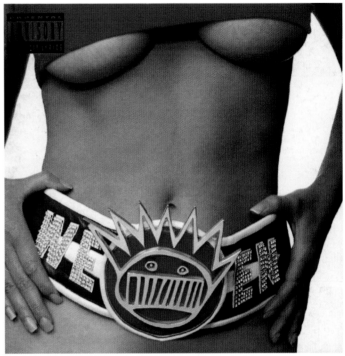

◀ Lazer Guided Melodies / Spiritualized

RELEASED 1997 | DEDICATED | UK | ORIGINAL ARTWORK MR UGLY LOGO | DESIGN ALBERT TUPELO | SLEEVE DESIGN BY ANDREW SUTTON FOR BLUE SOUR | MODELMAKER GAVIN LINDSAY | PHOTOGRAPHY BY PETE GARDNER | ALBUM PRODUCED AND MIXED BY J SPACEMAN AND BARRY CLEPSON

For this debut album, a whole cast of people worked on creating the alien or spectre-like models and photos for the front. Their next album came in a cardboard pillbox, the CD itself sealed in foil – but making the CD hard to take in and out. However, 2001's *Let It Come Down* was a truly remarkable package (page 247).

▲ What Another Man Spills / Lambchop

RELEASED 1998 | CITY SLANG | USA | SLEEVE DESIGN BY CRAIG ALLEN | ILLUSTRATIONS BY VIC CHESNUTT | ALBUM PRODUCED BY MARK NEVERS, KURT WAGNER AND PAUL NIEHAUS

Their record company calls them Nashville's most fucked-up Country band and no one seems to argue. Formed in 1993 in Nashville by Kurt Wagner, the membership of the band seems somewhat fluid. There is a large number of people who turn up at Lambchop recording sessions or gigs and play. Most of them appear to have full-time jobs doing other things. There is a definite Lambchop sound –

although it's hard to define. It's laid back, Country tinged, certainly, but there's also an element of Soul music in there. Mixing the rich musical and cultural heritage of their background, Lambchop seem determined not to be pinned down by any useless labelling. Their album sleeves are generally "odd" but this is brilliant. Printed on a kind of tough tracing paper, it contains various sketches by semi-paralyzed singer-songwriter Vic Chesnutt, with the band's name printed on it along with the message: "Visit the Country music hall of fame in Nashville, Tn." The track-listing is printed on the inner back sleeve and is barely visible beside the CD hinge.

▲ Chocolate & Cheese / Ween

RELEASED 1994 | FLYING NUN | USA | SLEEVE DESIGN BY REINER DESIGN CONSULTANTS, INC | PHOTOGRAPHY BY JOHN KUCZALA | ALBUM PRODUCED BY ANDREW WEISS

Gene and Dan Ween are very funny guys, and great students of all kinds of music. They mix Funk with Country, Punk with lounge and bluegrass with Reggae. Not all at once, but often enough. Ween album covers are almost all witty takes on other bands' sleeves. Here, they take on the Ohio Players in such a precise manner that it could almost be a Players cover. Only the childish Ween logo on the belt gives the game away.

1990s Sonic Youth

Formed in the New York No Wave scene in 1981, Sonic Youth began to create a new kind of music, one that was as noisy as Punk had been, as adventurous as Jazz and as indefinable as all the best kinds of music. They released their first "proper" album, *Confusion Is Sex*, on Glenn Branca's own label Neutral in 1983. The cover displayed a sketch by former art student Kim Gordon of her boyfriend (and future husband) Thurston Moore. It was clearly artistic and showed a definite Do It Yourself ethic that the band had inherited from Punk.

After a tour of the UK the band found that they were more popular there than at home and so signed a deal with Blast First, a label created in London specifically to release Sonic Youth albums. Their debut album for the label, *Bad Moon Rising*, had a photograph of a burning straw man on the cover. It was an unsettling image, reminiscent for UK audiences of a dark and odd British movie made in the late 1970s entitled *The Wicker Man*, and reflected the edgy sound of the band perfectly. For their next album, *EVOL*, they chose a still from a Richard Kern movie, *Submit to Me Now*, and used what was to become a trademark scrawled title. For their fourth album, *Sister*,

the band used an artistic collage made up of various images – one of which got them into legal trouble and another which made them fear legal trouble. On the original LP sleeve the band placed a Richard Avedon photo; he objected and threatened legal action against them and their US label (SST, home to Hüsker Dü and Black Flag) and so subsequent prints of the sleeve had the image blacked out. There's also an image of Mickey and Minnie Mouse at Disneyland on one side of the LP sleeve which the Mouse didn't object to, but for the CD the bar code was placed over it.

In 1988 the band released their first critically acclaimed album, *Daydream Nation*. A double vinyl release, it used paintings by Gerhard Richter (both entitled *Kerze*) on front and back. Not only did the music appeal to music critics, but the image of the burning candle also captured their imaginations. After one more independently released album, *The Whitey Album*, released as Ciccone Youth and a "tribute" to Madonna and Pop culture, the band signed to Geffen with a deal giving them complete artistic control. They then set about releasing albums that had some of their best artwork (and music), beginning with *Goo*. [BM]

▶ In the early eighties, there were a lot of artists involved with the music scene

KIM GORDON, SONIC YOUTH

▶ **Goo / Sonic Youth**
RELEASED 1990 | GEFFEN | USA | SLEEVE DESIGN BY KEVIN REAGAN | ALBUM PRODUCED BY SONIC YOUTH, NICK SANSANO AND RON SAINT GERMAIN
Kevin Reagan's sleeve features a drawing by Raymond Pettibon, with a similar drawing on the back. Reagan has taped what appears to be a Xerox copy of the drawing to the sleeve, letting the Scotch tape show, complete with small cat hairs stuck to it. Reminiscent of Andy Warhol's early Pop art drawings, such as *Dick Tracy*, the subject matter refers to Sonic Youth's early fascination with Charles Manson and other underground figures. "Even though my work is usually just one drawing," says Pettibon, "it is more of a narrative than it is a cartoon, with a punchline and a resolution and a laugh at the end." [BM]

▼ Washing Machine / Sonic Youth

RELEASED 1995 | GEFFEN | USA | SLEEVE DESIGN BY MIKE MILLS | PHOTOGRAPHY LANCE ACCORD | ALBUM PRODUCED BY SONIC YOUTH WITH JOHN SIKET

Early in 1995, Sonic Youth were reported as toying with the idea of changing their name to Washing Machine. Even if they were not serious, it led to this album sleeve. Lance Accord's Polaroid photograph of two fans wearing Sonic Youth Washing Machine t-shirts was taken after the band's April 28, 1995 show at Amherst College in Massachusetts. The shirt on the left was signed by support act Come. Sonic Youth liked the

photograph and wanted to use it as the album sleeve but Geffen would not use it without clearance from the fans. The band managed to contact them and get their permission through an MTV news bulletin. The band's use of distinctive imagery, simultaneously making a comment on consumer culture and giving the band a brand image, harks all the way back to Hipgnosis and their use of a cow on the sleeve of *Atom Heart Mother*. [BM]

▼ A Thousand Leaves / Sonic Youth

RELEASED 1998 | GEFFEN | USA | SLEEVE DESIGN BY FRANK OLINSKY | SLEEVE ART BY MARNIE WEBER COURTESY JESSICA FREDERICKS GALLERY, NYC | ALBUM PRODUCED BY WHARTON TIERS AND SONIC YOUTH

Marnie Weber's collage is called *Hamster Girl*, the lettering by Mark Borthwick. She combines a love of animals with deconstruction of the "cute" imagery of pets and little girls. The girl is sitting up in bed; images of females in bed often have a sexual connotation, so here she wears hamster ears, referring to a *Playboy* bunny and making the image a critique of porn and sexual exploitation. [BM]

▶ Dirty / Sonic Youth

RELEASED 1992 | GEFFEN | USA | SLEEVE DESIGN BY MIKE KELLEY | ALBUM PRODUCED BY BUTCH VIG WITH SONIC YOUTH

Sonic Youth never liked appearing on their album covers. While on a small independent label and releasing 12-inch vinyl albums they had created great sleeves (see *Daydream Nation*), but by the 1990s they were thinking about the smaller CD format. While *Goo* works brilliantly at 12-inch size, it doesn't transfer as well to CD format. This sleeve, however, works in both formats. Mike Kelly's finger puppets are slightly disturbing, humorous and enigmatic. Kind of like Sonic Youth, really.

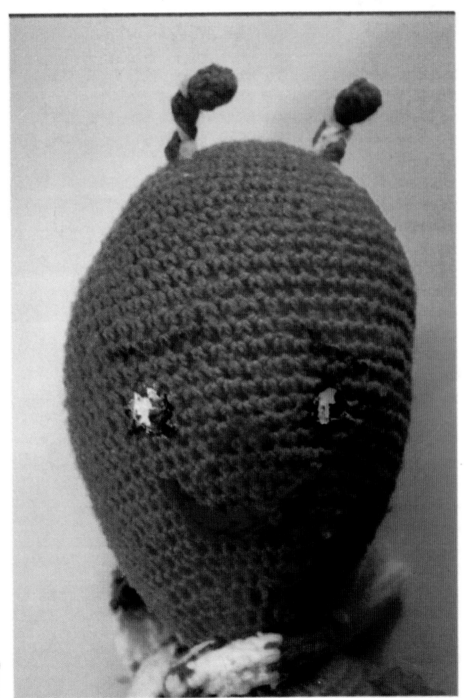

S O N I C

diRty

Y O U T H

1990s Grunge

It took ten years, but when Punk hit Seattle in 1986 the result was incredible. The city had no previous Rock history to boast of, but by the late 1980s there was a burgeoning music scene with similarly clad bands playing loud, fuzz-pedal-powered garage Rock. Initially the scene was led by Green River (who later became Mudhoney) and the Melvins, who were never to sample the fame enjoyed by many of their counterparts, despite being lauded by Nirvana's Kurt Cobain. New York's Sonic Youth would tour with Mudhoney and Nirvana in the late 1980s and were responsible for introducing the latter to Geffen (Youth's label). A home-based record company, the wittily named Sub Pop emerged to record and release the various and numerous local bands, among them Tad, Soundgarden (members of which had launched the label) and Mudhoney. Nirvana's debut album, *Bleach*, was released by Sub Pop in 1989, by which time the British music press had alerted the world to the growing Seattle scene dubbed "Grunge" by Green River and Mudhoney's Mark Arm.

Since the UK was by this time giving rise to the Rock-Dance hybrid of The Stone Roses and Happy Mondays, the section of the press that was more interested in loud, fast guitar music seized on the Seattle scene and promoted it heavily. That Grunge came with its own "look" in the form of biker boots, ripped jeans, checked shirts worn over t-shirts and beanie hats meant that before long clubs in London, Liverpool, Los Angeles, Lusaka and all points in between were soon filled with kids dressed for Seattle winters. Once Nirvana had scored a worldwide hit with Smells Like Teen Spirit – helped by heavy rotation on MTV of the accompanying video – in 1991, a genuine teen culture was born. For Cobain, fame and fortune sat uneasily; he wanted "credible" underground success like the Melvins had, and began to wear "Grunge Is Dead" t-shirts the same year that the world went crazy for it. Cobain's anti-success stance was part of its attraction for the millions of disaffected teenagers who loved the grunge sound and wanted to be "rebels". Post-Punk and Rap there seemed little for white Middle America to adopt as its own credo; Grunge provided a neat and attainable look and political stance. Album covers of grunge albums were varied and of varying quality. The ones included here represent the extent of the movement's reach and imagination.

▶ **One day, Dave and I were sitting around watching a documentary on babies being born underwater and I thought, 'Let's put that on the album cover'**

KURT COBAIN, NIRVANA

▶ **Nevermind / Nirvana**
RELEASED 1991 | GEFFEN | USA | SLEEVE DESIGN BY ROBERT FISHER | PHOTOGRAPHY BY KIRK WEDDLE | ALBUM PRODUCED BY BUTCH VIG AND NIRVANA
Initially for the *Nevermind* cover Kurt Cobain wanted a photo of a water birth, but designer Fisher thought this too graphic and so hired Weddle, an underwater photographer, to stage a shot. Weddle took four babies to be photographed and chose a shot of Spencer Elden – swimming for the first time, apparently – as the cover picture. The dollar bill on a fishing hook was Cobain's idea, and the cover has become the poster that adorns the bedroom walls of numerous 13-year-olds who "identify" with his nihilism.

◄ Superfuzz Bigmuff / Mudhoney

RELEASED 1996 | SUB POP | USA | PHOTOGRAPHY BY CHARLES PETERSON | ALBUM PRODUCED BY JACK ENDINO AND MUDHONEY

Of all the Seattle-based grunge bands who signed to Sub Pop, Mudhoney were probably the wittiest. They took their name from a Russ Meyer movie and as founder member, ex-Green River guitarist Steve Turner, put in the sleeve notes of their excellent 2000 compilation *March to Fuzz*: "In Seattle 1987 there was little reason to take being in a band seriously." Since Green River, with whom Mudhoney guitarist and singer Mark Arm had performed, were among the very first bands to create the sound that the world would later recognize as Nirvana's, it is apt that Mudhoney's first album for Sub Pop should look like this. It could be a 1960s garage band on the cover. The long hair, jeans and beads combined with vintage 1960s guitar and psychedelic-inspired lettering give it a distinctly vintage feel. The large, melting title frames the photo in such a way as to suggest a cramped but explosive sound coming from the guitarists. Which is exactly how the album sounds.

▶ Live Through This / Hole

RELEASED 1994 | GEFFEN | USA | SLEEVE DESIGN BY ROBIN SLOANE, JANET WOLSBORN | PHOTOGRAPHY BY ELLEN VON UNWERTH | ALBUM PRODUCED BY PAUL Q KOLDERIE, SEAN SLADE

Fashion photographer Ellen von Unwerth's hazy portrait of a mascara-streaked beauty queen on the front of *Live Through This* contrasts sharply with a family photo of Hole leader Courtney Love, aged around twelve in a checked shirt and black jeans, standing barefoot in a road, which smiles weakly out from the back. The front picture evokes a snatched moment of female victory as transient as beauty itself, while the girl on the back seems full of promise, vulnerable and smiling for daddy (who took the photo).

▶ No Code / Pearl Jam

RELEASED 1996 | EPIC | US | POLAROIDS BY E. VEDDER, J. AMENT, M. MCCREADY, B. AMENT, A. FIELDS, C. MCCANN, L. MERCER, DR PAUL J. BUBACK | SLEEVE LAYOUT BY BARRY AMENT, CHRIS MCCANN, JEROME TURNER | ALBUM PRODUCED BY BRENDAN O'BRIEN AND PEARL JAM

Unlike Nirvana, Seattle's Pearl Jam had little visual identity. Their first album cover looked like an afterthought, with the next two not much better. Which makes *No Code* even more arresting than it already is. Maybe there's an *Exile on Main Street* influence, but because this is all colour and so varied, the photos are more intriguing. There's no one topic (unlike *Exile*'s sex theme) and the range of close-ups of everyday things and human anatomy create a voyeuristic feel.

1990s Alt Rock

What exactly constituted Alt Rock in the 1990s was arguable and often argued over. By the 1990s Rock music had changed and the change was marked on both sides of the Atlantic. For the first time since the 1970s there were two distinctly different music scenes happening in Britain and America. In the UK new bands that would once have drawn on the Blues for inspiration now looked to dance music and the clubs which, it was estimated, attracted more than a million Brits every Saturday night.

Apart from Oasis and Blur, British bands that played live gigs on an ever-deflating circuit tended to identify visually and musically with people who went to dance clubs and took clubbers' drugs such as ecstasy and acid, both of which had grown more prevalent following the creation of the Rave scene in the UK in 1987. The rise in popularity of live stand-up comedy in Britain through the early 1990s had seen many former live music clubs switch their booking policies to the quieter and cheaper alternative. Many of the former venues would never open their doors to live bands again, thus making it more difficult for new, young bands to practise their live art anywhere in public.

There was no comparable Dance or Rave scene in America (although there were a few open-air Raves on the warmer West Coast). There was a still thriving live circuit but it had a rigid segregation between music types. For all Garth Brooks's sales, his fans didn't go to Red Hot Chili Peppers gigs and vice versa. The American Alternative Rock scene of the 1990s, particularly at the end of the decade, undoubtedly owed a debt to Grunge and in turn to Punk. By the end of the 1990s most of the big Alt Rock bands looked and sounded for the world like late 1970s Punks (unlike Guns N' Roses, who only sounded like them).

If there was a defining element to Alt Rock in the United States in the 1990s it was probably to do with age. All of the albums illustrated in this section are from bands whose fanbase was young – under 25 probably – and many of them reflect an element of childishness that had not been present in album design previously. The use of comic strip cartoon-style drawings and blatantly sexual images reflected the growing culture among young men as represented by the burgeoning popularity of prescriptive "men's" magazines such as *Maxim* and *FHM*.

▶ **I'm extremely proud of it. I said more in one of his covers than any novel could. It made people think *and* cringe**

PAUL BROWN, DESIGNER OF MECHANICAL ANIMALS

▶ **Mechanical Animals / Marilyn Manson**
RELEASED 1998 | NOTHING/ INTERSCOPE RECORDS | USA | SLEEVE DESIGN BY PAUL BROWN | PHOTOGRAPHY BY JOSEPH CULTICE | ALBUM PRODUCED BY MICHAEL BEINHORN AND MARILYN MANSON
To create Omega, Manson needed make-up, dyed hair, prosthetic breasts and airbrush, and the shock of the image was increased bcause it looked like a photograph. It would be nice to say that the cover was an indictment of America's growing obsession with sex in the form of porn and plastic surgery, but it's not. Manson claimed it was about sexlessness and vulnerability, and then went and spoiled it by adding: "Plus, I've always had an affection for prosthetic limbs."

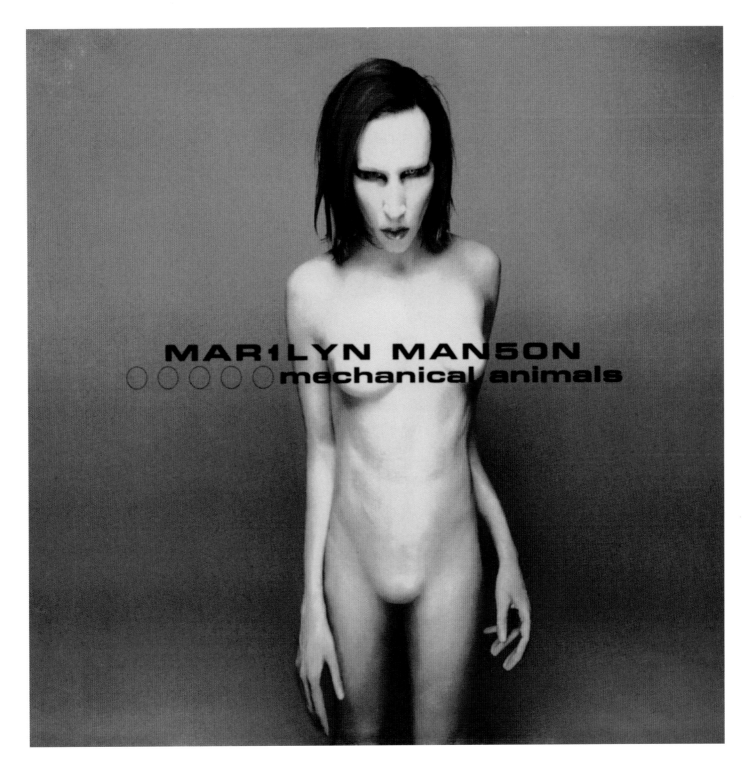

◄ Enema of the State / Blink 182

RELEASED 1999 | MCA | USA | SLEEVE DESIGN BY TIM STEDMAN AND KEITH TAMASHIRO | PHOTOGRAPHY BY DAVID GOLDMAN | ALBUM PRODUCED BY JERRY FINN | COVER MODEL JANINE LINDENMULDER

The first major label album to knowingly feature a porn actress on the cover, a very funny photo playing to pubescent sexual fantasies. It's a perfect example of 1990s Jock Rock, all smirking sexual subjectification and innuendo, rescued only by the fact that on the back the band look ludicrous in their shorts as they wait for a (hopefully painful) examination from "nurse" Janine.

▲ One Hot Minute / Red Hot Chili Peppers

RELEASED 1995 | WARNER BROS | USA | SLEEVE DESIGN BY ANTHONY KIEDIS, FLEA AND DIRK WALTER | ILLUSTRATION MARK RYDEN | ALBUM PRODUCED BY RICK RUBIN

For their sixth album, Californian Funk-metal superstars Red Hot Chili Peppers opted for a seemingly demure, artistic image, albeit one that suggests the creeping infantilism that had caught hold of the thirtysomething generation that they belonged to. The painting, by Californian fine artist Mark Ryden, is typical of his style. Reminiscent of a nineteenth- century children's book illustration there is something slightly worrying about the composition that's hard to put your finger on. That such an innocent-seeming painting should adorn an album by the Peppers is unnerving, of course. As is the presence of the Parental Advisory sticker in the bottom right-hand corner. Ryden's work is full of faux innocence, with dolls and small children often portrayed in somehow terrible situations – one work from 2003, entitled *Rose 42*, shows a big, sad-eyed girl in an oval frame, bleeding red tears – or with running, red mascara. He also illustrated a Stephen King novel and part of Michael Jackson's *Dangerous* album cover.

▲ Americana / Offspring

RELEASED 1998 | COLUMBIA | USA | SLEEVE DESIGN BY SEAN EVANS | ILLUSTRATIONS BY FRANK KOZIK | ALBUM PRODUCED BY DAVE JERDEN

Spanish-born artist Frank Kozik moved to Austin, Texas in 1976, making posters for local bands. Meanwhile in their four albums released prior to *Americana*, Offspring hadn't produced a decent sleeve or visual identity for themselves. Their music was California Punk, but previous artwork had seemed merely amateurish. With *Americana*, though, the band hit a visual high with Kozik's strident graphics. It perfectly reflects the 1990s post-Punk obsession with distorting innocent cartoon art.

1990s Rap

By the end of the 1980s there were two distinct US Rap communities, with emnity between the West Coast and East Coast fraternities leading to the death of two major stars, Tupac Shakur and Biggie Smalls. While the East Coast Rappers were spewing out political consciousness Rap (Public Enemy et al), the West Coast was developing Gangsta Rap (NWA et al) with its focus on sex, money and cop-killing. One thing about Gangsta Rap – there could never be a white imposter grabbing sales as Vanilla Ice had done with his execrable Rap in the 1980s.

Rap became a true part of the music industry in the 1990s. It even spread into Hollywood with Ice T, Ice Cube and L.L. Cool J developing successful film careers – others would follow. Rap's increasing glamorization of prison life in the form of clothes worn inside state penitentiaries had bizarre knock-on effects. Where once poor black guys had worn jeans several sizes too big because that was all they had – hand-me-downs from family and charities – rappers began wearing with pride the kind of denim trousers and work overalls that were issued in prison. They always bought sizes too big because in prison you were never given the right size and they wanted to be

authentic, to show that they were "street" and understood the sartorial shorthand used among the real O.G.s. So by the mid-1990s millions of kids around the world were wearing jeans a size too big with the cracks of their asses showing and the closest they'd ever been to an American prison was watching Rap videos. Major fashion houses made money out of selling prison chic clothes. Because rappers were willing to kill for the right sneakers (or at least Rap that they would), certain sneakers gained a worth well beyond their sale price. In parts of major American and European cities kids could be mugged for their shoes by kids who could afford their own pair, if they could find a store to sell them.

Rappers wore their hoods up in order to hide their faces from prying police cameras and CCTV; so too did millions of kids, even in towns without CCTV. Rap became the most influential musical movement of the decade. But because most rappers had inflated egos, their album covers were dull and repetitive, featuring full-on images of the stars wearing their favourite labels, or illustrations putting them in ghetto settings or fantastical situations. Which makes the following the best of the genre in the 1990s.

▶ **Mama Said Knock You Out / L.L. Cool J**

RELEASED 1990 | DEF JAM | USA | SLEEVE DESIGN BY THE DRAWING BOARD | PHOTOGRAPHY BY MICHAEL COMTE | ALBUM PRODUCED BY MARLEY MARL FOR MARLEY MARL PRODUCTIONS AND L.L. COOL J

With his (and Def Jam's) debut album *Radio* in 1985 (page 170), L.L. Cool J set the style of much that followed in Rap. At the start of the 1990s he almost did it again, with *Mama Said Knock You Out* showing one of the ways that Rap was going. (He wasn't a Gangsta rapper.) Fifteen years earlier, Isaac Hayes had featured black fashion and jewellery on his album covers, particularly *Hot Buttered Soul*, but not as aggressively as this. L.L.'s torso looks worked in the way that only guys in the joint have time to work their bodies. His Cool J pendant on a thick, chunky chain is held as if it could be used as either a kind of rosary or a knuckle duster– his hands are held fist in fist. You can't see his eyes (as on at least two Hayes covers) but you feel he's giving you a belligerent stare. Prior to this rappers wore their flashy attire with pride. After it, like L.L. they would seek to prove that they were worth more than the clothes they stood up in.

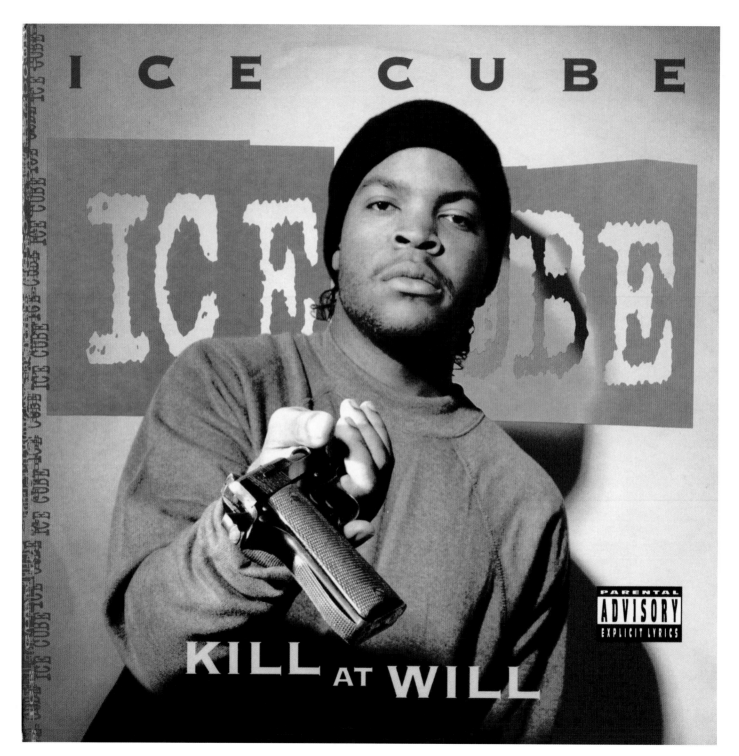

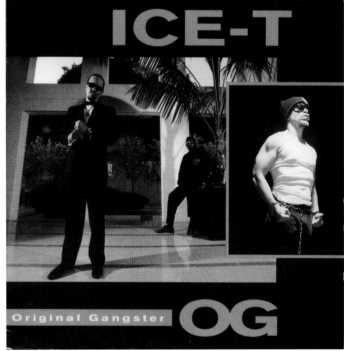

◀ Kill at Will / Ice Cube

RELEASED 1990 | PRIORITY RECORDS | USA | SLEEVE DESIGN BY UNKNOWN | ALBUM PRODUCED BY ICE CUBE, SIR JINX AND CHILLY CHILL

After being in LA's top Gangsta Rap crew, Niggaz with Attitude, in 1989 Ice Cube went solo with this mini LP. While he's full of attitude and anger, he's also a student of the civil rights movement, but tending more towards Malcolm X's take on matters than Martin Luther King's, and the sleeve shows this. Totally unglamorous, the unsmiling Cube stares out from the front offering you the gun. The title situated just below the butt of the gun adds more power to the image.

▲ Niggaz4life / NWA

RELEASED 1991 | RUTHLESS RECORDS | USA | SLEEVE ART DIRECTION BY KEVIN "DESIGN" HOSMANN | PHOTOGRAPHY BY PETER DORNS | ALBUM PRODUCED BY DR DRE AND YELLA FOR HIGH POWERED PRODUCTIONS | EXECUTIVE PRODUCER ERIC "EAZY-E" WRIGHT

NWA's fourth and final album is not their best, but the sleeve is. A disorienting murder scene with cops, Do Not Cross This Line tape, smoke and NWA reaching out of the picture, it reflects the cut-up beats and urgency of the raps on the album. There's no obvious central figure, with only the (white) cop standing with a (white) witness clearly in view.

▲ **The true success story of crime is being able to get into that suit. James Bond's best enemies were billionaires. So, it symbolizes I'm rich**
ICE T

▲ Original Gangster / Ice-T

RELEASED 1991 | SIRE RECORDS | USA | SLEEVE DESIGN BY TIM STEDMAN | PHOTOGRAPHY BY GLEN E FRIEDMAN | ALBUM PRODUCED BY ICE-T, DJ ALADDIN, AFRIKA ISLAM, DJ SIJ AND BILAL BASHIR FOR RHYME SYNDICATE RECORDS/AMMO DUMP PRODUCTIONS

As the cover of this, his fourth and breakthrough album shows, long-time rapper Ice-T (almost ten years older than Ice Cube) rapped about more than just being a gangsta. On the left stands T the successful criminal in front of his West Coast mansion wearing an evening suit; but on the right is T the jailbird, in chains, swamped by glaring white light.

1990s R 'n' B

Soul is dead, long live R 'n' B. The advent of Rap and its more technical brother Hip-hop, heralded many changes in the music industry. By the 1990s DJs and producers were as important as the artists, with live bands largely being made redundant in black music, replaced by samples taken from Soul and Funk records of the previous three decades. Prince was the biggest name at the beginning of the decade, and already an anomaly. He reworked the rhythms and attitudes of Sly Stone, James Brown, Bootsy Collins and George Clinton, but with a live band. He might have partied like it was 1999 but he played as if it was 1975.

Apart from Tony Toni Toné (who briefly looked as if they would carry on the live Soul legacy), most new black artists and producers also reworked the same sources, but directly from the original vinyl – James Brown's Funk Drummer beat became the most sampled riff in music. What was once Soul, now R 'n' B, was created with computers and electronic machinery rather than guitars, bass, drums and strings. The results were new, though tinged with nostalgia as older Soul fans found themselves singing along with snatches of modern music and realizing that it was Parliament, Marvin Gaye, Donna

Summer or similar hidden way back in the mix. New R 'n' B fans just thought that the tune was "phat" and liked it for what it was.

In the 1990s black music was the most influential and economically important part of the music industry. Female R 'n' B acts such as Mary J. Blige and Lil' Kim sold clothes to fans from the pages of glossy fashion magazines. Puff Daddy, a former rapper turned R 'n' B artist, designed his own clothes line, and is (wrongly) credited with inventing "Bling". In fact he was simply emulating the generation of Soul stars from the mid-1970s who wore what was then known as the Mack or Pimp style (James Brown, Isaac Hayes, Sly Stone and such).

However, in the 1990s there were infinitely more radio and TV stations than twenty years earlier; far more magazines and newspapers were writing about black music in the 1990s than they ever did in the 1970s. Across all aspects of the burgeoning entertainment business, image was becoming all important and more money than ever before was spent by record companies on creating an R 'n' B artist's image. This increase in marketing spend was reflected in the quality of the album cover designs of this time.

▶ **Journey with the Lonely / Lil' Louis & the World**
RELEASED 1992 | FFRR | UK | SLEEVE DESIGN BY RISA ZAITSCHEK | PHOTOGRAPHY BY DAVID LACHAPELLE | ALBUM PRODUCED, ARRANGED AND MIXED BY LIL' LOUIS
Lil' Louis Sims, son of Chicago Blues guitarist Bobby (who played with Bobby Blue Bland, among others), was one of the first stars of Chicago's late '80s House scene. After scoring in the UK in 1989 he took three years to make this album, now considered one of the lost classics of the era. It's not just the music that makes this great, with its mix of House and R 'n' B; it's also the artwork. This is one of David LaChapelle's first professional jobs. Not long out of university, LaChapelle was 23 years old, living in New York for the first time, and working for Warhol's *Interview* magazine. It isn't a classic LaChapelle photo (think Lil' Kim as a piece of Louis Vuitton luggage) but it's a great image. There's a nod to Robert Mapplethorpe in the flower, but the deep hues of the black-and-white printing make it contemporary, while the hand-drawn lettering hints at the elements of fun that the photographer would later incorporate into his work for other, more famous popstars.

Lil' Louis & the World

journey with the lonely

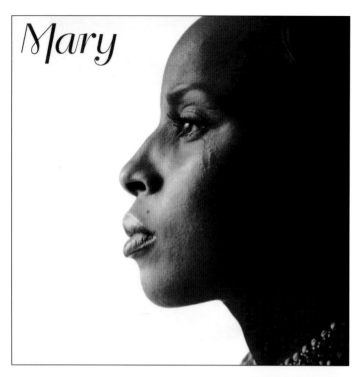

◀ Mary / Mary J. Blige

RELEASED 1999 | MCA | USA | SLEEVE DESIGN BY KENNY GRAVILLIS AND RUSSELL A ROBINSON 2 | PHOTOGRAPHY BY ALBERT WATSON | ALBUM PRODUCED BY MARY J. BLIGE AND KIRK BURROWES

Mary J. Blige had come out of the Rap-R 'n' B scene in the early 1990s, a protégée of Sean Puffy Combs. Her debut album was promoted by Uptown Records/MCA as being by "the original Queen of Hip-hop and Soul". On the cover of her second album My Life (1994) she's a tough street girl, all chunky chains and attitude. Three years later, however, and free of Puffy's influence, Mary is changing into a classy lady. By the end of the decade Mary J. Blige was arguably the biggest female R 'n' B artist in the world and this cover is a perfect demonstration of her status. Because the world's biggest stars are known simply by their first name, the album is titled simply Mary. The picture, taken by the fashion photographer Albert Watson, is powerful and clear. There is no attempt to hide Mary's scar which is, after all, proof of her street credibility, and her hair is scraped back to show her strong profile. The only adornment is her unflashy necklace which, as is to be seen on the photographs inside, is of an ethnic origin and contains no diamonds or other precious stones. Having done Bling, Mary is a statement of intent to be true to herself, to be "real".

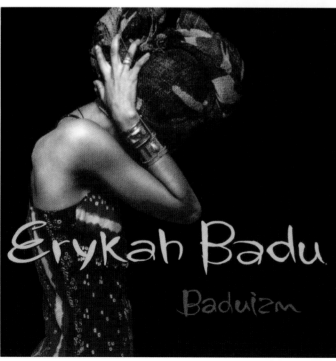

◀ Baduizm / Erykah Badu

RELEASED 1997 | UNIVERSAL | USA | SLEEVE DESIGN BY SANDIE LEE DRAKE, SUSAN BIBEAU FOR BEEHIVE PRODUCTIONS | PHOTOGRAPHY BY MARC BAPTISTE | ALBUM PRODUCED BY KEDAR MASSENBURG

By anybody's reckoning, Erykah Badu is a beautiful woman – which makes this album sleeve doubly intriguing. The image of the singer with her head completely covered by an African headdress provokes so many questions – not least, what does she look like? Flipping the CD, Erykah's face is revealed and then you get the idea that here is a singer who is interesting. Her voice has been compared to Billie Holiday, but then any female with a lower-register voice that can convey emotion is always compared to Ms Holiday. Born in Texas, Erykah Wright adopted Badu as her name in honour of the kind of scat singing from the 1940s and 1950s that she loved. In interviews she constantly refers to her Afrocentric views and hence her dress, but on record she sounds like a classic Soul singer – and apparently she carries a photo of her musical hero Marvin Gaye everywhere with her. It's far from certain whether Marvin would approve of this cover, though. Erykah clearly wants her music to sell her music rather than her physical beauty. Marvin had no such qualms.

▶ Maxwell's Urban Hang Suite / Maxwell

RELEASED 1996 | COLUMBIA | USA | SLEEVE DESIGN BY STACY DRUMMOND, JULIAN PEPLOE | PHOTOGRAPHY BY ERIC JOHNNSON | ALBUM PRODUCED BY MUSZE WITH STUART MATHEWMAN

Brooklyn born and raised, Maxwell grew up listening to classic Soul, West Indian music (his family's roots were in the Caribbean) and early Hip-hop sounds. For this, his debut album, he draws almost solely on the Soul sounds. So authentic are the sounds and songs on this album that it could have been recorded in 1971 and did as much as any album to prove that R 'n' B music was really Soul music. The cover is a brilliant variation on many 1970s Soul albums. The camera is lined up against a wall decorated with flock wallpaper of the kind to be found in less classy hotels. It is focused on a pair of high-heeled, golden mules that have been kicked off on a heavily patterned carpet, which similarly confirms this is a down-market setting. The message of the image is sex, while the typography and graphic layout says very firmly 1990s, with a nod to Barney Bubbles's design for Ian Dury's *Do It Yourself* (page 138).

▶ Things Fall Apart / The Roots

RELEASED 1999 | MCA | USA | SLEEVE DESIGN BY KENNY J. GRAVILLIS AND RUSSELL A. ROBINSON | ALBUM PRODUCED BY THE GRAND WIZZARDS

The Roots were formed in Philadelphia in 1987 by high school pals Tariq Trotter (who became Black Thought) and Ahmir Thompson (?uestlove). Over the next few years they built a local reputation by performing on street corners with Thompson drumming and Trotter rapping. In 1992 they released their debut album, *Organix*, with legendary Jazz bassist Jamaladeen Tacuma producing and with extra members Malik B and Rahzel. The Roots, as their name suggests, have a black consciousness sensibility and draw on the wealth of the history of black American music to create their sound. For this, their fourth album, The Roots make a definite statement of intent with the cover and title. The photograph was taken by a news reporter in the Bedford-Stuyvesant area of New York (Brooklyn) and shows two pre-pubescent girls (one is cropped from the image) in their Sunday best dresses running away from white cops who have their batons drawn. It was the second night of city riots that had begun in Harlem. The title, as well as being particularly apt for the image, is also the title of one of the most influential African novels of modern times, by Chinua Achebe.

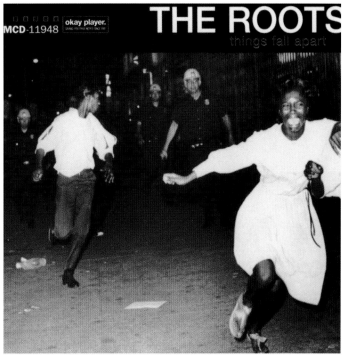

1990s Dance

While America was enjoying the R 'n' B, Rap and Hip-hop scene, Europe was dancing to a different beat. House, Garage and Hip-hop had made inroads into the UK and European club scene of the 1980s, but in 1987 a whole new movement erupted into the mainstream. Since the early 1980s there had been a growing trend for "squat" clubs to appear overnight, keep several hundred drugged-up people dancing, or raving, then melt away into the dawn. A "squat" club would open in any empty building into which a generator and sound system could be carried. Location would be circulated by word of mouth. As this rave scene grew, so too did the spread of the drug ecstasy, which had first appeared in the UK in 1983. Combining the effects of speed and LSD and creating a feeling of euphoria, it become the drug of choice for millions of British and European kids. As a result, DJs began to notice that dancers at rave clubs wanted more repetitive and faster and faster beats to move to.

There was little coming out that met the beats per minute requirement, so DJs began to put together electronically generated bass and drum tracks which did. By the end of the 1980s new acts had sprung up, all laying down fast electronic tracks with continuous, sequenced beats. The scene also developed a new graphic language. Because the clubs and raves often couldn't advertise where to meet, flyers were designed and printed to do so. As the scene grew to the point where two or three different raves were happening in the same area on the same night, the competing club organizers wanted to make themselves stand out from one another and so commissioned graphic artists to create an identity for their crew. Many of the creators of the flyers went on to design the covers for the bands that had emerged from the rave scene, and by the 1990s were releasing albums on major labels. By the time that acts such as Underworld, Orbital, Massive Attack and Prodigy were hitting the album charts, the CD had been around long enough for the designers creating the artwork to have bought nothing else. Vinyl and the 12-inch format were now confined to specialist, DJ-only releases, and many major album releases were not issued on vinyl at all. CD packaging was at last coming into its own.

Significantly from a design point of view, none of the sleeves in this section contains straight photographic content only; they are all graphically drawn.

▶ **Sometimes things are waiting for a context and I think there's a case in point with what we were doing here**

KARL HYDE, UNDERWORLD

▶ **Dubnobasswithmyheadman / Underworld**
RELEASED 1993 | JBO | UK | SLEEVE DESIGN BY TOMATO | ALBUM PRODUCED BY UNDERWORLD
Founder Underworld members Karl Hyde and Rick Smith were also in a successful art and design group, Tomato. The pair started making electronic Dance music in Smith's bedroom, and on their debut album they were the obvious choice to design the cover. Daringly black and white, the confusion of lines, words and different typefaces reflects the album's electronic beat and cut-up aesthetic. In fact, the sleeve is far more radical than the album sounded, and set a new standard of presentation for subsequent Dance albums.

> ◄ I loved [this] because I thought the picture had real attitude. It looks like the crab is saying, 'This is my beach'

LIAM HOWLETT, PRODIGY

◄ The Fat of the Land / Prodigy

RELEASED 1997 | XL RECORDINGS | UK | SLEEVE ART DIRECTION BY ALEX JENKINS AND LIAM HOWLETT | DESIGNED BY ALEX JENKINS | PHOTOGRAPHY BY KONRAD WOTHE/SILVESTRIS/ COURTESY OF FLPA-IMAGES OF NATURE | ALBUM PRODUCED BY LIAM HOWLETT

London's Prodigy stormed the singles and albums charts in 1992, with reviews that described them as Acid Punks. The music on their third album *The Fat of the Land* is as harsh and powerful as anything Prodigy had released. The sleeve is possibly the best use of a photograph of a crab ever to be used on an album cover. Designer Alex Jenkins distorted the background of the original picture to give the crab the appearance of "rushing" at the camera. Apparently the monstrous looking creature was only four inches long.

▲ Mezzanine / Massive Attack

RELEASED 1998 | VIRGIN | UK | SLEEVE DESIGN BY TOM HINGSTON AND ROBERT DEL NAJA | PHOTOGRAPHY BY NICK KNIGHT | ALBUM PRODUCED BY MASSIVE ATTACK AND NEIL DAVIDGE

Designer Robert Del Naja, known as 3D, was also member of the band. With their third album he was looking for a new direction, and found it with this picture by the fashion photographer Nick Knight, who had previously photographed insects for the Natural History Museum. The beetle was of an unnamed species discovered in South America and apparently large and dangerous. Knight added a metallic edge to the image by combining several colour copies together and photographing them. 3D added the type and the result was as near as perfect an album sleeve as there could be.

Funkstörung

Additional Productions

Exterior productions put through the Funkstörung audio process.

730003802829

Visit Venus. Visited by Funkstörung
East Flatbush Project. Tried by Funkstörung
Various Artists. No.9,5 by Funkstörung
Björk. In love with Funkstörung remix
Finitribe. Made up by Funkstörung
DJ Craze mit Funkstörung
Wu-Tang Clan. Reunixed by Funkstörung
S'Apex. Synkopic reprogrammed by Funkstörung

Included inside, your Funkstörung Aesthetic Standards Manual. Specifications and guidelines for the integration of the Funkstörung aesthetic into the global marketplace.

▲ Additional Productions / Funkstörung

RELEASED 1999 | STUDIO K7 | GERMANY | SLEEVE DESIGN BY THE DESIGNERS REPUBLIC LIMITED GRAPHIC DESIGN ASSOCIATES | ALBUM PRODUCED BY MICHAEL FAKESCH AND CHRIS DE LUCA OF MUSIK AUS STROM

In this collection of remixes, including work by Björk and the Wu Tang Clan, the melodies are darker and the beats even harder than Funkstörung's previous work and the cover takes you on a similar journey. Strong believers in creative freedom, they allowed the designers to bring together a series of intense abstract photographs with highly evolved instructions laid out as if the cover were a scientific or engineering manual. This combination of the abstract emotive image and cold hard fact is the perfect metaphor for the strange music inside. [GS]

▶ Dots and Loops / Stereolab

RELEASED 1997 | DUOPHONIC | UK | SLEEVE DESIGN BY HOUSE @ INTRO | ALBUM PRODUCED BY STEREOLAB WITH JOHN MCENTIRE AND ANDI TOMA

There are very few bands with which you could choose any of their covers and say they are all equally successful. Stereolab are one of that few. Combining the sound of melodic 1960s Pop with an Art Rock sensibility, their attention to detail has created a body of cover artwork which could easily be judged as a whole. Led by Tim Gane and Laetitia Sadier, their trademark sound was one of a hypnotic rhythm track overlaid with melodic, singsong vocals, often sung in French and – bizarre though it sounds – promoting revolutionary Marxist theory. Throughout their career they relied heavily on primitive methods of recording, using analogue synthesizers and electronics as well as sampling hi-fi test records. In 1997 the release of *Dots and Loops* saw them working with members of American ambient soundscape band Tortoise and the German techno Pop refugee Jan St Werner of Mouse on Mars. This collaboration brought a much fuller dance sound to their work. Stereolab have always chosen an illustrative format for their album sleeves, often with the use of hand-drawn typography. On *Dots and Loops*, their fifth studio album, this works particularly well to provide a strong and graphic cover. [GS]

STEREOLAB DOTS AND LOOPS

1 Brakhage 2 Miss Modular 3 The Flower Called Nowhere 4 Diagonals 5 Prisoner of Mars 6 Rainbo Conversation
7 Refractions in the Plastic Pulse 8 Parsec 9 Ticker-tape of the Unconscious 10 Contronatura

DUOPHONIC ULTRA HIGH FREQUENCY DISKS D-UHF-CD17

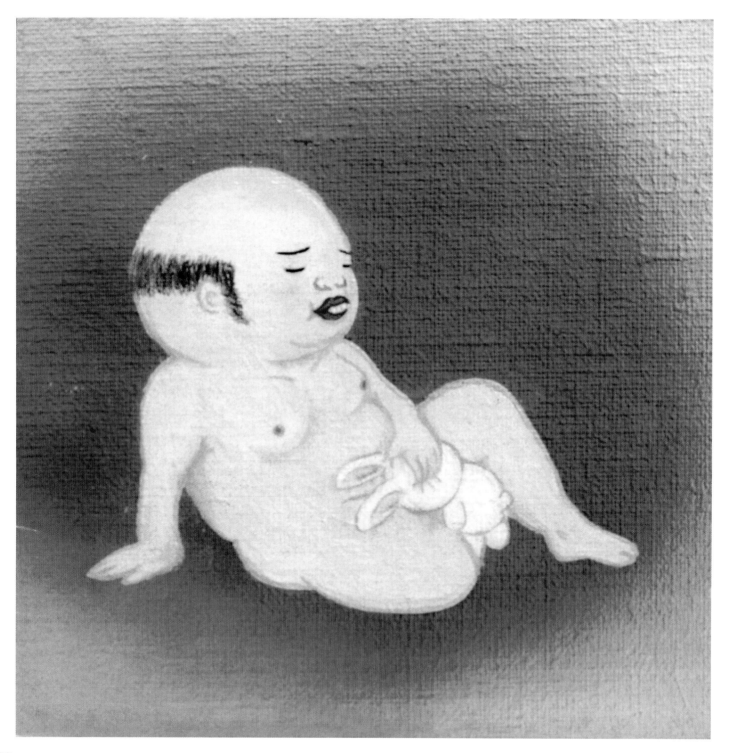

◀ Eureka / Jim O'Rourke

RELEASED 1999 | DOMINO | UK | SLEEVE ART BY MIMIVO TOMOZAWA | ALBUM PRODUCED BY JIM O'ROURKE

O'Rourke's worked throughout the 1990s with sound, improvising acoustic instrumentals and recording with used music tape. But he was highly self-critical – the music rarely met his high standards, and it had little commercial appeal. It was not until the release of *Eureka* that O'Rourke's voice was heard and commercial success was immediate. With the cover of *Eureka* he established a strong visual identity for his work, using the same strong colours and non-specific figures. [GS]

▼ Peel Session / Boards of Canada

RELEASED 1999 | WARP | UK | SLEEVE DESIGN BY DESIGNERS REPUBLIC | ALBUM PRODUCED BY MICHAEL SANDISON

The one cover BOC didn't design themselves was for this mini-album taken from recordings for John Peel's BBC Radio 1 show. Looking like a library card, there's no image, since the band like to create their own, just a block, pastel colour, and the title perfectly positioned. The sleeve is clean, minimal and, despite the colour, somehow very definite. It looks unlike any other BOC cover, but since it's only 20 minutes long and was recorded live, perhaps that's deliberate. [GS]

I often buy albums based on the cover art. I figure if I like the impact of the artwork, then I'll probably like the music, though that's not always the case. Sometimes the art director is better than the band

BOB GRUEN, ROCK PHOTOGRAPHER

▼ Music Has the Right to Children / Boards of Canada

RELEASED 1998 | WARP | SLEEVE DESIGN BY MICHAEL SANDISON AND MARCUS EOIN | ALBUM PRODUCED BY MICHAEL SANDISON AND MARCUS EOIN

With its faceless, soft-focus figures and over-saturation of colour, the cover perfectly reflects the soundscapes within. Typography is clean, precise and understated, delivering a message without intruding on the main image. As original and uncompromising as the music, this cover works extremely well because it has been conceived as part of the creative process by the band themselves, the people who understand it best. [GS]

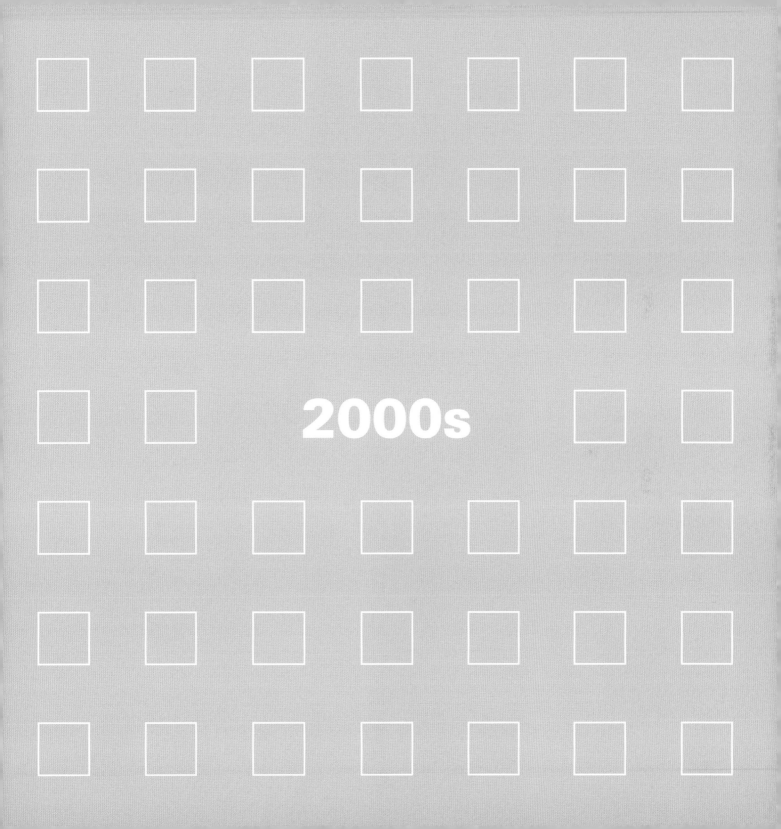

2000s

2000s Dance

As the twenty-first century began, it seemed the music industry had distilled to just four vibrant musical genres. While Country was self-contained and stable, the singles and albums charts in America and the UK were a churning mass of shifting styles, dominated by Dance sounds. Rappers worked with Hip-hop and R 'n' B producers to produce yet another new genre – Urban – usurping both R 'n' B and Rap in sales. Music from around the world was combined with spaced-out, slow Hip-hop beats to make chill-out sounds. Rock was dead and there was only Alt Rock, which seemed to include any record that had guitars on it. And then there was Dance music. Still predominantly electronic, it now included anything that had a groove and could be played in clubs as well as on radio.

In the UK, Dance acts had become headline performers at major music festivals such as Glastonbury, where the tents now resembled the rave clubs of the late 1980s. While the performers of Dance music were largely faceless, white and almost middle aged, their product and band identity were always tightly drawn and highly visible. Orbital, Underworld, The Chemical Brothers, and Fatboy Slim were nobody's poster pin-up boys, but each of them had a clearly

defined image and their cover art was easily recognizable to fans. The British scene had begun to make inroads into America off the back of Hollywood movies. In 1996, U2's Larry Mullen and Adam Clayton reworked the *Mission: Impossible* theme and put the kind of high-energy Electro Punk-Funk that acts such as Orbital and Leftfield had been making for some time into shopping malls across the States. Orbital's own thumping reworking of *The Saint*'s theme tune for the 1996 movie starring Val Kilmer pushed them into the US market too.

The result of British bands making it into the clubs of the US was that a generation of American DJs and Hip-hoppers began to include samples from their music in what was to become a US dance scene. As with the music, so with the imagery. The British use of non-human images for album covers began to be replicated in the US – see Money Mark's Push the Button and Change Is Coming (page 229) and Yo La Tengo's The Sounds of the Sounds of Science (page 233). In the UK the use of non-human imagery to sell music made on machines for humans to dance to began to mutate into a particularly British sense of humour. See page 231 for an excellent example of this.

> ▶ **We want to make the records as gorgeous and precious and collectable as possible. That's the joy of it: to make an artifact**
>
> **FRED DEAKIN, LEMON JELLY**

▶ **lemonjelly.ky / Lemon Jelly**
RELEASED 2000 | IMPOTENT FURY | UK | SLEEVE DESIGN BY FRED DEAKIN AT AIRSIDE | ALBUM PRODUCED BY NICK FRANGLEN
There's no lettering anywhere on the sleeve, which folds out into a three-part canvas. Jelly's Fred Deakin designed it, clearly influenced by psychedelia. Where there would have been shifting areas of colour on a 1960s album, he uses more regular, pointed blobs, though in typically psychedelic yellow, red and green. The shapes look as if they should have some kind of industrial use and serve as an intriguing design highlighting the music's naive charm. As the cover hints, this is a fun album with drug-related overtones.

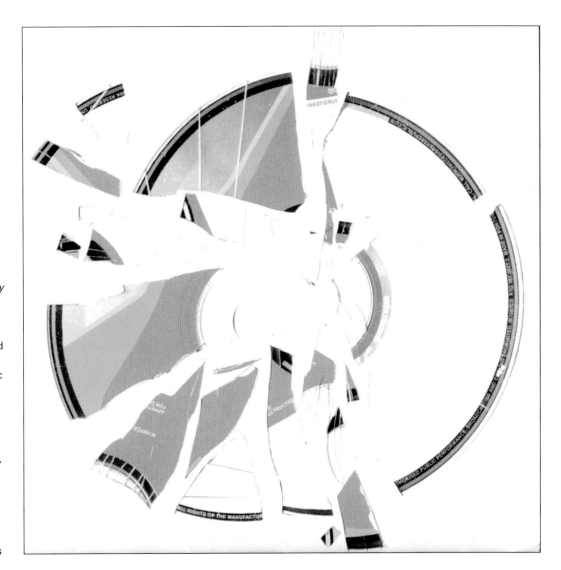

◀ Lost Horizons / Lemon Jelly
RELEASED 2002 | IMPOTENT FURY |
UK | SLEEVE DESIGN BY FRED
DEAKIN AT AIRSIDE | ALBUM
PRODUCED BY NICK FRANGLEN

For Lemon Jelly's second, but
first "proper" album (*lemonjelly.ky*
consisted of previously released
EPs) *Lost Horizons*, there is
still no lettering anywhere to be
found on the sleeve, nor any kind
of identifying stamp. Instead
there is brightly coloured graphic
artwork showing what look like
perfectly regimented fields
leading down to a perfectly blue
sea. Fold out the sleeve (again it
is in three parts) and the scene
rolls back to a dark but uniformly
arranged industrial town. Less
obviously naive and childlike
than their first album, with *Lost
Horizons* Deakin and Franglen
employ people to read for them
and sample fewer tracks. There's
a dark edge to the album which
is reflected in the sleeve. There's
still whimsy as demonstrated in
the track Ramblin' Man, but
there's danger too. Experiment
Number Six is a spoken word
piece read from a (supposedly)
genuine experiment in which
a man is given a hallucinogenic
drug that leads to his death.

**▲ Appetite for Disctruction /
Funkstörung**
RELEASED 2000 | STUDIO !K7 |
GERMANY | SLEEVE DESIGNED BY
THE DESIGNERS REPUBLIC LIMITED
GRAPHIC DESIGN ASSOCIATES |
ALBUM PRODUCED BY MICHAEL
FAKESCH AND CHRIS DE LUCA

Funkstörung is German for
interference but it is also a
Germanic play on words, as
"Funk" is the word for radio
and "Störung" the German for
disturbance. With 2000's *Appetite
for Discstruction* (a pun on the
Guns N' Roses album title) they
spent as much time on the cover
as was required (design matters
to them, see page 218) to ensure
that the resultant artwork became
as of one with the music. The
highly stylized finished product,
which shows the destruction of a
compact disc, brings a controlled
and considered resolution to an
explosive act. [GS]

FUTURE LOOP FOUNDATION ®

CAT NO. PCKCD001   TITLE: DIGITAL AUDIO PRODUCT

01. APRES SKI
02. SUN COMES FILTERING THRU
03. I LOVE HER MORE IN SUMMERTIME
04. WHAT'S YOUR NAME?
05. FREETOWN
06. LUCKY BLUE
07. HEADPHONE MUSIC
08. YOU & ME
09. MY MOVIE IS LIKE LIFE (WITH MICHAEL CONN)
10. I LOVE HER MORE... (PART 3)
11. WHEN NIGHT BECOMES DAY
12. THE BOY WITH THE GUN

(handwritten) THIS IS HOW I FEEL

PEEL

THANK YOU: MUNCHKIN, TA TA, SEAN, TINA, JOHNNY R (OR X ?), ROSS, MICHAEL CONN, RICHARD @ TITANIUM, EUGENIE, MUM & DAD, CLAUDIO, KHUDAI, MIKE P. DENNIS VENOHR, WOLFRAM, GENETIC DRUGS, BOB PAT & LUCINDA @ SIX DEGREES, ANDY CLIVE NIKKI ADAR AND ALL THE INTERGROOVERS, JAMIE @ DARLING DEPT., GUY @ WAXWORKS, DUNCAN & STEVE @ ZZONKED, ANDY RONAN & LISA @ FUTURE PUBLISHING, MICHAEL, BANCO, THE FLAVA, SIM @ 23, GREY DAD, GARETH, MOCCU, KEITH, IAN & ED @ SOUND TECH., CHRIS @ GMEDIA, COLIN @ EVOLUTION, JASON @ PIONEER, MICHAEL @ ABELTON, ANTONI @ PSP, RICHARD @ LACIE, ENRICO'S (I & M) @ IKMULTIMEDIA, DAVE @ MUON, DANNY @ JOE MEEK, IAN & DAVE @ THE DESIGNERS REPUBLIC.

◀ This Is How I Feel / Future Loop Foundation

RELEASED 2002 | PAN-KAY RECORDS | UK | SLEEVE DESIGN BY DESIGNERS REPUBLIC | ALBUM PRODUCED BY MARK BARROTT

Mark Barrott, who is Future Loop Foundation, grew up in Sheffield at a time when early electronic acts such as Human League and Cabaret Voltaire were just breaking in the U.K. His obsession with synthesizers began then and he immersed himself in music by Kraftwerk. After releasing three Drum 'n' Bass albums in the U.K. in the mid to late 1990s he moved to Berlin. There he DJed and moved from the harsher Drum 'n' Bass to ambient music. It was that shift which inspired him to write and record *This Is How I Feel* – which is clearly kind of fuzzy and mellow but still electronic. The versatile and often brilliant Designers Republic (see page 218 for another of their designs) created what at first sight looks like a demo recording cover. The fuzzy image of a pre-teenage boy is almost concealed by the track-listing (which actually folds over the package and has to be ripped to get the CD out), on to which the title is handwritten as if it's a postcard to someone.

▲ Change Is Coming / Money Mark

RELEASED 2001 | EMPEROR NORTON | USA | SLEEVE DESIGN BY SOAP DESIGN CO | LA PHOTOGRAPHY BY B+ | ALBUM PRODUCED BY MARK RAMOS-NISHITA

Former Beastie Boy Money Mark's second album uses a pun in the title and visually too. He has always been hard to label, mixing old-fashioned Funk played on modern synths with more exotic beats. Like the Beasties, he doesn't take things too seriously but feels as if he should (hence the title), and despite claiming he had no political motive, the cover was his idea. The money on it is in different currencies collected by Money Mark from around the world. He also folded the bird-like figures which inside the cover burns up – having set it alight himself. The title also refers to the Sam Cooke song A Change Is Gonna Come.

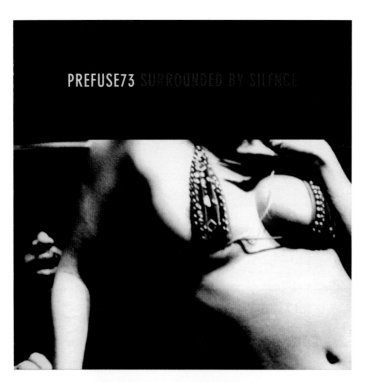

◀ Surrounded By Silence / Prefuse 73

RELEASED 2003 | WARP | USA | SLEEVE ART DIRECTION GRACIA VILLAMIL, GUILLERMO SCOTT HERREN & ESTRO | PHOTOGRAPHY BY GRACIA VILLAMIL | ALBUM PRODUCED BY PREFUSE 73

"Prefuse 73" (Guillermo Scott Herren) refers to pre-fusion Jazz of 1973. The cover gives more of idea of where Herren's coming from. Neither of the people there are him, but are current take on the early 1970s Mack Daddy figure that runs through this album. Glorious Soul and Funk melodies flow through a Hip-hop soundtrack, mixed and switched between Raps and classic choruses. The artful image of the cover is stark but clearly constructed in homage to an earlier time, just like Prefuse 73.

> ▶ For me a record sleeve is an integral part of the album experience. It's one of the most enduring and unfettered platforms for an artist to make a statement, the place where icons are created
>
> MATT ROSS
> MUSIC EXECUTIVE

◀ Bunkka / Oakenfold

RELEASED 2002 | MUSHROOM RECORDS/PERFECTO RECORDS | UK | SLEEVE DESIGN BY MICHAEL NASH ASSOCIATES | PHOTOGRAPHY BY MATTHEW DONALDSON | ALBUM PRODUCED BY PAUL OAKENFOLD AND VARIOUS

By the time Oakenfold released this he was known worldwide as a DJ. However, this is a dull and confused album. Its saving grace is the cover, a fantastic piece of photo manipulation that turns the female model into a cartoon-like superhero, complete with mask and rubber suit. It was produced by the same company responsible for INXS's *Welcome to Wherever You Are* and a Roxy Music compilation, but does most of its work for the retail trade. It doesn't have anything to do with the contents but it's truly striking.

▶ The Altogether / Orbital

RELEASED 2002 | FFRR | UK | SLEEVE DESIGN BY FARROW DESIGN | DIGITAL IMAGING BY MARK BULLEN | ALBUM PRODUCED BY P & P HARTNOLL

Orbital covers tended to be as anonymous and minimal as the music of one of their heroes, the minimalist composer Steve Reich. This, their ninth album, is the first to use a picture of the band, albeit an X-ray image. On stage, they wore headsets with lights attached so they could see the keyboards as the set was in darkness or bathed in strobe light. The lights here refer to the Jolly Roger pirate flag, the clinical aspect of the image reflecting the sterile environment of the studio in which the Hartnoll brothers make their powerful and moving electronic music.

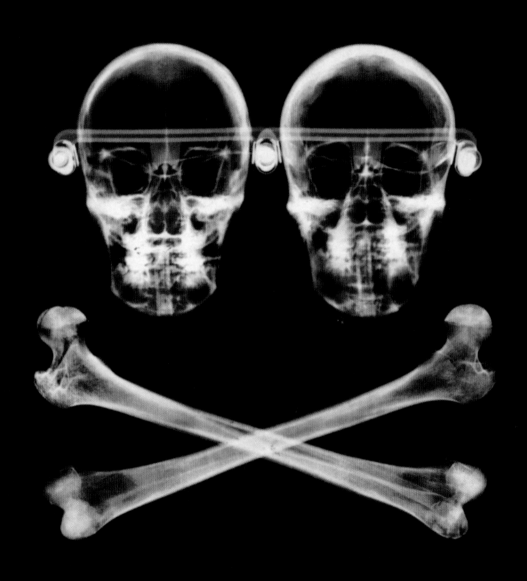

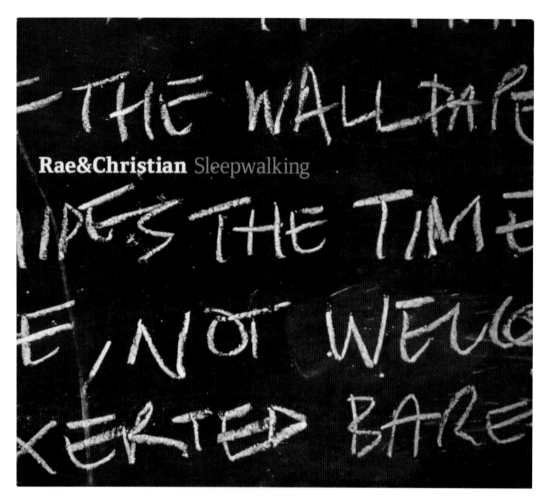

**▲ Sleepwalking /
Rae & Christian**

RELEASED 2000 | GRAND CENTRAL
RECORDS | !K7 RECORDS |
GERMANY | SLEEVE DESIGN BY
BLUE SOURCE | ALBUM MIXED AND
ENGINEERED BY STEVE CHRISTIAN

Mark Rae and Steve Christian are
often referred to as being the
godfathers of the new Northern
Soul. Hailing from Manchester,
the two men separately and
together did more to promote

British Hip-hop than possibly
anyone else. Rae managed
the Fat City Record store in
Manchester and then launched
Grand Central Records in 1995
which launched Tony D and the
Funky Fresh Crew. It was as a
duo that the pair scored their
greatest success and this, their
second album, was arguably the
greatest musical and design
statement. Why no one had
previously thought of using a

blackboard as a cover device is
odd, because this looks fantastic.
It's fresh and unique within the
genre, simple but strong. Those
are track titles written across the
board, by the way, and the CD
cover folds out to reveal more of
the writing, though not every title
is displayed in full.

**▶ The Sounds of the Sounds
of Science / Yo La Tengo**

RELEASED 2001 | MATADOR | USA |
PHOTOGRAPHY BY JEAN PAINLEVÉ |
ALBUM PRODUCED BY GREG CALBI

Formed back in 1984 in
Hoboken, New Jersey, Yo La
Tengo comprise the husband
and wife team Ira Kaplan on
guitars, vocals and keyboards,
and Georgia Hubley playing
drums and singing, with their
friend James McNew on bass
and everything else. The group
wrote two soundtracks for
Sundance Film Festival selected
films *Game 6* (directed by
Michael Hoffman, written by
Don DeLillo) and *Junebug*.
However, it was in 2001 with their
ground-breaking performances
of this piece of music that they
took experimental soundtracks
into a whole new arena. In a
series of performances in both
the United States and Europe,
they created and played highly
original instrumental music to
accompany the remarkable
underwater films of the French
documentary film maker Jean
Painlevé, which were projected
on a screen above them as they
performed in near total darkness.
Originally designed just to be
sold in small quantities at the
end of the concert, the album
cover features a still from one
of Painlevé's spectacular films
and has an eloquent and graceful
beauty which takes a humble film
still into a completely different
area of interpretation. The
typography is both refined and
restrained allowing the image to
shine in its own right. [GS]

Yo La Tengo The Sounds of the Sounds of Science

2000s Urban

As popular music has splintered into numerous sub-genres, so music stores have sought to keep track of it. So they have come up with catch-all musical genres, such as this one, Urban. Exactly what constitutes an Urban record is hard to define. It seems to be a grittier style of black R 'n' B that mixes Rap with Hip-hop beats and Soul samples, and has "adult" lyrics. It's almost wholly an American music.

Unlike Raphael Saadiq (ex Tony Toni Toné), D'Angelo or Maxwell, who are all Soul artists and who get racked in the R 'n' B section, Urban artists are rappers who sing, such as Nas or Missy Elliott. But Adina Howard and Jill Scott, who are Soul singers who work with Rap producers and who sing about sex and adult relationships, are also racked in the Urban section.

Presumably it's the experience of being born and raised in the inner city that makes an artist Urban. Although there is no rural category, there is a tradition of music mutating when musicians move to cities – the Blues became electric with the migration of former field workers to industrialized cities in America in the early twentieth century. Those musicians who remained in rural Mississippi rather than moving to Kansas, Chicago or New Orleans in search of work became known as Country Blues singers. The electrification of the Blues gave birth to Rhythm 'n' Blues and then Rock 'n' Roll, of course. Maybe the introduction of the Urban musical genre is a completion of a circle that was first begun almost a hundred years ago.

However, it's more likely just a way for music stores to rack similar sounding music together without having to create too many genre separaters. Of course, Ms Scott did record with The Roots (Urban was pretty much a twenty-first-century invention) which can have perhaps helped in her being allocated a position in this Urban section of the book.

Visually the musical mixing of styles and methods is reflected in the varied and varying quality of cover art that adorns many Urban releases. The harder, masculine Rap end of the genre tends to be focused on the artist and portrays them as comic-book style superheroes or in their fine, tattooed glory, usually with arms and torsos showing. The feminine Urban artists are somewhat softer in their presentation, both musically and visually. Urban has proven to be a rich and fertile area of graphic development.

▶ **Dead Prez / Dead Prez**
RELEASED 2004 | COLUMBIA | USA | SLEEVE DESIGN BY CHRIS FELDMAN | ALBUM PRODUCED BY STIC, M1 AND SEAN C
Dead Prez are two rappers, Stic.man and M-1 who rap Black consciousness and positive action lyrics and a "revolutionary but Gangsta" message. Their debut album *Let's Get Free* used a striking photo of African revolutionaries with rifles raised in the air. For this, their second album, Dead Prez commissioned graphic artist David Santana to create a Gangsta scarf as worn by the notorious Los Angeles gangs the Crips and the Bloods to identify which gang they belonged to, but to make it original to Dead Prez. So it's green, black and red like the national flag of Malawi. (They often start a live show asking "where are my African people?".) The quality of the illustration is such that it looks as if it's made of cloth. The sleeve folds out to reveal a poster on which the Dead Prez present the RBG Code – 1 No Snitching, 2 Protect self, family, and community at all times, 3 Each one, teach one, 4 Be organized, 5 Be productive. The package is a rare complete part of the album and works perfectly within context but also stands alone.

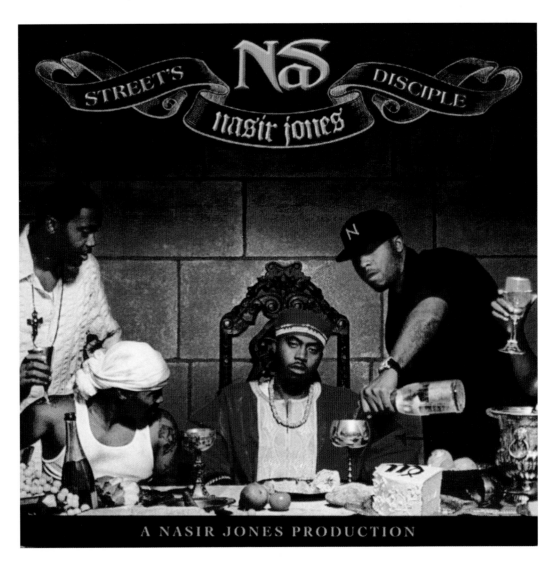

◄ Keep Right / KRS-One

RELEASED 2004 | GRIT RECORDS |
USA | SLEEVE DESIGN BY KEITH
CORCORAN FOR SOULSHOT |
ALBUM PRODUCED BY KRS-ONE
AND OTHERS | EXECUTIVE
PRODUCER SIMONE PARKER
AND INEBRIATED RHYTHM

KRS-One was one of the original
wave of rappers to emerge in
the 1980s as half of Boogie Down
Productions, along with Scott
La Rock. After La Rock was shot
in 1987, BDP found a political
conscience and, having
previously glorified Gangsta
style, began to preach against
it. *Keep Right* is his tenth solo
album since going solo in 1993
and it's full of hard-edged,
stripped-down Raps preaching
the gospel of Hip-hop. It includes
contributions from fellow
members of the Temple of Hip-
hop, such as Minister Server,
the Minister of Hip-hop Kulture
and Afrika Bambaataa. The
fantastically strong and direct
cover is so simple it's almost
genius. It combines the rapper's
message to the young (he also
uses the moniker of the Teacha)
which the temple of Hip-hop is all
about (www.templeofhiphop.org)
and makes a reference to his
roots – he is a former graffiti
artist. The 12-inch vinyl version
of the sleeve is a work of art that
could grace any gallery.

▲ Street's Disciple / Nas

RELEASED 2004 | SONY URBAN
MUSIC | USA | SLEEVE ART BY
CHRIS FELDMANN | PHOTOGRAPHY
BY DANNY CLINCH | ALBUM
PRODUCED BY NASIR JONES,
SALAAM REMI & L.E.S.

For this, his sixth album, rapper
Nas looks like Jesus in a version
of Leonardo da Vinci's *The Last
Supper*. Other rappers have done
a Christ-like pose, but usually on
the cross. Maybe the success of
The Da Vinci Code prompted the
idea. This expensively assembled
photo bears only a passing
resemblance to the original –
there are five disciples to his left
and seven to the right, whereas
they're evenly split on the Da
Vinci. And no one in the original
is pouring Christ a glass of Cristal
champagne while smoking a
cigar – which is airbrushed out
on the cover image but clearly
visible on the poster that comes
with the double CD album.

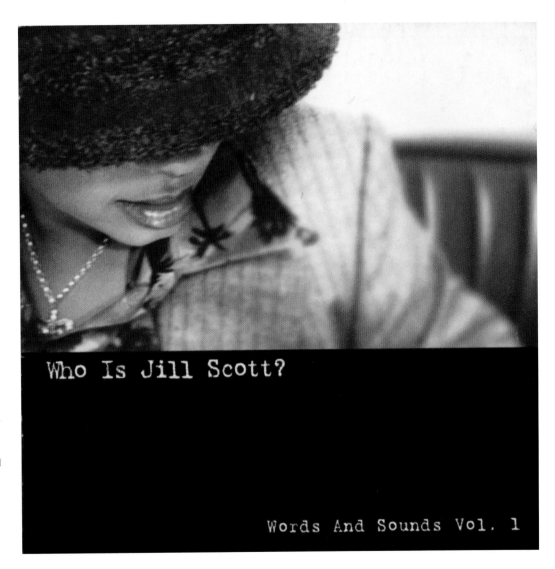

Who Is Jill Scott?

Words And Sounds Vol. 1

◀ The Second Coming / Adina Howard

RELEASED 2004 | RYKO | USA | SLEEVE DESIGN BY SHERI WILLIAMS, J. WESLEY KNOWLES, SPECTRUM TYPE & ART | PHOTOGRAPHY BY RANDEE ST NICHOLAS | ALBUM PRODUCED BY ADINA HOWARD, MAX GOUSSE AND THE PLATINUM BROTHERS

On the cover of her debut album *Do You Wanna Ride?* in 1995, singer Adina Howard had straightened black hair, was wearing tight hotpants and pointing her butt at the camera as she leaned on the hood of a BMW. The songs on that and this, her third album (her second, Welcome to Fantasy Island, showed her naked, short dyed blonde hair and a snake wrapped around her), are sexually explicit in a way that few female singers, with the exception of Millie Jackson, had been. The photograph was taken by the man who put Shelby Lynne in denim hotpants on the cover of *Love, Shelby*. St Nicholas likes to draw out the sexuality of his subjects (never a problem for Ms Howard), but what's great about this is the relaxed sensuality the singer is exuding. She's almost naked in the studio, which is silly, but her direct stare gives this a jolting impact.

▲ Who Is Jill Scott? / Jill Scott

RELEASED 2000 | EPIC | USA | SLEEVE DESIGN BY LYZEL WILLIAMS, THORNELL JONES | ALBUM EXECUTIVE PRODUCED BY STEVE MCKEEVER AND JAZZY JEFF TOWNES

This, Jill Scott's debut album and the first to be released by Hidden Beach. It's not wholly a Soul album, although there's a lot of Soul in it and it's certainly a slightly retro-looking album. Like Erykah Badu (page 212) Jill Scott is a beautiful woman who seems determined not to sell her music on her looks. While the photo and title work well as a visual pun, the courier-style type on a stark black background gives the impression that it is a secret dossier of some kind. The blue hues of the seat and jacket in the photo are set perfectly against the singer's hat and lipstick. It could almost be a painting, not a photograph.

2000s Chill Out

One of the legacies of the 1980s rave culture in Britain was the opening of "super clubs" in major cities across Europe, from Cream in Liverpool to Hedonism in Ibiza. Another was the introduction of longer opening hours for clubs. Because the original rave generation had been hyped up on ecstasy various other amphetamine-laced drugs, they didn't stop dancing until dawn. In unlicensed clubs this wasn't a problem, and soon legal, licensed clubs began to keep their DJs working until the sun came up, too. In the 1990s clubs didn't close until dawn, and even then many continued to spin discs, but they weren't playing dance tunes; they were playing what became known as Chill-out records. At first DJs would play seamless albums from the 1970s by bands such as Pink Floyd, with gently rolling soundscapes, acoustic guitars, and a mellow mood. Then DJs and producers began to create Chill-out records from scratch – the first hugely successful one being The Orb's *Adventures Beyond the Underworld*, released as a double 12-inch album in 1991. It sampled Pink Floyd, Joni Mitchell and other 1970s hippie performers, setting them against a Dub bass which oozed rather than banged and was the

perfect background soundtrack as people eased themselves down from a dancing high before going home.

Chill-out sounds were classed as ambient, which prompted the release of Ambient compilation albums so that fans could relax at home in a style akin to that of the chill-out rooms which had been installed in many of the super clubs. These rooms had bean bags, sofas, "lava-lamp" light shows and even incense burning.

There are a few essentials for Chill-out music. If there's a vocal it has to mumble or repeat bits of evocative sentences. A Chill-out track needs to be long with consistent beats per minute, the music has to evoke relaxation without putting people to sleep, and if there's an exotic element, all the better. Smooth Jazz, Cuban, and even African-influenced albums work in chill-out rooms. Chill-out packaging should be similarly abstract but not disturbing, ideally making a visual connection with a chilled mood or place. Because Chill-out albums have been primarily released on CD, their designs work at a smaller size than ones that stoned 1970s hippies listened to and gazed at, looking for meaning in the sci-fi landscapes that were perfect for rolling joints on.

▶ **The Intercontinentals / Bill Frisell**

RELEASED 2003 | NONESUCH RECORDS | USA | SLEEVE DESIGN BY DAYLE PARTNERS | PHOTOGRAPHY BY TOM SCHIERLITZ | ALBUM PRODUCED BY LEE TOWNSEND

Bill Frisell is one of the most prolific and hardest-working men in the music business. Although from the 1970s Jazz scene, he makes a unique kind of American music on his own albums and contributes his trademark guitar playing skills to pretty much anyone who asks him to. A quiet, diffident man, he seems as concerned with how his releases look as how they sound, and has issued some interesting and well-designed albums. For this, a Grammy-nominated release (for Best World Music), the long established New York design agency Doyle Partners used a photo of an old amplifier (by a *New York Times* and commercial photographer) on the booklet front and a record deck on a cardboard outer sleeve to convey the idea that here is an album that is all about the sound, not the people making it. As indeed it is, the music clear, chilled and intriguing with Frisell's plaintive acoustic guitar intertwining with Sidiki Camara's calabash and djembe.

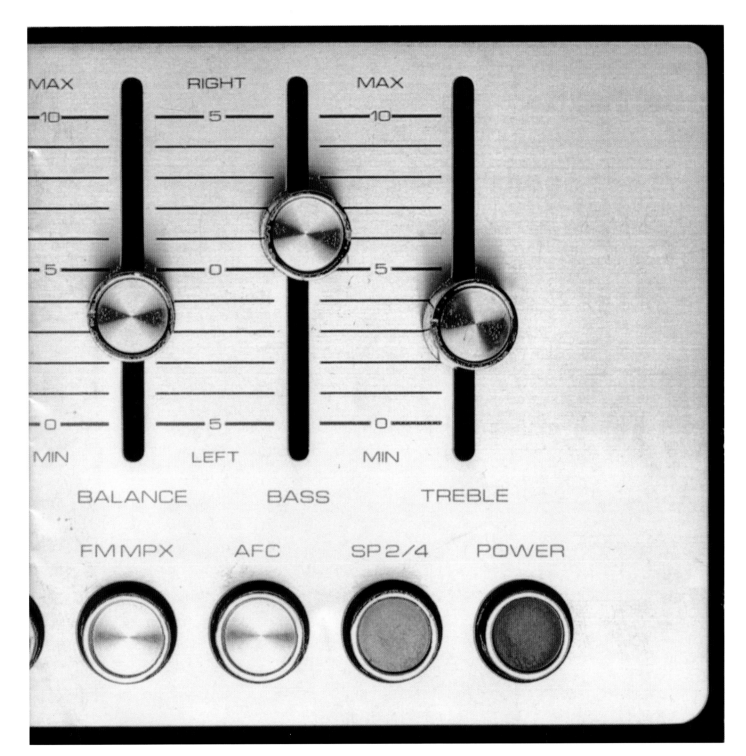

Pieces in a Modern Style
William Ørbit

◀ Pieces in a Modern Style / William Orbit

RELEASED 2000 | WARNER BROS | USA | SLEEVE DESIGN BY FARROW DESIGN | PHOTOGRAPHY BY JOHN ROSS | ALBUM PRODUCED BY WILLIAM ORBIT

This album, released after Orbit's work with Madonna, was a new way to treat classical music. His electronic take on minimalist pieces by Cage, Satie and Gorecki are set against similar versions of Beethoven, Handel, Ravel, Barber and Vivaldi. Designer Mark Farrow's use of Ross's flower image perfectly reflects the sweeping orchestral music. Like the music the flower looks hyper-real, an imitation more vibrant than the real thing.

▲ Mambo Sinuendo / Ry Cooder, Manuel Galbán

RELEASED 2003 | NONESUCH RECORDS/WARNER BROS | USA | SLEEVE DESIGN BY DOYLE PARTNERS | PHOTOGRAPHY BY CINDY LEWIS | ALBUM PRODUCED BY RY COODER

Building on the success of *Buena Vista Social Club*, Ry Cooder and Cuban guitarist Manuel Galbán continued their collaboration on *Mambo Sinuendo*, fusing Jazz, Country Rock and Cuban popular rhythms. The 1959 Cadillac El Dorado on the cover is one of the most perfect emblems of this period and is perfectly suited, both to the Cuban love of flash and style, and the 1950s feel of the music it encloses. [BM]

▲ liverpool sound collage / Paul McCartney, Youth and Super Furry Animals

RELEASED 2000 | LIVERPOOL TATE GALLERY | UK | SLEEVE DESIGN AND COLLAGE BY PAUL MCCARTNEY | ALBUM PRODUCED BY PAUL MCCARTNEY

In the spring of 2000, artist Peter Blake, of *Sgt Pepper* sleeve fame, had a show entitled *About Collage* at the Liverpool Tate Gallery and invited his old friend Paul McCartney to create a collage soundtrack to go with the show. This is the result: an avant-garde collaboration involving McCartney, Super Furry Animals and the mix artist Youth. The hour-long CD is really all one piece, a collage of studio outtakes and interview fragments recorded by The Beatles between 1965 and 1969, and Paul interviewing people on the streets of Liverpool. It is mixed by Cian Ciaran from Super Furry Animals and given a final tweak by Youth. Although the invitation came from Peter Blake, McCartney's collage owes everything to Richard Hamilton, who made the fold-out poster collage that came with The Beatles' White Album. McCartney attended Hamilton's studio every day while it was being made and learned a lot about composition and white space from the master. [BM]

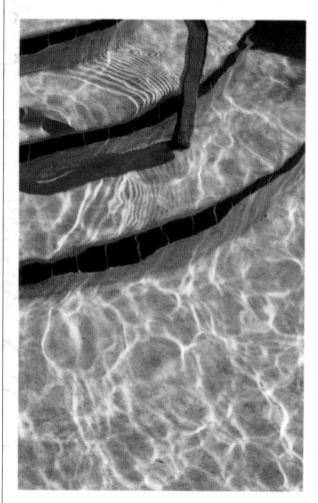

Arthur Russell

THE WORLD OF ARTHUR RUSSELL

Soul Jazz Records

▲ **The World of Arthur Russell / Arthur Russell**
RELEASED 2004 | SOUL JAZZ RECORDS | UK | SLEEVE DESIGN BY ADRIAN SELF & RODNEY PILE UP | ALBUM PRODUCED BY ARTHUR RUSSELL AND OTHERS
Russell played cello on several records by Allen Ginsberg before moving to New York where he was almost a founder member of Talking Heads, for whom he wrote horn arrangements. He studied the deep structure of Dance music, and his tapes and 12-inch mixes always got them dancing at the uber-trendy Studio 54. Arthur died of Aids in 1992 leaving behind a series of unique tracks that fuse weird avant-garde textures with Disco heaven. His love of the gay Disco scene is skilfully evoked by a reference to David Hockney's swimming pool paintings and the Pop lettering of Disco albums in an otherwise formal sleeve. [BM]

▶ **Strawberries oceans ships forest / The Fireman [Paul McCartney]**
RELEASED 1993 | PARLOPHONE | UK | SLEEVE DESIGN BY PAUL MCCARTNEY | ALBUM PRODUCED BY YOUTH AND PAUL MCCARTNEY
In the 1990s Paul McCartney was well aware that his songs were not being played in the clubs but he didn't want someone to come in and just put drums and rhythms all over his songs. He brought in Chillin' Room mixer Youth. "The brief was we would let him source from anything off the album, (*Off the Ground*) or anything he would want me to give him live here," said McCartney. "But it had to be us. It couldn't be a rhythm box or anything unless we'd used a rhythm box." Youth decorated McCartney's studio with Indian hangings, lit joss sticks and candles, installed a light machine and looped and chopped McCartney's tapes until 7am. The result was an album with a cover that perfectly reflects the content. It was a staple of Chill-out rooms well into the twenty-first century. [BM]

strawber

2000s Alt Rock

As in the previous decade, Rock music in the twenty-first century is a disparate genre. Many of the dinosaurs of Rock continue to record and tour – Robert Plant and Jimmy Page still play gigs and make records together, often drawing on the Led Zep catalogue in doing so. In 2005 the original line-up of Cream, Eric Clapton, Ginger Baker and Jack Bruce, re-enacted their Royal Albert Hall concert of 1968 and, to cash in, Polydor released a double album of original material in a very dull and un-Cream like sleeve. Also in 2005 Queen re-formed with former Free and Bad Company singer Paul Rodgers not quite donning Freddie Mercury's leotard, but attempting to hit some high notes in Freddie's absence. R.E.M. and U2 continue to tour and release increasingly irrelevant albums in much the same way that Bob Dylan and Bruce Springsteen do. They all attempt to wrap their new albums in contemporary packaging, but rarely do any of the major acts produce a good-looking album.

The Rolling Stones, who are the only band to have several sleeves in this book and in four out of the six decades, might well release an album with a good cover because clearly the packaging matters to

them – the music stays the same as it ever did, of course. And so the only really innovative area of Rock music is what is loosely termed Alt Rock. A new wave of American guitar acts emerged in the early part of the decade who referenced the 1960s musically, but were entirely contemporary in their packaging. In the U.K. a new wave of guitar bands emerged who reference the early 1980s original Alt Rock scene, each of whose albums sound like lost tapes recorded by XTC, Gang of Four and Wire 25 years earlier. Franz Ferdinand, Bloc Party and Kaiser Chiefs not only sound like it's 1981, but unfortunately produce sleeves that look like it, too.

Most of the acts contained in this final section are American, and while musically they don't sound as if they would appear on the same bill, graphically they share a true inventiveness and originality.

▶ **Let It Come Down /
Spiritualized**

RELEASED 2001 | ARISTA | UK | SLEEVE DESIGN BY FARROW DESIGN | SPACEMAN SCULPTURE YOKO BY DON BROWN | ALBUM PRODUCED BY J. SPACEMAN AND J. COXON

In 1997 Spiritualized released their second album *Ladies and Gentlemen We Are Floating in Space* to huge success and praise for its eclectic mix of genres. It also had original packaging. The follow-up album *Let It Come Down* three years later proved to be very different musically but just as diverse, with influences drawn from Ray Charles to The Beach Boys with a more Rock sound overall. A big-scale production recorded in the Abbey Road studios with more than a hundred musicians, it needed a cover that was similarly impressive. The result was achieved by Farrow Design, who also created William Orbit's *Pieces in a Modern Style* (see page 242), vacuum-forming a thin, cream plastic to create a three-dimensional artwork with a narrow pocket at the rear for the CD to sit in. Just as the music has a weight and grandeur, the casing has a similar presence, which stands out from its more conventionally packaged contemporaries. [GS]

◀ Yankee Hotel Foxtrot / Wilco

RELEASED 2002 | NONESUCH RECORDS | USA | SLEEVE DESIGN BY LAWRENCE AZERRAD | PHOTOGRAPHY BY SAM JONES | ALBUM PRODUCED BY WILCO

In 2002 Wilco released this, a kind of Radiohead version of Alt Country with guitar solos intercut with snatches of radio static, and a melancholy that is pure Wilco. The sleeve for *YHF* reflected the different and difficult nature of the album. Founder of the LA Design company Azerrad had previously created the *Summerteeth* cover which had begun to hint at the alienation and other-worldliness that Tweedy certainly seemed to be feeling. This is a work of pure art, full of space and warped perspective, displaying a sense of alienation that has meant it quickly became widely available as a poster.

▶ And Then Nothing Turned Itself Inside Out / Yo La Tengo

RELEASED 2000 | MATADOR | USA | SLEEVE PHOTOGRAPHY BY GREGORY CREWDSON | ALBUM PRODUCED BY ROGER MOUTENOT

As Yo La Tengo's music became less obvious and more cinematic, their covers began to feel more like stills from an unseen movie. The dark, enigmatic, atmospheric scene here hints at the dark American underbelly and illicit late-night relationships. This is an approach to photography which is often referred to as "Fine Art" and can be seen hanging in pristine white galleries, but as with many great covers, when seen while listening to the album it takes on new meanings not necessarily noticed when in an exhibition space. [GS]

▶ It's Like This / Rickie Lee Jones

RELEASED 2000 | ARTEMIS | USA | SLEEVE DESIGN AND PHOTOGRAPHY BY LEE CANTELON | ALBUM PRODUCED BY RICKIE LEE JONES AND BRUCE BRODY

For *It's Like This* photographer, film director and designer Lee Cantelon photographed Rickie Lee Jones's life in stark black and white, processing the images as if they were news photographs. This, the photos show, is how it is in Rickie's world. The album itself, like 1991's *Pop Pop* (page 182), is made up of cover versions, although they are more contemporary than the earlier album. Rickie Lee Jones albums have been consistently well designed and thought out over the past twenty years; this is just one example of that.

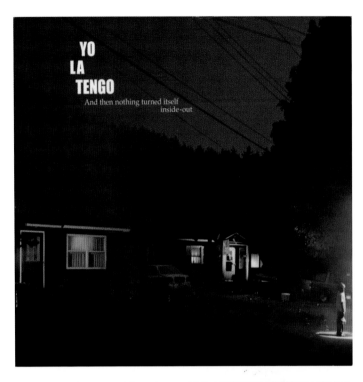

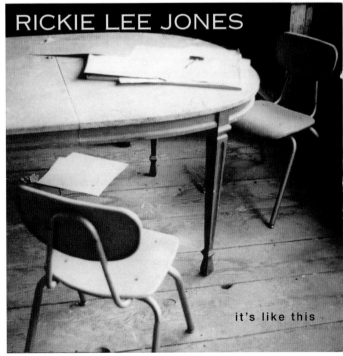

◄ America's Sweetheart / Hole

RELEASED 2004 | VIRGIN | USA | SLEEVE ARTWORK BY OLIVIA | ALBUM PRODUCED BY MATT SERLETIC, JOSH ABRAHAM, JAMES BARBER

Anybody with even the slightest knowledge of who Courtney Love is and how she is perceived would immediately see that the title of this album is pure irony, and that the graphic interpretation of the title takes this to its purest logical conclusion. Courtney Love is not and never will be America's Sweetheart and yet the idea of her plastered on to the side of a B-52 bomber is less hard to imagine. The recognized master of this style of illustration from the 1940s onwards was Alberto Vargas who brought an idealized version of the all-American woman to the world via *Esquire* and *Playboy* magazines (see page 97 for his work on The Cars' *Candy-O*). His work was much copied on to clothing and military vehicles until his death in 1982. This is very much a pastiche of his work but it is carried out with such attention to detail and lightness of touch, from the right choice of clothing through to the hand-drawn typography, that it works. In a world of Photoshop perfection this cover takes an airbrushed gloss to a troubled idol. [GS]

▶ Is This It / The Strokes

RELEASED 2001 | ROUGH TRADE | UK | SLEEVE PHOTOGRAPHY BY COLIN LANE | ALBUM PRODUCED BY GORDON RAPHAEL

Amid great music industry excitement The Strokes, a group of twentysomething New Yorkers, released their debut album *Is This It* in 2001. The cover featured a sexy, Helmut Newton-/Guy Bourdin-influenced photograph of a woman's nude behind and hip, with a leather-gloved hand suggestively resting on it. In Britain shops such as Woolworth's and HMV objected to its controversial nature, and for the American version the cover was changed for an abstract pattern on the front. It's either a stylish and graphically strong cover or a sexist *Smell the Glove* travesty. [GS]

▶ Sea Change / Beck

RELEASED 2002 | GEFFEN | USA | SLEEVE DESIGN BY KEVIN REAGAN AND BECK | PHOTOGRAPHY BY AUTUMN DE WILDE | ALBUM PRODUCED BY NIGEL GODRICH

Deeply pesonal, reflecting the sadness at the ending of a relationship, this was never going to be a commercial hit. But despite this, no costs were spared in its packaging. Released with four different versions of the same artwork, each one in a different colour palette, all four covers could be seen when you purchased any version as the sleeve folded out into a four-panel mural showing Beck being swallowed by successive layers of vividly coloured liquid. The idea is brilliant, subtle, and memorable – a perfect metaphor for such an album. [GS]

THE STROKES IS THIS IT

◀ Renegades /
Rage Against the Machine

RELEASED 2002 | EPIC | USA |
SLEEVE DESIGN BY RAGE AGAINST
THE MACHINE, RICK RUBIN AND
AIMÉE MACAULEY | ALBUM
PRODUCED BY RICK RUBIN, RAGE
AGAINST THE MACHINE

Rage Against the Machine
are that rare thing, a genuinely
politically motivated American
Rap-Rock band. They play
benefits for causes that they
believe in and make statements
that don't always come off
(attempting to hang an inverted
US flag on their amps got them
kicked off a network TV show, for
instance), but they care and try to
make a difference. Their albums
and website offer reading lists
and direct action group contacts
for anyone who wants to follow
their lead. And they have
Number One selling albums, too.
This, their fourth since forming in
1991, is an album of surprising
and obvious cover versions. The
surprises are the older tracks –
The MC5's Kick out the Jams,
the Stones' Street Fighting Man,
Springsteen's Ghost of Tom
Joad, and Dylan's Maggie's
Farm, but they're the ones that
prompted the cover design. In
1967 Pop Artist Robert Indiana
created a series of screen prints
which used the letters LOVE in a
tight square, in a range of colours
including black and white. This
clever reworking of Indiana's
original idea uses a palette that
he didn't use but is based on the
best-known version, Sky Love.

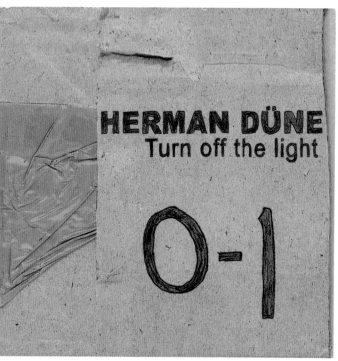

◀ Turn off the Light /
Herman Düne

RELEASED 2000 | PROHIBITED
RECORDS | SWEDEN | SLEEVE
DESIGN BY DAVID-IVAR HERMAN
DÜNE AND DON NINO | ALBUM
PRODUCED BY F. LOR

Swedish-born and Paris-based
brothers André Herman Düne,
David-Ivar Herman Düne, and
Omé Herman Düne formed
Herman Düne in 1999. In their
music they present a view of
the world with a delicate and
honest cynicism in tightly scored
musical vignettes. The haunting
and beautifully disjointed, low-
budget backing to their ragged
stream-of-consciousness songs
is joyfully hypnotic. With the
influences of their heroes Bob
Dylan, Neil Young and Sonic
Youth obvious in the music, this
Swedish band and their Swiss
drummer sing often out-of-tune
songs with half-tuned, cheap
guitars. They have released five
albums and written more than
four hundred songs so far, but
it is with *Turn off the Light* that
their music is most effectively
reflected in the cover artwork.
Feeling and looking like an art
student project on a brown
parcel wrapping, it has a naive
charm and directness which is
at the same time both refreshing
and effective. [GS]

▶ The Covers Album /
Cat Power

RELEASED 2000 | MATADOR |
UK | SLEEVE SCULPTURE BY
JOAN GIORDANO 1978 | ALBUM
PRODUCED BY CAT POWER AND
JIM WHITE

Cat Power is the alter ego of
shy American singer-songwriter
Chan (pronounced Shawn)
Marshall. With her first album
Moonpix in 1998 she clearly set
out the introspective, abstract
and deeply personal territory
which she would explore
throughout the rest of her career.
Her use of rudimentary guitar
and piano playing, as well as her
cracked, raw vocals, tap into the
traditional porch Blues of her
native Georgia. This is a fact
most clearly seen in her live
performances, which are stripped
back to a very basic staging with
Chan nervously stalking the stage
almost begging her audience to
let her finish and leave as soon as
possible. Fragile live versions of
songs by Bob Dylan and Lynyrd
Skynyrd, and her love for the
work of Dylan, Lou Reed, and
Moby Grape led to the obvious
conclusion that she should
release a covers album. Simply
and honestly entitled *The Covers
Record*, the choice of artwork is
similarly straightforward – just a
piece of original art that Chan
liked. A simple cover for a simple
album, which simply works. [GS]

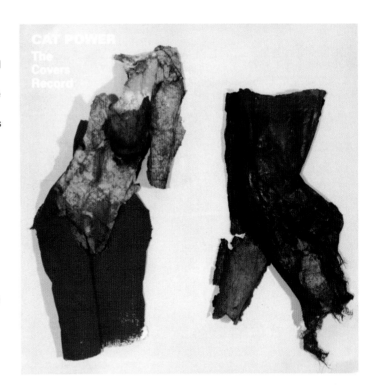

▶ The Concretes /
The Concretes

RELEASED 2004 | LICKING FINGERS
AB/EMI | SWEDEN | SLEEVE DESIGN
BY LISA MILBERG | ILLUSTRATION
BY LISELOTTE WATKINS | ALBUM
PRODUCED BY JARI HAAPALAINEN

There is a long tradition of
people from art schools joining
and forming bands, and then
going on to design their own
covers – with varying degrees of
success. Continuing this tradition
are The Concretes. There are
eight full-time members of the
Swedish band and the designer
of their albums, Lisa Milberg, is
one of them. A drummer and
trained graphic designer, with
their debut album *The Concretes*,
released in 2004, she immediately
created an identity for the band
which was strong enough to
be developed and expanded
on, in the style of their videos,
website and other releases.
By using a simple and direct
colour palette and the distinctive
illustrations by Liselotte Watkins
she has avoided the need to
shout with the design through
the use of gimmicks and flashy
photography. The music is based
on their Swedish background
with an awareness and love of
everyone from Diana Ross to The
Velvet Underground. Similarly
the cover echoes the strong
design heritage of Sweden and
particularly the work of the
Merrimeko company, while not
slipping into pastiche or corny
tweeness. [GS]

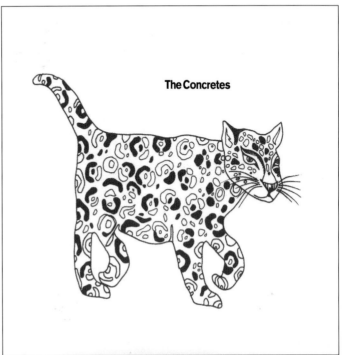

The Concretes

Index

Author Barry Miles was a central figure in the development of the hippie movement in the 1960s. He was a guest at both the live recording of the Beatles' 'All You Need Is Love' international television broadcast in 1967 and the cover photo shoot for *Sgt Pepper's Lonely Hearts Club Band*. Miles has written several seminal books on the Beat generations, including biographies of Ginsberg, Burroughs and Kerouac, and in October 2002 published his memoirs of the decade entitled In The Sixties (Jonathan Cape). He is the author of the bestselling Hippie (Cassell Illustrated).

During his highly successful career art directing several leading magazines, including *Tatler* and English *Elle*, Grant Scott worked with photographers such as William Klein, Jean Loup Sieff, David Bailey and Don McCullin. He has also compiled various photographic monologues including John Swannell's *On Twenty Years* and Trevor Leighton's *Jokers*. He was the art director for *Hippie* (Cassell Illustrated). A professional photographer, Scott was winner of the John Kobal Portrait Awards 2000 and has been exhibited at the National Portrait Gallery. His book, *At Home With the Makers of Style*, was published by Thames and Hudson in 2005.

Music journalist and writer Johnny Morgan has contributed articles on different styles of music for a number of different music magazines. Before becoming a writer in the late 1980s he was a professional musician and band manager. He has contributed to a number of reference books on popular music, among them the Collins Gem *Hit Singles* and Collins *Gem Hit Albums*. He is the author of *Ocean Colour Scene Belief* is All (Andre Deutsch).